Tourism Business Frontiers

I never think of the future. It comes soon enough.

(Albert Einstein)

Tourism Business Frontiers

Consumers, products and industry

Edited by Dimitrios Buhalis and
Carlos Costa

ELSEVIER
BUTTERWORTH
HEINEMANN

AMSTERDAM BOSTON HEIDELBERG LONDON NEW YORK OXFORD
PARIS SAN DIEGO SAN FRANCISCO SINGAPORE SYDNEY TOKYO

Elsevier Butterworth-Heinemann
Linacre House, Jordan Hill, Oxford OX2 8DP
30 Corporate Drive, Burlington, MA 01803

First published 2006

British Library Cataloguing in Publication Data
A catalogue record for this book is available from the British Library

Library of Congress Cataloguing in Publication Data Control Number: 2005928301

ISBN 0 7506 6377 4

For information on all Elsevier Butterworth-Heinemann
publications visit our website at www.elsevier.com

Working together to grow
libraries in developing countries

www.elsevier.com | www.bookaid.org | www.sabre.org

ELSEVIER   BOOK AID
            International   Sabre Foundation

Typeset by Charon Tec Pvt. Ltd, Chennai, India
www.charontec.com
Printed and bound in Great Britain by Biddles Ltd, King's Lynn, Norfolk

Cover photographs by D. Buhalis

Contents

List of figures

List of tables

List of case studies

Editors

Dimitrios Buhalis, University of Surrey, Guildford, UK

Dr Dimitrios Buhalis is Course Leader MSc in Tourism Marketing and Leader of eTourism Research at the School of Management, University of Surrey. Dimitrios is also Adjunct Professor at the MBA in Hospitality Management at IMHI (Cornell University–ESSEC) in Paris. Dimitrios has been an active researcher in the areas of ICT and tourism, and also serves as Vice Chairman on the International Federation of Information Technology and Tourism (IFITT) Board. He has editorial roles in a number of academic journals, and he has written, edited or co-edited eight books on eTourism, tourism strategic issues and distribution channels of tourism. Dimitrios is working closely with the World Tourism Organization, the World Travel Tourism Council and the European Commission on a number of eTourism-related projects.

Carlos Costa, Universidade de Aveiro, Aveiro, Portugal

Dr Carlos Costa is Associate Professor at the University of Aveiro. He has been Director of the Tourism teaching programme since 1996, which includes a BSc on Tourism Planning and Development and an MSc on Tourism Management and Development. He holds a PhD and MSc on Tourism Management from the University of Surrey. He is also Editor of the *Tourism & Development Journal*, the first tourism journal that was launched in Portugal. Dr Costa has also been involved in several projects and in consultancy work for the Portuguese Government and other Portuguese organizations. He is currently a Visiting Professor in several universities around the world, and has taught tourism courses in Finland, the UK, Greece, Cuba, Brazil and Goa.

Contributors

Pierre Benckendorff, James Cook University, Townsville, Queensland, Australia
Pierre Benckendorff is a Lecturer in Tourism Management in the School of Business, James Cook University, Australia. Pierre has completed his PhD dissertation on strategic planning and the future of tourist attractions. He has particular interests in tourism futures, visitor attraction management, tourism and leisure technologies, and space tourism.

Jim Butcher, Department of Geography and Tourism, Canterbury Christ Church University College, Canterbury, Kent, UK
Jim Butcher lectures at the University of Greenwich in London. He has a PhD from the University of Birmingham on the subject of NGOs and development thinking. Jim's principal interest is the sociology and politics of tourism development. His book, *Sun, Sand ... and Saving the World: The Moralisation of Tourism*, was published by Routledge in 2003.

Richard Butler, University of Surrey, Guildford, Surrey, UK
Richard Butler is Professor of Tourism in the School of Management, University of Surrey. He is co-editor of the *Journal of Tourism and Hospitality Research*, and the author of publications in tourism and resources management, particularly in the areas of destination development and sustainability.

Chris Cooper, The University Of Queensland, Australia
Chris Cooper is Foundation Professor and Head of the School of Tourism and Leisure Management at The University of Queensland, Australia. He has a PhD from University College London, and worked in market planning and research for the tourism industry before entering higher education. Chris Cooper has worked closely with the World Tourism Organization helping to raise the profile and standards of tourism education globally. He has acted as a consultant and researcher in every region of the world.

P. De Knop, Vrije Universiteit, Brussels, Belgium, and Tilburg University, The Netherlands
Paul De Knop is a full-time Professor at the Vrije Universiteit Brussel, and part-time Professor at the Tilburg University. He holds a PhD in Physical Education and

an MSc in Sports Sociology and Sports Management from the University of Leicester (UK). He is Chairman of the Board of BLOSO (the Flemish Sport Administrative Body).

Hilary du Cros, The University of Hong Kong, Hong Kong, SAR, China
Dr Hilary du Cros works at the Department of Geography, The Hong Kong Polytechnic University, China. She is an Australian cultural heritage management analyst and academic based in Hong Kong. Her research interests are cultural heritage management in Asia, world heritage and cultural tourism. Together with Bob McKercher she authored the book *Cultural Tourism: The Partnership between Tourism and Cultural Heritage Management*.

Daniel R. Fesenmaier, Temple University, Philadelphia, Pennsylvania, USA
Daniel R. Fesenmaier is a Professor in the School for Tourism and Hospitality Management, and Director of the National Laboratory for Tourism and eCommerce, Temple University. His main research and teaching interests focus on the use of information and the Internet in travel decisions, the use of information technology for tourism marketing, and the development of knowledge-based systems for tourism marketing organizations.

Anne Graham, Senior Lecturer, University of Westminster, London, UK
Dr Anne Graham is a Senior Lecturer in Air Transport and Tourism at the University of Westminster. Anne has a first-class BSc degree in Mathematics, an MSc degree in Tourism, and a PhD in air transport and tourism management. She specializes in the research of air transport economics, regulation and management. The second edition of her recent key textbook, *Managing Airports: An International Perspective*, was published by Elsevier in 2003.

Ulrike Gretzel, Texas A&M University, Texas, USA
Ulrike Gretzel is an Assistant Professor of Tourism at Texas A&M University. She received her PhD in Communications from the University of Illinois at Urbana-Champaign, and holds a Masters degree in International Business from the Vienna University of Economics and Business Administration. Her research focuses on persuasion in human–technology interaction, the representation of sensory and emotional aspects of tourism experiences, and issues related to the development and use of intelligent systems in tourism.

Antti Haahti, University of Lapland, Rovaniemi, Finland
Dr Antti Haahti, MBA, BSc is Professor of Tourism in the Faculty of Business and Tourism at the University of Lapland, Finland. His special areas of interest are entrepreneurship in tourism, destination marketing management, marketing research and business models for heritage, rural and village tourism. Professor Haahti is a member of the executive body of the Finnish University Network for Tourism Studies.

C. Michael Hall, University of Otago, Dunedin, New Zealand, and Umeå University, Umeå, Sweden
Michael Hall is a Professor in the Department of Tourism, University of Otago, New Zealand and a visitor in the Department of Social and Economic Geography,

Umeå University, Sweden. Co-editor of *Current Issues in Tourism*, he is the author of a number of publications in the areas of tourism, mobility and regional development.

Dimitri Ioannides, Southwest Missouri State University, Springfield, Missouri, USA
Professor Dimitri Ioannides teaches in the Department of Geography, Geology, and Planning at Southwest Missouri State University. He is also Senior Research Fellow at the Centre for Regional and Tourism Research in Denmark. His research includes economic geography of tourism, sustainable development, and regional policy for island regions.

Peter Jones, School of Management, University of Surrey, Guildford, Surrey, UK
Professor Peter Jones is the International Flight Catering Association (IFCA) Chair of Production and Operations Management and the Subject Leader of Hospitality in the School of Management at the University of Surrey. His research interests include yield management, menu development, operational performance improvement, and innovation. He has also published numerous articles in academic journals such as the *Journal of Production and Operations Management*, the *International Journal of Service Industry Management*, the *Journal of Hospitality and Tourism Research*: the *Surrey Quarterly Review* and many others.

John Kester, Programme Officer, Market Intelligence and Promotion Department, World Tourism Organization, Madrid, Spain
John Kester works at the World Tourism Organization (WTO) in Madrid (Spain) as Senior Research Officer in the field of market research and promotion. He has worked on the *Tourism Economic Report*, 1st edition (1998) and the *Methodological Supplement to World Tourism Statistics*. Since 1999 he has worked in the Market Intelligence and Promotion Department. Among his main duties is participation in the preparation of the yearly *Tourism Market Trends* series of regional reports.

Raija Komppula, University of Joensuu, Joensuu, Finland
Dr Raija Komppula is Professor of Marketing (Acting) in the Department of Business and Economics at the University of Joensuu, Finland. Her special areas of interest are product development in tourism, SMEs in tourism, networking in tourism, and rural tourism. Dr Komppula is also a member of the executive body of the Finnish University Network for Tourism Studies.

Adele Ladkin, International Centre for Tourism and Hospitality Research, School of Services Management, Bournemouth University, Poole, Dorset, UK
Adele Ladkin is Professor of Tourism Employment in the International Centre for Tourism and Hospitality Research, School of Services Management, Bournemouth University. She has worked in education and research for the last ten years and is currently the Head of the Meetings, Incentives, Conferences and Exhibitions Research Unit (MRU). She is currently Assistant Editor-in-Chief for the *International Journal of Tourism Research*, and co-author of *Tourism Employment: Analysis and Planning*.

Vaios J. Lappas, University of Surrey, Guildford, Surrey, UK
Dr Vaios Lappas is Lecturer at the Surrey Space Centre of the Department of Electrical Engineering in the University of Surrey. He teaches various technical

courses in space engineering, and mainly conducts research on the controls and stability of spacecraft and missiles. He also assists the School of Management on seminars related to Space Business and Space Tourism.

Mara Manente, CISET – Ca' Foscari University, Venice, Italy
Mara Manente is Director of CISET. Her main fields of interest are the macroeconomics of tourism, the study of the economic impact of tourism, tourism demand analysis and forecasting, and tourism statistics. She is a consultant for many national and international tourism institutions in Italy and abroad (ISTAT, Eurostat, World Tourism Organization, etc.) and member of the AIEST (Association Internationale des Experts de Sciences Touristiques) and TRC (Tourist Research Centre).

Bob McKercher, The Hong Kong Polytechnic University, Hong Kong, SAR, China
Dr Bob McKercher is Associate Professor in the School of Hotel and Tourism Management, The Hong Kong Polytechnic University, China. He specializes in cultural tourism, marketing and product development. He worked in the Canadian tourism industry before joining academia. Together with Hilary du Cros he authored the book *Cultural Tourism: The Partnership between Tourism and Cultural Heritage Management.*

Tanja Mihalič, University of Ljubljana, Ljubljana, Slovenia
Tanja Mihalič is a Professor in Tourism Economics and Management at the University of Ljubljana, Faculty of Economics. Her research covers a wide range of tourism-related economic and management issues, and focuses on environmental policy measures and labelling. She wrote *Environmental Economics in Tourism* (in Slovenian and, with Claude Kaspar, in German), and lectures on environmental economics and management in tourism.

Valeria Minghetti, CISET – Ca' Foscari University, Venice, Italy
Valeria Minghetti is Senior Researcher at CISET. After specializing in Tourism Economics at Ca' Foscari University, she now coordinates various national and international projects for CISET. Her main fields of interest are tourism demand analysis, the economic impact of tourism, tourism and transports, tourism and information technology. She is a Board member of IFITT (the International Federation for Information Technology and Travel & Tourism) and member of the Scientific Committee of ENTER, IFITT's Global Travel & Tourism Technology and eBusiness Forum.

Richard Mitchell, Department of Tourism, University of Otago, Dunedin, New Zealand
Richard Mitchell is a Senior Lecturer in the Department of Tourism, University of Otago, New Zealand. He has previously worked at La Trobe University and the University of Western Sydney in Australia. Richard has interests in wine marketing and consumer behaviour, and conducted an extensive longitudinal study of wine tourism in New Zealand for his doctoral research.

Gianna Moscardo, James Cook University, Townsville, Queensland, Australia
Dr Gianna Moscardo is a Senior Lecturer in the School of Business at James Cook University. Her doctorate in applied social psychology explored the nature

of visitor experiences in heritage attractions. Her research interests are analysing visitor experiences and the variables that influence them.

Joseph T. O'Leary, Texas A&M University, Texas, USA

Joseph T. O'Leary is a Professor and Head of the Department of Recreation, Parks and Tourism Sciences at Texas A&M University. His main research and teaching interests focus on the data mining for tourism marketing and knowledge systems for destination marketing organizations.

Philip Pearce, School of Business, James Cook University, Townsville, Queensland, Australia

Philip Pearce is the Foundation Professor of Tourism at James Cook University in Australia. His research interests include understanding tourist motivation and satisfaction, aspects of emerging and established tourism markets, and tourism–community relationships.

Aurora Pedro, University of Valencia, Valencia, Spain

Aurora Pedro is Senior Lecturer in the Department of Applied Economics, University of Valencia, Spain. She has been a consultant for the World Tourism Organization, and often delivers the WTO Tourism Policy Strategy Course. She has written a number of articles for academic journals and books.

Yvette Reisinger, Florida International University, Miami, Florida, USA

Dr Yvette Reisinger is Associate Professor of Tourism in the School of Hospitality and Tourism Management at Florida International University, Miami. She is a specialist in tourism marketing and conducts research in the area of cross-cultural differences in tourist behaviour, cross-cultural communication, and socio-cultural impacts of tourism. She is the author of the books *Cross-Cultural Behaviour in Tourism: Concepts and Analysis* and *International Tourism: Cultures and Behaviour*. Dr Reisinger is also a Regional Editor (Australia and Asia) of *Tourism – An International Interdisciplinary Journal* and editorial board member of *International Journal of Culture, Leisure and Tourism Research*; *Tourism Review International*; and *Journal of Vacation Marketing*.

Greg Richards, Fundació Interarts, Barcelona, Spain

Greg Richards is Coordinator at Fundació Interarts, Barcelona, Spain. His main research interests are the relationship between culture and tourism, the development of creative tourism and new travel styles.

Noel Scott, School of Tourism and Leisure Management, The University of Queensland, Australia

Dr Noel Scott is a lecturer at the University of Queensland, Australia. His research interests involve strategic destination management and marketing. Prior to his academic career Noel was Strategic Services Manager for Tourism Queensland, where he acquired extensive knowledge of the tourism industry in Australia. He has also worked as a consultant on a number of tourism projects, and is a past Chairman of the Market Research Society (Queensland).

Melanie Smith, University of Greenwich, Greenwich, London, UK
Melanie Smith is a Senior Lecturer in Cultural Tourism Management at the University of Greenwich. She has been Director of both the BA Tourism Management and the MA Cultural Tourism Management there. She is also currently Co-ordinator of ATLAS Europe, and her recent publications include the book *Issues in Cultural Tourism Studies* (Routledge, 2003).

Dorota Ujma, University of Luton, Luton, Bedfordshire, UK
Dorota Ujma is a Lecturer at the University of Luton. Previously she taught at the Krakow University of Economics, Poland. She completed her Masters degree in Krakow, and her PhD at the University of Luton. Her current research interests are focused upon tourism marketing, specifically distribution in tourism and hospitality, health resorts and tourism associations and their role in the travel trade.

Julie Wilson, Department of Geography and History, Universitat Rovira i Virgili, Tarragona, Spain; University of the West of England, UK
Julie Wilson is a Research Fellow at the Universitat Rovira i Virgili, Tarragona, Spain, with research and teaching interests in the geography of youth and independent travel, urban tourism and tourism imagery.

Foreword

Over the past few years, the travel and tourism industry has had to contend with a series of unprecedented challenges. Political uncertainty, terrorism, consumer wariness and economic turbulence have all placed enormous pressure on our industry. These events have left their mark – not only on the balance sheets of industry players and on global employment, but also in terms of changes in consumer demand and behaviour. In an effort to adapt to the shifting marketplace, the travel and tourism industry has had to restructure and refocus its efforts. While business plans have become increasingly short term, more and more governments are realizing that they cannot leave travel and tourism growth to chance. This emerging global consciousness represents a great opportunity for our industry.

In response to this opportunity, the World Travel & Tourism Council (WTTC), the forum for global business leaders in travel and tourism, has created a new vision and strategy. This vision of 'New Tourism' is set out in the Council's *Blueprint for New Tourism*, and calls for a coherent partnership between the private sector and public authorities. New Tourism is geared to delivering commercially successful products, but in a way that ensures benefits for everyone. It looks beyond short-term considerations and focuses on benefits not only for people who travel, but also for people in the communities they visit, and for their respective natural, social and cultural environments.

Through the *Blueprint*, the travel and tourism industry has declared its readiness to do its part. Now we call upon other stakeholders to commit to the policies set out in the *Blueprint* and to join us in building a new vision of tourism which will bring benefits to the wider world. Therefore:

1. Governments should recognize travel and tourism as a top priority, and
   - show leadership by defining coherent and streamlined management structures that can efficiently drive New Tourism
   - elevate travel and tourism to strategic national level with senior-level policy-making
   - factor travel and tourism into all policies and decision-making, to promote growth that respects both business needs and the well-being of citizens.
2. Business should balance economics with people, culture and environment, and
   - adapt strategic thinking so as to develop tourism with benefits for everyone
   - extend and diversify product offerings to improve yields and social value

- spearhead innovative management and help to spread best practice through corporate social responsibility.
3. Tourism and travel stakeholders should develop a shared pursuit of long-term growth and prosperity by
   - cooperating in identifying opportunities for growth
   - focusing on building travel and tourism that opens up prospects for people – from employment to development
   - working together to remove impediments to growth – from infrastructure shortcomings to pollution, and from outdated legislation to unmet health and security concerns.

With these issues and priorities in mind, we are particularly pleased to welcome the *Tourism Business Frontiers* and *Tourism Management Dynamics* books, which explore not only developments in the supply and demand of tourism but also a wide range of trends and management tools. The books, written by renowned researchers from around the globe, provide contemporary thinking and contribute to the exploration of the future for empowering the tourism industry. The books provide an insight into the travel and tourism industry's transformation, and support our vision for realizing our industry's potential for growth and ensuring maximum and sustainable benefits for everyone involved.

Jean-Claude Baumgarten
President, World Travel & Tourism Council

Preface

As this book was written, the Athens 2004 Olympic Torch Relay travelled the globe proclaiming: 'Pass the flame, unite the world'. The Olympic flame is the primary symbol of the Olympic ideals: noble competition, friendship and peaceful coexistence. Apart from sport, education and tourism are the only other ideals that promote similar principles and can contribute to a more peaceful, prosperous and equitable world. Tourism is one of the most dynamic and challenging global industries. Its international nature, in combination with the need to coordinate the needs of a number of stakeholders, makes peaceful and constructive collaboration essential for the successful development of tourism products and destinations. Tourism is also increasingly responsible for poverty alleviation and for a greater understanding of our world – leading to peace and global prosperity.

Exploring the future of tourism not only enables businessmen, politicians, managers and academics better to understand the key trends and developments, but also prepares tourism organizations and destinations to devise strategies and policies to strengthen their competitiveness and ensure their future prosperity. *Tourism Business Frontiers* and its affiliate publication *Tourism Management Dynamics* look into the future of tourism and explore six key areas that will determine how the industry will develop globally. These include trends, management techniques, tools, consumers, products and industry. The books aim to provide analytical tools to enable both tourism professionals and researchers to identify trends and predict the future in order to strengthen the competitiveness of the industry. They should also assist tourism destination organizations around the world to take advantage of predictions and prepare their regions for enjoying better advantages from tourism. Finally, the books aim to educate younger generations of tourism professionals, who are currently studying in courses around the world.

We hope that you will enjoy the two books, and we are looking forward to the feedback, contributions and debates that will inform future editions, and the meetings that we will organize on the topic. Predicting the future of tourism is a dynamic process that will keep all of us busy for many years to come.

Have a great tourism future! Happy 'Pass the flame, unite the world...'.

Dimitrios Buhalis and Carlos Costa
June 2005

Acknowledgments

Tourism Business Frontiers and *Tourism Management Dynamics* have a long history. We, Carlos and Dimitrios, first met at the University of Surrey, looking for knowledge and challenging the world. Many people were instrumental in our professional development. We are particularly grateful to Chris Cooper for leading the development of our academic career, and for providing inspiration and solid frameworks for further research. Years later, over a beer at seaside Estoril, we were looking for material to systematize knowledge and explore the emerging global changes for our students. Ideas were floated and the key concepts for the book projects emerged. Before we knew it, colleagues, friends and leading researchers from around the world (most all three!) were invited to contribute to the project. Sally North, Kathryn Grant, Francesca Ford and their colleagues at Butterworth-Heinemann adopted the project, provided helpful guidance and offered a cheerful friendship that made the author–publisher relationship a great pleasure. A project of this nature is a huge undertaking; bringing together 50 contributions from 72 authors spread across 20 countries was to prove both an academic challenge and an immense pleasure. We are grateful to all colleagues and friends who contributed to this project, and would like to thank them for the academic debates and stimulation we enjoyed through the process.

During the preparation period of these books a number of things affected us, both personally and professionally. The project survived the best-ever organized EURO2004 Football Cup in Portugal … when the Greeks won the cup after beating the Portuguese team twice. Both nations celebrated together – demonstrating in practice what noble competition, friendship and peaceful coexistence are all about. We were also saddened by the premature loss of Dr Felix Martins of the University of Algarve, a great friend and colleague, reminding us where the future lies for all of us. We were also extremely sad about the tragic loss of life of both tourists and local residents and the disaster that the tsunami caused in Asia, demonstrating the power of nature. And we watched our children grow, bringing hope, dreams and inspiration for the future. We must acknowledge the contribution of our families, Maria and Stella in Guildford and Graça, Sebastião and Lourenço in Aveiro, who have suffered from our absence, looked after us when we were editing, and often reminded us that there is more to life than tourism research.

1

Introduction

Carlos Costa and Dimitrios Buhalis

Tourism as a phenomenon is constantly pushing its frontier forward, expanding its importance and involving more people globally. Tourism is now the world's largest industry. Evidence clearly demonstrates that the industry of the twenty-first century will move further than it has ever thought. From the 'mere' 25 million international arrivals registered in the 1950s, tourism had climbed to the impressive figure of 700 million international travellers by the turn of the century and generated a considerable proportion of the GDP in most countries of the world. More importantly, tourism is critical for peripheral, rural, alpine and insular regions, which find it difficult to develop alternative industries. Regrettably, tourism is often seen by governments and development organizations as a 'soft' investment industry, and authorities tend to underestimate its significance until major crises demonstrate the scale of its contribution and complexity. In spite of the world's recession towards the end of the twentieth and beginning of the twenty-first centuries, prompted by the turmoil caused by the terrorists attacks of 11 September 2001 in the United States, the Afghanistan crisis, the two Iraq wars, the bombings in Bali, Egypt and Spain, the escalation of oil prices, SARS, foot and mouth disease, the devastating earthquakes and tsunami in Southern Asia, and the collapse of a number of airlines, all forecasts demonstrate that the number of international travellers will sharply increase in the near future.

Over the next two decades it is predicted that tourism will more than double, reaching 1.6 billion international arrivals by 2020, representing an average rate of growth of more than 4 per cent per year. Despite this unprecedented scale of expansion, these figures are not surprising when taking into account the fact that the expansion of tourism is linked to improvements in the living standards of the world's population and to the availability of disposable income, especially in the developing world. Gradually expenditure on leisure will overtake the amount of money spent on housing, food and transport, demonstrating that leisure and tourism are becoming essential parts of modern life. To take advantage of this expansion, governments, investors and stakeholders in general need to develop a comprehensive appreciation of the trends and issues that will shape the future of tourism. They should design suitable infrastructures and superstructures, as well as comprehensive planning and management responses, to ensure that they will benefit from this expansion.

Tourism Business Frontiers provides an insight into the future dimensions of the tourism industry. It concentrates on the demand and supply sides by analysing the most significant consumer trends, as well as the product developments and industry restructuring. This edited publication has been written by some of the most well-known and internationally widely-quoted tourism academics and researchers who, based on empirical evidence, analyse past trends, describe the state of the art, and provide vision for the future of tourism as it is emerging around the globe. As demonstrated in Figure 1.1, an understanding of the demand and supply trends

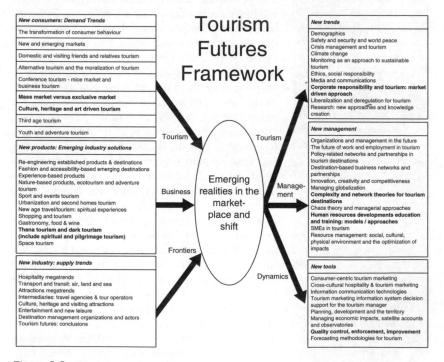

Figure 1.1 The framework of tourism futures

2

enables the development of suitable management techniques and tools for taking advantage of emerging trends. While the focus of this book is geared towards the demand and supply trends that will shape the future of the tourism industry, and in particular of its consumers, products and industry, the affiliate book, *Tourism Management Dynamics*, examines the techniques and tools that will shape the evolution of the tourism sector in terms of its megatrends, management and tools.

Tourism will expand greatly in the future, mainly due to the enormous transformations that are taking place on both the demand and the supply sides. The changing profile of the world population, improvements in living standards, more disposable income, fewer working hours, growing leisure time, better-educated people, ageing of the world population and a more curious youth market will decisively fuel tourism demand. The expansion of the tourism markets will come not only from well-established and mature tourist regions, which have almost reached their plateau stage, but also from new territories where tourism is still in its infancy. For example, economic growth and socio-political changes in China and India, which together have a population of more than 2.5 billion people, are expected to contribute significantly to the growth of international tourism. Even small rates of growth in these two countries will have strong repercussions on the world tourism market.

Expected growth rates as well as the transformation of consumer behaviour and industry structures will also be evident in mature markets and in better-off world regions. The benefits of domestic tourism arc also becoming more evident, and this market is growing in a number of well-established tourist destinations to become as important as international tourism. The expansion of domestic and residential tourism around the Mediterranean, and in particular in Spain, Portugal, Greece and Italy, provides a good example. Both international and domestic tourism are likely to be fuelled by a number of presently 'smaller' and niche market segments. Visiting friends and relatives (VFR), conference tourism, third age, youth, educational and adventurous tourism will boost the industry, as new consumers are changing their behaviour and attitude towards the tourism sector and are looking for these 'new' forms of leisure.

Part One of this book discusses the new consumers. The development of the 'new' tourist signifies consumers who are becoming knowledgeable and are seeking exceptional value for money and time. The new, sophisticated traveller has emerged as a result of experience and knowledge. Tourists from the major generating regions of the world have become frequent travellers, are linguistically and technologically skilled, and can function in multicultural and demanding environments overseas. Special interest activities and independently organized tourism will increasingly grow at the expense of mass tourism and package tours, which are based on low prices and low quality. Consumers enabled by information available on the Internet can develop their own experiences, based on dynamic packaging and flexibly created individualized itineraries. Hence a new, experienced, sophisticated and demanding tourist is emerging, looking for authentic and environmentally friendly experiences and exceptional value for both time and money.

However, the expansion and transformation of tourism will not only come from the demand side. New policies and developments launched from the supply side also shape the future of the tourism product and industry, and Part Two discusses these new products. While developed destinations in Europe, America, Australia and Asia strengthen their positions, opening and diversifying their markets to make them more competitive, formerly closed markets and less-developed tourist territories will join the tourist sector and make their offering greater, more diversified and more competitive. Tourism growth is becoming an inevitable regional development option, as most places around the world – and in particular insular and peripheral areas – seek to take advantage of and attract tourism demand in order to increase their prosperity. This is the case for most regions, even those that have not previously been regarded as potential destinations – such as urban centres (e.g. Bradford, Liverpool, Leeds), remote and hostile regions (e.g. Antarctica, Alaska, Greenland), disaster sites (e.g. battlefields, natural disaster areas) and industrial sites (e.g. nuclear stations, factories and mines). There is also a proliferation of smaller, purpose-built or converted 'attractions/leisure facilities', such as theme parks, staged experiences (e.g. Canterbury Tales or London Dungeon), agricultural farms, snake farms, factories, rebuilt traditional villages etc.

In Europe, the enlargement of the EU frontiers and the strengthening of the single currency will make the oldest continent even stronger. In North America, the USA and Canada will also flex their muscles with their 'natural' appeal to attract larger numbers of national and international travellers. In South America, the enlargement of the Mercosul towards the Caribbean, the launching of new agreements targeting the movement of capital and human resources, and a greater specialization on eco- and cultural tourism will also augment the region's capacity to attract more tourists. The growth of tourism in countries such as Brazil, Cuba and Ecuador provides a good example. Down south, Australia and New Zealand will affirm their distinctness with a special appeal for adventure, beach, sports, and anthropological tourists. In Asia, despite the economic crisis in the early 2000s and the massive disaster caused by the 2004 earthquakes and tsunami, tourism will continue to grow rapidly. Established destinations such as Indonesia, Thailand and Malaysia will continue to expand, and the industry will steadily spread to developing countries such as Burma, Vietnam, Laos, China and India. In many places, tourism will be the only form of economic activity to bring direct benefits to local communities.

The arrival of increasing numbers of consumers, better-educated and more sophisticated will prompt the tourist industry to launch new products and brands and reinvent traditional markets. Established destinations founded on the 'sun–sea–sand' products will have to re-engineer their offerings and design new and more sophisticated products to complement, diversify, and improve the attractiveness and quality of their traditional offers. Alongside beach tourism, the tourism sector will register a steady development of new products based on natural, business, leisure, anthropological, gastronomic and spiritual resources. Such a tendency will be strengthened in the future as tourists increasingly look for new and fashionable products and destinations, and also because the tourist sector will be seeking to differentiate its offering in order to charge premium prices.

Focusing on value rather than volume, the industry should be using renewable resources to generate unique experiences and to attract more business benefits from smaller amounts of tourist growth. The growing awareness that tourism ought not to exceed sustainability limits will gain accrued importance in future. This means that one of the major challenges that will face destinations in the future will be to introduce better organized and sustainable products that will support regional development without threatening the long-term prosperity of the destination. Hence tourism production should increase its efficiency and generate more profit and value-added for all stakeholders, but at the same time minimize the resource consumption. High margins and low volumes should be the strategy followed, especially by new destinations, to support sustainability and impact optimization. Tourist products need to adjust and become more complex and rewarding, supporting a better-organized tourist industry. Such a trend will be underpinned by the fact that tourists' average length of stay at destinations will continue to shrink. Conversely, spending may tend to increase because tourists will need less time to 'consume' the place. Tourists will increasingly be looking for stronger, more remarkable and more rewarding experiences. Destinations will have to be planned and designed to ensure that unique, fashionable and differentiated products are offered, and that the majority of the tourist expenditure remains in the region.

New consumers and new products will therefore lead to the transformation of the tourist industry, and this is what Part Three looks at. The future of the tourism industry will be dominated by two megatrends. On the one hand, there will be a tendency leading to the creation of mega-attractions, with a strong capacity to attract large numbers of tourists into the area. These honey-pots, or 'tourism intensive poles', will be characterized by the offer of attractive, fashionable and rewarding products, with the capacity to impact on the tourists' imagination. They will be underpinned by clustered tourist industries which will be interconnected with the outside world by efficient 'transit regions' led by well-organized networks of transportation and an extremely dynamic range of intermediaries. This new emerging tourist industry will require more complex management of operations and logistics, as well as support from professional destination management organizations. New forms of tour operation, retail and intermediation will emerge to take advantage of the ever-changing technological capabilities and also to reflect the demand trends.

The tendency towards the creation of growth poles will also boost the creation of smaller and adjunct offers, spinning off from these poles and towards neighbouring areas. Most of the present lighter, unstructured and niche tourist offers will gradually become networked and anchored to big businesses, enabling product enhancement and expansion. Forms of nature, heritage, adventure, education, scientific, business and spiritual-based tourism, as well as youth and senior tourism, will gradually be developed to supplement and enhance the mainstream tourism business, offering additional value to specific market segments. Most of these niche markets will be managed in a more professional way, thus enhancing and complementing tourist offers located at large poles. They will assist the optimization of the tourism industry profitability, stimulate diversification, and improve the levels of occupancy of infrastructure, superstructure and equipment that currently remain under-utilized for most of the time owing to the seasonal characteristics of the tourism industry. In addition, such niche offers will be supported by more professional forms of management that appreciate and serve better the needs of particular segments.

As a result of the growth and enhancement of tourism supply, competition will increase, making it much more difficult to achieve success. Destinations and enterprises at the declining stage of their lifecycle will find it much more difficult to survive. The inevitability of tourism development and competition will have positive and negative impacts throughout the world. As a consequence, tourism destinations and enterprises will need to rationalize their strategic and operational planning and management in order to satisfy their main stakeholders, optimize their tourism impacts and/or profitability, and ensure sustainability. Tourism research provides a comprehensive range of tools for tourism management and planning. Hopefully, governments and international organizations (EU, WTO, the World Bank etc.) will recognize tourism as the driving force of economies and therefore be willing to invest in and support development.

Tourism Business Frontiers aims at providing an insight into these new realities and trends that are emerging worldwide. The book comprises a blend of 24 chapters concerned with specific niche markets and contributed by globally renowned academics, who provide empirical evidence and vision for the future of the tourism industry. The chapters are rooted in a structure that comprises:

1. A brief overview of the historical evolution of the area, as far as knowledge, issues trends, managerial implications and paradigms are concerned
2. A comprehensive explanation of the 'state of the art' of the issue
3. An exploration and discussion of emerging trends, approaches, models and paradigms
4. A provision for the future vision of the tourism industry
5. A presentation of emerging and leading (best) practices in the tourism sector.

With the objective of supporting academics and practitioners to explore the issues easily and schematically, a range of pedagogic material (powerpoint slides, web pages, discussion points and questions) helpful for both business meetings and classroom discussions is provided in the accompanying material available on the Internet. This book is also complemented by *Tourism Management Dynamics*, which explores the emerging management techniques and tools required for addressing the emerging megatrends in the marketplace.

A companion website containing material for both tutors and students can be found at http://books.elsevier.com/hospitality?ISBN=0750663774

Part One: New Consumers

2

The transformation of consumer behaviour

Ulrike Gretzel, Daniel R. Fesenmaier and Joseph T. O'Leary

Introduction

The emergence of new information and communication technologies (ICTs), higher levels of wealth, more leisure time, and changes in values and lifestyles due to a new consciousness regarding one's own needs as well as regarding social responsibilities, have led to a new breed of tourism consumers. The new consumers of tourism products and services are more informed, more independent, more individualistic and more involved (Poon, 1993). In addition, the new travellers are used to having many choices, expect speed, and use technologies to overcome the physical constraints of bodies and borders. However, consumer behaviour has also become increasingly contradictory (Marobella, 2004). Many travellers are 'trading up' (Silverstein and Fiske, 2003), and are more willing than ever to pay for luxury travel experiences. At the same time, they will fiercely search the Web for 'the best deal' on hotel rooms and flights. Travel behaviour has also become more unpredictable: a traveller who bought an organized

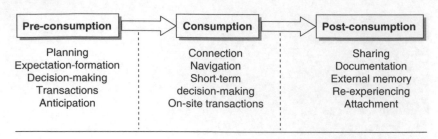

Pre-consumption	Consumption	Post-consumption
Planning	Connection	Sharing
Expectation-formation	Navigation	Documentation
Decision-making	Short-term	External memory
Transactions	decision-making	Re-experiencing
Anticipation	On-site transactions	Attachment

Figure 2.1 Communication and information needs in the three stages of tourism consumption

city sightseeing tour the previous year might engage in a month-long trekking adventure the year after.

In contrast to many consumer goods and services, the consumption of travel experiences involves often extensive pre- and post-consumption stages in addition to the actual trip, which itself can spread over several weeks or months. These stages of the tourism consumption process are typically information intensive. Internet-based technologies have come to play a significant role in supporting consumers throughout this multi-stage process. The specific way in which the various technologies are used in the different stages depends on the particular communication and information needs they are expected to serve (Figure 2.1). Internet technologies are used in the pre-consumption phase to obtain the information necessary for planning trips, to formulate correct expectations, to evaluate, compare, and select alternatives, and to communicate with the providers of tourism products and services in order to prepare or execute transactions. In contrast, the functions served by these technologies during the actual consumption of tourism experiences are more related to being connected and obtaining detailed information relevant to a specific place and moment in time. During the post-consumption phase, Internet technologies are used in ways that allow for sharing, documenting and reliving tourism experiences through storytelling, as well as establishing close relationships with the places, attractions or product/service providers – such as in the case of Frequent Flyer programmes.

The new travellers are empowered by the Internet, which provides them with easy and cheap access to various information sources and extended communities (Rifkin, 2000; Windham and Orton, 2000). Further, the Internet is a highly personalized medium and new consumers expect marketers to address and cater to their complex personal preferences. Consequently, new travellers are 'in control' and have become central players in the process of creating and shaping brands and experiences. This chapter outlines those aspects of travel-related consumer behaviour that establish the foundation for most of the transformations that can currently be observed. Specifically, three roles that consumers play when they travel have been identified as critical for understanding current and predicting future travel behaviour:

1. Travellers as users of new technologies
2. Travellers as co-producers of meaningful experiences
3. Travellers as storytellers.

Travellers as users of new technologies

New Web-based and mobile technologies have become important drivers of change in travel behaviour. They provide travellers with greater access to information, and facilitate the purchase of remote tourism products. They also offer greater transparency, and thus supply travellers with increased negotiating power in the market, as well as new levels of connectedness before, during and after trips. The specific influences of new technology on consumers' information search, decision-making, trip experience and trip recollection have to be understood within the framework of the 'five Ws' of technology use:

1. Who uses these new technologies?
2. What emerging technologies and types of content/information are used?
3. When do consumers use new technologies?
4. Where does the use of new technologies occur?
5. Why are new technologies used?

Who uses these new technologies?

Regardless of what specific technology one looks at, a general pattern that can be recognized in most important origin markets is the increasing extent of use as well as increasing usage across different consumer segments, whether defined by age, income, education, etc. Internet use among Americans aged 65 or older, for example, jumped by 47 per cent between 2000 and 2004 (Pew Internet & American Life Project, 2004). With this growing use of information technologies across demographic and social groups, specifying who the users are in terms of traditional variables is becoming increasingly irrelevant. Many interactions are now mediated through user profiles (e.g. destination recommendations are made based on a user's saved preferences), agents (e.g. a traveller's query at a destination portal website is answered using the index of destination-specific pages compiled by a Web robot, or a traveller signs up for an alert at an online travel agency website to receive an email when a travel product is added that meets particular specifications) or avatars (e.g. travellers create their own virtual personas to interact with fellow travellers in virtual communities or through instant messaging services). Thus, it appears to be especially important to think about users as representing ever-changing preference structures and to envision the implications of mediated rather than direct interactions with potential visitors. Defining a traveller in terms of dynamic preferences rather than rigid socio-demographic characteristics opens up new ways of thinking about appropriate marketing strategies. With the growing availability and use of spiders, Web robots and other types of intelligent agents, it will also become ever more important to present tourism products in a way that makes them accessible for these computer programs.

What emerging technologies and types of content/ information are used?

The role of travellers as users of technology has changed, with users increasingly interacting with the medium as creators rather than just passive receivers of information. Consumers are not only accessing content on the Web, but also engaging in creating and sharing content through digital cameras, Web cams, picture phones, virtual community websites, Web blogs, etc. In the context of tourism, this active participation of consumers is becoming especially prevalent through websites that provide consumers with the opportunity to save and print their own travel itineraries, or to purchase tourism packages dynamically assembled based on their personal preferences. Consequently, technologies that allow for an active participation in the creation, presentation and sharing of travel information have grown and will continue to grow in importance.

The Internet provides travellers with a greater amount as well as variety of information than any other information source. However, search engine usage statistics show that consumers rely heavily on intelligent search technologies to navigate the abundance of information available on the Web. Almost 85 per cent of US Internet users seek information through search engines (Emarketer, 2004), and a recent UK-based study indicates that over 40 per cent of travel website visits come via search engines (Travelmole, 2004). In addition, the rising popularity of recommendation systems suggests that consumers do not always have a clear idea of what they are looking for and still need the kind of advice they used to receive from real world travel agents. Emerging technologies used on many retailing websites have also led to higher expectations regarding the ability to inspect products before they are purchased. Tourism websites increasingly recognize consumers' need to imagine and thus pre-experience a trip through the help of virtual tours, videos, suggested itineraries and personal testimonials of other travellers. However, current approaches are still very limited, and will not be able to satisfy the increasing demand for online product trial experiences.

When do consumers use new technologies?

The '24/7' quality of the Internet has important implications for information accessibility in general. As Web content is available all the time, users begin expecting the same from communication, feedback and other services provided by the tourism industry, both online and offline. The Internet changes the concept of time, which leads to new communication and consumption patterns that require fundamental organizational adjustments as well as new marketing strategies and approaches.

Travellers increasingly use ICT throughout all phases of their trip, starting with information search and booking before the trip. Mobile technologies, hand-held devices used in museums, interactive kiosks and Internet access provided by Internet cafés or accommodation establishments enable technology use while *en route*. Personal websites, virtual communities, email newsletters, blogs etc. create opportunities to remember and re-experience trips after their completion. This growing usage of technology throughout all phases of a trip implies that consumers are not only more informed but also more engaged. The challenge for the tourism industry lies in translating the enhanced contact with a customer into greater satisfaction and relationship-building/loyalty and, ultimately, greater profitability.

Where does the use of new technologies occur?

The locus of technology use has shifted tremendously. Mobile devices afford uses outside the realm of offices or homes, and the development of wearable computing is expected to push this trend even further. Computing has become embedded and is increasingly ambient in nature. For instance, calls can be made from almost anywhere, trains, taxicabs and airlines are starting to provide Internet access, GPS technology has become indispensable for orientation in remote locations, and mobile phones allow for restaurant tables and hotel rooms to be reserved while on the road. It can be expected that this ubiquity of information access and communication possibilities will have an enormous influence on travel planning behaviour and travel patterns – for example, more travel decisions will be made while *en route* and booking cycles will become increasingly shorter.

Why are new technologies used?

The Web has evolved from a shopping catalogue-like platform for one-way broadcast communication to an interactive medium that affords many forms of communication, interaction and transaction. Knowledge creation and learning in an online context are increasingly supported through technologies that help users build social capital, which illustrates another function of technologies – community building. Whether using cell phones, instant messenger, or message boards and chat-rooms in virtual communities, the purpose of using the technology is often to connect with family members or peers. Yet another reason for using the Internet is the value such technologies provide by allowing users to have and share experiences. Travel research has only recently started to investigate the hedonic, emotional and social in addition to the functional aspects of information search and technology use (Vogt and Fesenmaier, 1998; Blythe *et al.*, 2003). The popularity of online gaming confirms that consumers seek flow experiences, fantasies, feelings, friends and fun, in addition to functional benefits, when engaging with technologies.

The reasons for using technology often depend on the context of life and the specific needs of the user at a point in time. The 'new' traveller has many wants and needs that change rapidly. Finding ways to use existing and emerging technologies for need identification and individualization of content and design has become crucial. Imagining why travellers use technology in certain situations can greatly assist the tourism industry in anticipating future needs and wants, and consequently in defining what specific functions to support and what information to present.

Travellers as co-producers of meaningful experiences

Marketing researchers and economists alike have drawn attention to the experiential nature of goods and services (Pine and Gilmore, 1999; Holbrook, 2000). Hedonic values and emotional responses to consumption situations are especially relevant for marketing tourism, given the inherently experiential nature of tourism products and services. Also, the Internet is a highly personalized medium, and new consumers expect marketers to address and cater to their complex personal preferences. Engagement is key to superior experiences from which personal meaning can be derived (Shedroff, 2001). Thus tourists have evolved from pure consumers to co-producers of meaningful experiences, for instance through using dynamic packaging and creating personalized online itineraries. Consequently, new travellers are 'in control' and have become important players in the process of creating and shaping their experience at destinations and attractions (Gottdiener, 1997).

In search of meaning

Norton (2003) argues that consumer demand has evolved from a focus on products and services that conveyed a certain brand image in the 1980s, and themed brand experiences in the 1990s, to a new emphasis on meaningful consumption experiences in the new millennium. This shift has resulted from a general decline in cultural capital (family, health, safety, well-being, etc.). Whereas consumption was previously a means for building and displaying wealth, consumers increasingly seek opportunities to create cultural capital through the purchase and use of products and services. The consumption of tourism products has traditionally played a significant role in providing experiences that can increase cultural capital by delivering opportunities for the creation of personal meaning, such as connecting with one's family, becoming emotionally attached to a place, or increasing one's sense of self by discovering a piece of personal history. Thus tourism experiences are becoming ever more important for the new travellers who are constantly in search of a purpose for their lives. Accordingly, there is also a rise in the use of tourism for adding meaning to the consumption of other consumer goods – for instance, through a tour of a factory in which the family car was produced or a favourite brand of beer is brewed. The new travellers, with their highly individualized and often hybrid motivations and needs, can derive unique meanings from many different experiences in a variety of ways. The only prerequisite for meaning creation seems to be active mental and/or physical involvement in the experience. This constitutes an opportunity as well as a challenge for the providers and marketers of tourism products, as they need to encourage involvement and facilitate these highly personalized consumption experiences.

Embodied cognition

The consumption of products such as destinations is a rich source of sensory, affective and cognitive associations that result in memorable and rewarding brand experiences (Schmitt, 1999). Thus purely cognitive models of consumers can provide only limited explanations for the holistic and often largely hedonic consumption experiences that form the basis of pleasure trips. What is needed is an extended conceptualization of consumption that takes sensory experiences and emotions into account. Such a model is based on the notion of 'embodied cognition' (Rosa and Malter, 2002), which assumes that higher-level cognition is dependent on our bodily experience of the world around us, and thus recognizes that information derived from our senses has to be considered when trying to understand how consumers anticipate, plan, experience and remember trips (see Case study 2.1).

Case study 2.1 Discoverhongkong.com, Hong Kong, China

The website of the Hong Kong Tourism Board has translated many of the consumer needs discussed here into actual website features. It encourages tourists not only to visit Hong Kong but also to 'sense it', 'taste it', 'love it', 'live it' and 'share it'. The website supports the creation of meaningful experiences through stories told by Hong Kong residents as well as a list of guided walks that visitors can join to interact with locals and learn about life in Hong Kong. It provides consumers with opportunities to experience the destination before their trip through tools such as Web cams, videos, sound files, an interactive map linked to virtual tours of the sights, etc. It thus engages several of the human senses instead of providing a simple visual experience of the city. In addition, the website allows for social interactions by offering a 'Tell a Friend' feature that can be used to conveniently email content discovered on the website to others who might be interested. A treasure hunt game and an interactive gallery ensure that website visitors have fun while planning a trip to the area. The website also fosters relationship-building through the possibility of subscribing to a Hong Kong E-zine.

Important trends in this context are the heightened awareness of the significance of their senses among consumers, and an increased recognition among marketers of the sensory and emotional components of pleasure (Le Bel *et al.*, 2004). Aromatherapy dishwashing detergents and artificially produced 'new car smells' are examples that illustrate the wide-reaching implications of this new demand for superior sensory experiences. E-commerce has contributed to this new emphasis on the senses by making problems associated with the lack of additional sensory information in the communication of product aspects apparent. At the same time, new technological developments promise inexpensive and readily available substitutes for real-world product trials that are particularly important for experience goods (Klein, 1998). Thus, especially for Internet-based tourism marketing, these trends suggest that the integration of sensory information on websites plays an important role in supporting information search and decision-making processes by providing the sensory cues essential for the conceptualization and evaluation of travel-related consumption experiences. Integrating sensory information is particularly important for developing more human-centric user modelling strategies, especially in the context of destination recommendation systems. Sensory experiences associated with destinations are complex but not idiosyncratic, and therefore can be used to communicate certain tourism experiences to specific groups of travellers (Gretzel and Fesenmaier, 2003). With a growing awareness of their senses, travellers are expected increasingly to value communication strategies that address their need for sensory information.

Travellers as storytellers

People love to tell and hear stories. Most of the knowledge we use in our day-to-day communication and reasoning is comprised of stories (Schank and Berman,

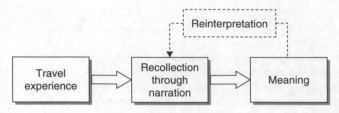

Figure 2.2 The role of stories in the process of deriving meaning from travel experiences

2002). Stories help us make sense of the world. Telling others (and ourselves) stories about an experience is an important means of transforming various isolated pieces of sensory and cognitive information into a coherent whole, making the experience more memorable and allowing us to derive meaning from it. Packer and Jordan (2001) define a narrative as something that reflects the associative tendencies of our mind, drawing attention to previously undetected connections and links between disparate ideas and elements. Accordingly, stories play an important role in the recollection of travel experiences, which are usually comprised of many different impressions and emotions (Figure 2.2). We reconstruct what happened during a trip so that it sounds good as a story to tell others. We include or omit details or stress certain aspects depending on the needs of our listeners. Thus our story might change each time we tell it, and as the story changes so does our memory of the travel experience – and possibly also the meaning we attribute to it.

Communication of travel experiences using stories

People are especially sensitive to information in narrative format, in that stories are particularly entertaining and are very effective in encouraging mental imagery (Green and Brock, 2002). Thus, stories are important for communicating complex travel experiences. Traditional travel information search is dominated by narrative situations, such as asking family and friends or consulting a travel agent. These human travel information providers typically supply contextual information and emphasize particular experiential aspects in a way that enables the information seeker to establish mental connections among the various trip elements. Therefore, stories make it easier to imagine what a trip would be like. In addition, travel stories play an important role in our social relationships: we tell them to impress, to entertain, to relate to others, etc. Tourists take pictures (and videos) and purchase souvenirs to support their storytelling activities. Some travellers keep journals or write blogs to capture details and feelings encountered during their trip, not only to support their own memory but also to be able to relive and share the moment with fellow travellers or loved ones.

Consumers have always engaged in storytelling to communicate tourism experiences. What is different now is the greater recognition and understanding of the value of storytelling that stems from a stronger focus on social networks and community-building in society. Another important factor to consider is the availability of more easy-to-use and ever-cheaper technology that facilitates story creation and telling, and also expands the potential audience for such stories through virtual communities that connect travellers around the world.

New technologies for storytelling

Email and cell phones are increasingly used to provide access to our friends and family during and after trips, providing a near spontaneous means by which to share our experiences. Personal Web pages and Web space provided within virtual communities are popular means for travellers to tell stories of their trips, supported by digital images or even streaming video. Chat rooms and bulletin boards allow for a synchronous sharing of stories with others, whether these are real or virtual friends and acquaintances. Blogs offer new levels of interactivity and immediacy in broadcasting a story as it evolves. Many tourism websites now feature testimonials of tourists to the area, and sometimes integrate stories of residents to convey the essence of the destination. Interactive storytelling technology is currently being developed that will be able greatly to enhance story construction, telling and 'listening'. These technological developments imply that storytelling has experienced a new revival in our social life, and plays a major role in our travel culture.

Conclusions: the new traveller and the future of travel behaviour

Tourism is an information-intense product that is consumed at a distance from home, and therefore relies heavily on the use of technology. Consequently, the Internet has had and will continue to have a tremendous impact on the way consumers search for, purchase, consume, and remember tourism experiences. However, the Internet is not the only channel through which consumers obtain information, communicate or complete transactions; rather, it is one of many options currently used by tourism consumers. Word of mouth, for instance, remains the most popular way of gaining access to first-hand knowledge about travel destinations and tourism experiences. Also, travel magazines and movies continue to be significant sources of inspiration. The success of mobile telephones stresses the importance of being able to talk with another person anytime and anywhere. The concept of the 'hybrid' consumer, who uses many media and technologies simultaneously, is especially applicable to the context of tourism. Nevertheless, many current technology developments aim at convergence, and the creation of one channel that can satisfy all information search, transaction and communication needs, and therefore this situation might change in the near future.

The Internet and its many different applications have provided travellers with unparalleled access to choices, opportunities for comparison shopping and control over the many processes related to the consumption of tourism experiences. The success of auction models where the consumers name prices rather than accepting the industry-imposed price indicates that the market has shifted from a supplier- to a consumer-centric market. Tourism has always been characterized by many alternatives, yet many travellers lacked the necessary information to take advantage of the variety of tourism offers available. The Internet has, to a large part, closed this information gap.

We live in an electronic media-dependent culture, and thus the nature of travel can only be understood within the framework of the affordances of emerging technologies, their impacts on society and, most importantly, the uses to which travellers put these new tools. Thus when analysing the impact of ICTs on travel behaviour, it is important constantly to remind oneself that the technology is still evolving and that its impact on tourism consumers can be only partly grasped but not yet fully understood. It is impossible to know how travel behaviour will change in the future, but it is possible to prepare for future change by extracting knowledge from present experiences. The three aspects of travel behaviour outlined in this chapter (travellers as users of new technologies, as co-producers of meaningful experiences and as storytellers) provide an important basis for thinking about how current realities will shape the future of travel behaviour.

3

New and emerging markets

Chris Cooper, Noel Scott and
John Kester

Introduction

The study of new and emerging markets is a critical
issue for companies, destinations and indeed countries involved in economic activities, and this is no different in tourism. New product development and
innovation in tourism is essential for sustainable
competitive advantage. Effectively, these processes
depend upon the accurate and timely identification
of new markets. However, in the tourism sector the
process of new market identification has tended to be
reactive, and only in recent years has the sector taken
a professional and disciplined approach. In the future
a disciplined approach to new product development
will be essential, due to further competition between
destinations and to increasingly sophisticated customers. This approach involves the identification of
external factors to tourism that drive the formation
of new markets, as well as the recognition of the com-
petencies of the tourism sector to both understand
and serve these new markets.

Definitions and approach

When we speak of new and emerging markets, it has to be recognized that there are in fact varying degrees of newness and innovation involved. For example, some new markets involve relatively simple elaborations of existing products, whilst others represent a radical change to the system of production and consumption, often driven by technological or social change. In order to understand new tourism markets, it is essential to define markets and recognize how to identify a new market.

In terms of definitions, Bourgeois *et al.* (1987: 370) see markets as:

> The area of actual and potential exchanges, between consumers and producers, involving the offerings of producers, and the wants of customers, and with respect to a particular situation.

Because the wants of consumers 'cluster' into specific types of demand, tourism producers tend to offer products that share similarities. Commercial tourism involves an exchange transaction between a supplier and a visitor. Tourism exchanges are generally considered to involve some combination of attractions (or leisure and recreation), accommodation, hospitality and transportation. This exchange takes place at the destination, and is set within environmental, political, economic and social resource environments. The nature of services as interactions between suppliers and visitors makes each particular exchange transaction unique. By using various classification techniques, these transactions (and the people and suppliers they involve) can then be grouped into markets (Figure 3.1).

The identification of a tourism market is an exercise in classification. In identifying types of tourism markets, we generally use a 'special classification' approach.

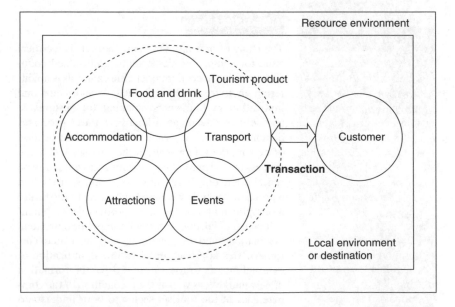

Figure 3.1 A tourism market involves suppliers and visitors with a resource environment

This involves identifying a type of tourism market based upon particular specific characteristics. For example, in ecotourism, although there is debate over the exact features to choose, we identify ecotourists by characteristics that include their behaviour in a natural environment, or the type of support facilities they choose – such as accommodation or transport. Similarly, heritage tourists may be identified on the basis of the type of attractions they visit (for example museums).

Other characteristics used to classify new markets include:

■ geographical origin (e.g. Chinese tourism)
■ geographical destination (e.g. Antarctic tourism)
■ type of attraction (e.g. culture-heritage tourism; Boyd, 2002)
■ accommodation type (e.g. resort tourism)
■ type of transport (e.g. drive tourism).

Often a new type of tourism will involve some combination of transport, geographical location, and attraction characteristics. Some authors describe these new markets as 'niches'.

The implications of this approach to defining new markets are that:

1. The definitional issue of what is, say, ecotourism is better understood because the different definitions are based on the special classifications approach of individual tourism exchanges
2. It suggests that new tourism markets are in a sense arbitrary and can be defined on the basis of the characteristics of the supplier(s), customers or destination
3. It suggests the idea that, depending on the amount of difference in the supplier(s), customers or destination, we may identify markets that are similar or different.

The evolution of tourism markets

The evolution of tourism has been characterized by a strong overall expansion coupled with continuous diversification. Since 1945 domestic and international tourism have experienced almost uninterrupted growth, fuelled by a continuous amplification of markets as new customers have entered the market and existing customers have travelled more often. In this same period, the options available for and chosen by travellers increased spectacularly. A significant diversification has taken place in destinations visited, in the source markets of travellers, attractions offered, motivations and activities undertaken, the means of transport taken, accommodation used, and trip organization.

On the demand side, tourism growth has been fuelled by various factors, including:

■ economic growth in major source markets
■ an increase in disposable leisure time and a longer life expectancy with sufficient health to travel
■ changes in living conditions, particularly the change from agricultural to industrial and post-industrial society, as city dwellers are far more inclined to engage in tourism than are people in the countryside

- rising educational levels and increased access to information, stimulating curiosity
- increasing international integration of life with enhanced international inter-action in trade, politics, communication, media and emigration.

On the supply side, tourism growth has been made possible through:

- the quantitative and qualitative development of and investment in infrastruc-ture, in specific tourism stock and in transport
- continuous tourism product development
- the elimination of legal limitations on and practical obstacles to travel.

In quantitative terms, between 1950 and the early years of the twenty-first cen-tury the number of international tourist arrivals multiplied from a mere 25 million to around 700 million – an average growth of 6.6 per cent a year. In 1950, the first 15 destination countries concentrated 97 per cent of all international tourist arrivals, and there were less than 10 destinations recording over a million arrivals a year. By contrast, in 2002 the share of the first 15 destinations had declined to 60 per cent and a total of 75 destination countries received over a million international arrivals.

In fact, the share of the world population taking part in tourism and the trip fre-quency is still rather modest. Relative to population, worldwide 11 arrivals per 100 of population were generated in 2000, up from less than 1 in 1950, while for the year 2020 the number is expected to have risen to 21 arrivals per 100 of population. There is a considerable variation between regions. Europe currently generates 46 arrivals per 100 of population, and this is expected to grow to 81 in 2020. All other regions generate a significantly lesser number of arrivals per 100 of population.

According to the WTO's long-term forecast, *Tourism 2020 Vision*, tourism con-tinues to grow (WTO, 2001a). There is still a huge potential to unleash, first in many developing markets and secondly also in mature markets, as saturation seems not yet to be near. Economic growth will enable many new customers to start enjoying travel, extending tourism to a larger stratum of the population. An increase in the frequency of trip-taking will further boost volumes. Worldwide, the number of international tourist arrivals is expected to more than double to 1.6 billion in 2020, corresponding to an average growth of 4.1 per cent a year for the period 1995 to 2020. In geographic terms, growth is very much fuelled from emerging economies in Asia, and above-average growth rates are anticipated in the Middle East, Southern Africa, Southern America, and Central and Eastern Europe. For the more mature regions of North America and Europe, below-average growth rates are expected of around 3 per cent a year (WTO, 2003).

For marketers, this environment signifies a comparatively comfortable starting point: instead of having to fight to maintain a share in a consolidated market, the focus can be on capturing a fair share of this ever-increasing market. The chal-lenge is to identify those emerging markets, match them with suitable products, and apply the appropriate marketing and promotion. This is not necessarily an easy task, as the number of suppliers is also expanding and competition is fierce. For this reason, the ongoing development of new products is of major impor-tance, as well as continuous and up-to-date market research. This is especially true for the more mature markets of the developed world, as it is easier to lure the experienced and demanding customer with new products that differentiate from the rest. However, no market is completely mature or virgin. Segmentation must be taken into account in each market, and new segments and niches can also be found in mature markets, whilst markets continually evolve and the interests and desires of customers may shift in time.

Case study 3.1 describes the emergence of a new tourism market in China.

Case study 3.1 The Chinese tourism boom

China perfectly exemplifies the opening up of a new market (WTO, 2003). As a result of the rapid economic growth experienced in recent decades, living standards have risen, awakening a strong appetite for travel among the Chinese – in the first place to explore their own country, but increasingly also internationally. Although the majority of the population is still confined to the booming domestic tourism sector, already an expanding upper class and a rapidly growing middle class have developed that can afford to travel internationally. Of a population of 1.3 billion, the number of Chinese with sufficient disposable income to engage in international tourism is estimated at some 50 million, mostly originating from the developed urban centres of Beijing, Shanghai and Guangzhou. China is a particularly significant case of a new market due to the size of its population. As still only a proportionally small number of Chinese travel abroad, the fraction of Chinese taking part in international tourism only has to increase moderately to produce a large increase in numbers.

Traditionally, outbound tourism from China has been strongly regulated. Travel is still mostly limited to group tourism to countries that have signed a so-called Approved Destination Status (ADS) Agreement. In the early days, travel was predominantly directed to the Special Administrative Regions of Hong Kong and Macau. In 1987 travel started in the border areas of China from the adjoining provinces, first to the Democratic People's Republic of (North) Korea, followed by the Russian Federation, Mongolia, Kazakhstan, Kyrgyzstan and Vietnam. In the late 1980s Chinese citizens were allowed to travel to Thailand, and later also to Singapore, Malaysia and the Philippines, to visit family and relatives, provided their relatives paid for their expenses and offered a guarantee for them. Travel to Australia, New Zealand and the Republic of (South) Korea was approved in 1999, soon followed by Japan, Vietnam, Cambodia, Myanmar and Brunei. Since 2002 a growing number of countries outside China have gained ADS, including Egypt, Malta, Turkey and South Africa. The European Union signed the agreement in 2004, and by the end of that year the ADS list consisted of 55 countries (www.tourismchina-ca.com/news_r.html). Table 3.1 shows the rapid growth in outbound travel by Chinese citizens. Recently constraints on individual travel have also been eased with the introduction of individual travel permits from China to Hong Kong and Macao in July 2003. As a result, Chinese outbound tourism surpassed 20 million trips in 2003, yet Chinese outbound tourism is still very much in its infancy – expenditure per capita (travellers and non-travellers) on international travel is only US$12. According to the WTO's *Tourism 2020 Vision*, China is expected to become the fourth major generating market, with an estimated 100 million outbound trips in 2020 (Figure 3.2).

Table 3.1 The rapid growth in outbound travel by Chinese citizens

China Outbound tourism by country of destination

	Trips abroad (1000)			share (%)	% change 1998–2002	
	1998	2000	2002		total	average
Total	**8 426**	**10 649**	**16 602**	**100**	**97**	**18.5**
Asia and the Pacific	**7 166**	**8 952**	**14 412**	**86.8**	**101**	**19.1**
Hong Kong	3 373	4 142	7 771	46.8	130	23.2
Macao	1 598	1 644	2 783	16.8	74	14.9
Japan	502	596	760	4.6	52	10.9
Thailand	568	707	689	4.1	21	5.0
Republic of Korea	214	401	551	3.3	158	26.7
Singapore	193	263	289	1.7	50	10.7
DPR Korea	98	195	248	1.5	154	26.2
Malaysia	79	87	231	1.4	192	30.7
Australia	93	127	199	1.2	115	21.1
Taiwan	70	86	112	0.7	60	12.5
Other	380	704	777	4.7	105	19.6
Europe	**818**	**1 123**	**1 447**	**8.7**	**77**	**15.3**
Russian Federation	434	606	691	4.2	59	12.3
Germany	84	113	166	1.0	98	18.6
France	63	96	137	0.8	117	21.4
UK	36	61	128	0.8	251	36.9
Other	201	247	326	2.0	62	12.8
Americas	**397**	**523**	**618**	**3.7**	**56**	**11.7**
USA	319	395	419	2.5	31	7.1
Canada	58	100	148	0.9	154	26.2
Other	20	28	52	0.3	163	27.4
All Africa	**40**	**48**	**74**	**0.4**	**86**	**16.7**
Not specified	**4**	**4**	**51**	**0.3**		

Source: World Tourism Organization (WTO)

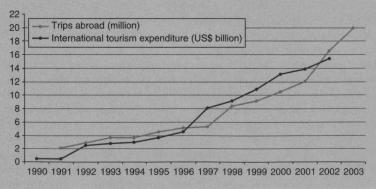

Figure 3.2 China: outbound tourism growth 1990–2003

Tourism markets today

As tourism markets have matured, they have also fragmented. It is therefore useful to examine new tourism markets from the perspective of market segmentation.

Demographic and geographic segments

The major developed tourism markets of Europe, America, Japan and Australia are all experiencing an ageing population. This is leading to changing tourism markets, such as the Grey Nomads in Australia and Snowbirds in the USA, who take regular extended drive holidays after retirement. In contrast, developing countries such as India and the People's Republic of China have comparatively young growing populations that are interested in urban nightlife and coastal tourist destinations.

Lifestyle and psychographic segments

A review of recent trends clearly demonstrates the fact that tourism markets are fragmenting. The economic and social freedom experienced by Western and increasingly by Eastern nations is leading to a desire for self-expression that is delivered through diverse tourism experiences. Adventure tourism, cultural tourism and ecotourism are markets created by tourists choosing types of tourism that match their lifestyle. Increasingly we can see other segmentation approaches evolving that identify benefit- or psychographic-based markets – the idea of hard and soft adventure is an example here (Frochot and Morrison, 2000). However, these types of tourism markets primarily represent Western values that may not reflect those of the growth markets of, say, China or India, except to the extent that they are absorbing these values from mass communication channels such as television and the Internet. New markets are emerging that determine visitor behaviour in terms of attitude to the environment and the ethical behaviour of both the visitors and the suppliers (see Case study 3.2).

Case study 3.2 Whale-watching in Hervey Bay, Australia

The development of whale-watching in Hervey Bay, Australia, is an example of a new market that has emerged on the back of significant lifestyle shifts in society and changes in community attitudes to the environment in the 1970s and early 1980s. Increasing concern for the environment is attributed to a reaction against the rampant developmental ethos of the 1960s, and was heralded by the publication of *Silent Spring* (Carson, 1963), which partly led to the demonstrations that resulted in the humpback whale becoming a protected species worldwide in 1966.

The overall growth of whale-watching from its commercial introduction in Hawaii to 1998 has been rapid (Figure 3.3). Hoyt (2001) estimates that whale-watch numbers grew by around 14 per cent annually between 1994 and 1998, such that by 1998 whale-watching around the world provided direct expenditure of

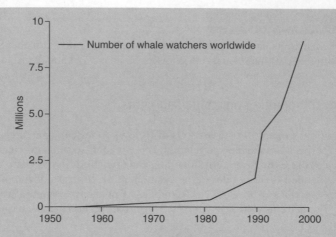

Figure 3.3 Growth of whale-watching worldwide
(Source: Hoyt, 2001)

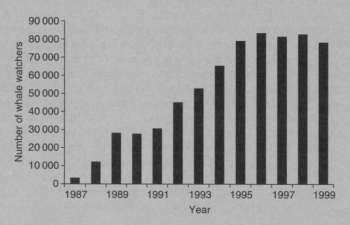

Figure 3.4 Whale-watch passengers in Hervey Bay 1987–1999
(Source: Queensland Parks and Wildlife)

USD$300 million with over 9 million visitors undertaking commercial whale-watching.

In Hervey Bay, whale-watching began in 1988 when a fishing tour operator encountered whales. His entrepreneurial actions in immediately offering whale-watching tours were widely communicated in the media, which was receptive to stories related to the environment. Since that time, whale-watching in Hervey Bay has grown dramatically (see Figure 3.4).

Most recently, market growth has slowed due to increasing competition from other destinations along the East Coast of Australia as well as internationally. Operators in Hervey Bay have not developed new products to match the changing situation, a clear example of the imperative to innovate in tourism to maintain competitive advantage.

Technographic segments

There is an increasing divide between skilled users of technology and those who are unable to utilize, or less skilled at using, technology to purchase and search for tourism information. The technology of the Internet and World Wide Web is maturing and increasingly providing value for consumers and enterprises alike with innovations such as lifestyle travel portals, which allow the personal customization of products.

The dimensions of future tourism markets

The external drivers of future tourism markets are the changing social, economic and technological issues in society. These are impacting on all of the tourism markets discussed here. The external environment for tourism is one of turbulence and rapid unexpected change; this has led to revolutionary changes in tourism markets and supply, particularly in terms of safety and security following the terrorist attacks in America on 11 September 2001. In this 'new normality', it is important to begin not only to understand and forecast the tourism markets of the future but also to better manage and indeed seek proactively to anticipate unexpected events and to influence the future. This requires a more sophisticated approach to the business of tourism than has been evident in the past.

Sector vision

Markets are becoming more complex and competitive, resulting in a need for a broader, strategic picture for the tourism sector that involves both private and public sector participants and extends across the economic sectors. Whilst tourism is by its very nature an international industry, it is not necessarily one that has embraced the process of globalization; and particularly the marketing implications of globalization. Indeed the trend is perhaps the opposite, as globalization is paradoxically focusing political attention on regional and local issues, and the competitiveness of tourism destinations. In a maturing market, destinations at the regional and local scale have to choose their development path rather than being able to expect growth. This involves taking a fine line between adopting the advantages offered by globalization, whilst also recognizing that tourism is delivered within a local destination context. There is a need therefore to consider not only the implications of developing new markets in terms of community reaction but also, increasingly, the interaction between markets.

Sector practices

If tourism is to take advantage of new and emerging markets, then more disciplined and enlightened business practices will be needed. These include innovative approaches to supplying markets to gain competitive advantage, deep and meaningful market research to understand the changing consumption patterns of the 'new normality', quality in delivery, the use of technology, and sophisticated segmentation approaches. These skills, common in other sectors of the marketplace, are now required by destination managers and private sector operators. Cooperative branding campaigns involving mass media advertising, quality benchmarking and assurance techniques, risk assessment and crisis management processes, purposeful product development rather than relying on serendipitous entrepreneurial activity, and strategic planning rather than tactical budgeting are all being adopted in tourism destinations around the world. Perhaps as important as these innovations is the changing mindset of destination enterprises and members of the tourism value chain, where the concept of 'coop-etition' and the sharing of resources are slowly being accepted. In fact, the existing model in tourism of markets being found and exploited may be outdated. In some countries, efforts are being made to develop new products in a similar manner to the new product development process used in other industries. Examples include the product clubs of Canada (Boyd, 2002) and the development of book towns in the United Kingdom (Seaton, 1999). Similarly, technology enables the creation of extended virtual value chains that shape markets and suppliers. As a result we should consider the idea that markets are created and shaped, not found and exploited. This brings into play the idea of strategic planning and knowledge management. The future will not be the same as the past, in part because of the megatrends of globalization and population growth, terrorism and religious fundamentalism, safety, and risks of disease – the 'new normality'.

Case study 3.3 discusses the issue of space tourism.

Case study 3.3 Space tourism

Although we are aware of the concept of space tourism, the cost, technology and safety mean that the market has yet to be realized. Space tourism is defined by the Space Tourism Society as including:

1. Earth orbit and suborbital experiences
2. Beyond Earth orbit (such as Lunar and Mars) experiences
3. Earth-based simulations, tours, and entertainment experiences
4. Cyberspace tourism experiences.

The first commercial space tourist in orbit was Denis Tito, who visited the International Space Station in 2001, followed by Mark Shuttleworth in 2002. Commercial Earth-based simulations, tours and experiences are available, including simulated 'weightlessness' experiences in a plane diving from 35 000 to 25 000 feet in 30 seconds, a ride 'to the edge of space' in a Russian MIG fighter jet and a space training course, as well as visits to museums and space launch sites, and also theme park rides.

While currently a vacation on the moon is not possible, space agencies are realizing that tourism will help to pay for the cost of their space flights. A variety of market studies have examined the price elasticity of space flight, leading to the question – is space tourism a dream or a reality? Richard Branson has signed a deal to build five space planes (see http://www.bbc.co.uk/cgi-bin/education/betsie/parser.pl/0005/news.bbc.co.uk/1/hi/sci/tech/3693020.stm).

Conclusions

The world is undergoing a period of rapid and unexpected change. In these times, a disciplined business and marketing approach is vital if tourism organizations and destinations are to remain competitive. A significant part of this process is the understanding of new markets and their consumers, and of their evolution. This chapter has demonstrated that tourism has grown significantly since 1945, driven by social, economic, environmental and technological factors. These factors are dissolving traditional market segments and reforming them into leisure lifestyles, with the consequent development of new products, such as whale-watching. Demographic factors have also driven the growth of tourism, and in countries such as China they will continue to do so. Yet whilst the tourism sector has responded to these changes in the external environment through the development of new products, there is still a need for the sector to embrace contemporary approaches to new markets – approaches that recognize the need for deep and meaningful market research, marketing strategies that recognize the challenges and opportunities of globalization, and, of course, the realities of a deteriorating security environment for tourism. In the future, new and emerging markets will be best served by a disciplined, professional and visionary tourism sector.

4

Third-age tourism

Gianna Moscardo

Introduction

One of the most common demographic trends identified across the globe is the ageing population of most nations. Substantial academic, government and media interest has been focused on this phenomenon, with many predictions made about the likely impact of this demographic trend on a number of sectors, including tourism. This chapter will analyse the phenomenon of third-age or senior tourism, and explore a number of different aspects of this growing tourism market. The analysis will highlight the importance of applied tourism research, providing insights into and evidence about the changing nature of tourism markets to support improved practice in the tourism sector as a whole.

These themes will be explored in more detail with tourism industry practice examples from around the world, and with empirical data from an ongoing programme regarding the patterns and characteristics of tourism to Australia's Great Barrier Reef (GBR). There is currently only limited research evidence about various features of senior travel, and the GBR data allow for a more complete picture to be drawn. According to Pearce (1999: 36), 'it is a part of the spirit and mission of tourism research to use academic and analytical observation and skills to assist emerging business developments while at the same time enhancing our understanding of tourism phenomena'. This chapter therefore has the dual objectives of reviewing the latest available information on senior travel, and testing some of the predictions made about this travel segment with the GBR tourist data to further our understanding of this phenomenon.

Setting the scene – ageing populations and tourism demand

Table 4.1 provides a summary of the some of the key population statistics that have been presented with regard to ageing. As can be seen, the demographic ageing trend is a widespread phenomenon. In addition to these simple statistics on the numbers of older people in various countries, it has been argued that these older population segments will live longer, be healthier and more active, have more income and time, and expect a higher quality of life than similar age groups in previous decades.

These shifts in characteristics, activities and motivations have been described as the core elements of the concept of the 'third age'. The label 'third age' comes from sociology, and is used to describe a change in the way in which retired people see themselves. The core idea is that with greater wealth and higher living standards, people begin see their retirement as an opportunity for personal development and fulfilment. Thus the labels 'senior' and 'third age' are not necessarily interchangeable (Gilleard and Higgs, 2002) – not all seniors in all places and under all circumstances will see their retirement as a 'third age'. In the case of tourism, however, the focus is on those seniors who travel, and thus it seems appropriate to use either term.

Table 4.1 Selection of population age statistics and predictions

Reference	Summary of ageing statistics
Fleischer and Pizam, 2002	In 1996 in Israel, 16 per cent of the people were aged 55+ and 9.6 per cent 65+ years; these rates will be 22 per cent and 13.2 per cent, respectively, by 2020
Hossain, 2003	In Australia, between 2001 and 2011 a 44 per cent increase in the population aged 55–64 years is expected (an increase from 1.8 million to 2.6 million) while the number of people aged 65+ is expected to increase by 26 per cent (from 2.4 to 3 million)
Ritchie *et al.*, 2003	Globally, the number of people aged 60+ was estimated to be 600 million in 1999; this is projected to grow to 2 billion by 2050, when the population of older persons will be larger than the population of children (aged 0–14 years) for first time in human history In 1997, the percentage of the population aged 55+ in specific countries was as follows: USA, 21 per cent; Taiwan, 15 per cent; UK, 26 per cent; France, 25 per cent; Germany, 28 per cent; Italy, 28 per cent
Sakai *et al.*, 2000	Japan is the fastest ageing society in world; by 2025 the number of people aged less than 30 years is expected to decline by 11 million, while those aged 50+ are expected to increase by 15 million

There is evidence of a strong current demand for travel from seniors. According to Shoemaker (2000), United States residents aged 55–64 years spend an average of 7.1 per cent and those aged 65 and older spend 10.8 per cent of their household income on travel. In Australia in 2001, those aged 55 and older made nearly 16 million overnight trips, accounting for 21 per cent of all overnight trips made (Hossain, 2003). Predictions about future demand are, however, more speculative. These predictions are often based on the simple assumption that the global ageing trends will translate into larger proportions of senior travellers. Table 4.2 provides a summary of the age profiles for five different regions of origin for tourists visiting the Great Barrier Reef region of Australia. These data are derived from an ongoing research programme into patterns of tourism to this major Australia destination (see Moscardo, 2004, for details regarding the methods used to collect these data). When looking at the total sample of visitors, the predictions about an ageing population of travellers appear to hold true for this destination. However, this pattern does not apply to all the groups in the table. Japanese and Australian groups have aged as predicted, but the North Americans, Europeans and Chinese visitors are younger in 2001 than in 1996. These figures highlight the difficulties in translating global trends into destination specific patterns.

What is currently known about senior travel?

While it is quite common for authors to claim that present and future senior travellers will be wealthier, healthier, more active and have more time than their predecessors (Shoemaker, 2000; Horneman et al., 2002; Kim et al., 2003), very little empirical evidence is available on the characteristics that distinguish senior travellers from other age groups. Many studies do not actually provide comparisons between age groups, but rather just profile senior travellers. In addition, the samples of senior tourists used in this research are often restricted to particular types of senior tourist, such as those taking a package tour (Huang and Tsai, 2003) or long-distance drivers (Pearce, 1999).

Horneman et al. (2002) provide one of the few reviews that distinguishes between studies that have profiled seniors only and those where seniors have been compared to other groups. This review suggests that senior travellers stay longer at their destination, spend more time planning, and visit friends and relatives more often. In addition, there is some evidence that seniors are attracted to certain types of travel. Pearce (1999), for example, describes the phenomenon of long-distance driving often associated with lengthy stays in warmer locations during winter. Fleischer and Pizam (2002) report strong associations between senior travellers and package tours, especially motorcoach and cruise ship options.

Table 4.3 shows the results of a series of comparisons of senior and non-senior reef tourists, and provides a summary of those characteristics found to be significantly different between the two age groups. Some of these results are consistent with claims made about seniors, including a focus on couples and family groups as the main travel parties, and a higher concentration of seniors in package tours. Some of the findings are not, however, quite so clear. While seniors were significantly less physically active than younger age groups, nearly half of the senior sample went snorkelling and more than one in ten went diving, which could be

Table 4.2 Percentage of each age group of visitors to the Great Barrier Reef, by geographic origin, in 1996 and 2001

Age group (years)	Japan		China		USA/Canada		Europe		Australia		Total	
	1996	2001	1996	2001	1996	2001	1996	2001	1996	2001	1996	2001
<21	7	9	13	6	5	23	11	9	6	3	8	9
21–30	48	22	30	28	32	23	29	54	34	18	34	30
31–40	23	30	24	35	27	17	21	16	27	22	25	20
41–50	11	25	23	27	28	15	16	9	17	21	17	17
51–60	7	10	8	4	10	11	12	8	11	19	10	13
61–70	2	2	2	1	7	8	11	3	5	9	6	7
>70 years	1	2	–	–	–	3	–	1	–	8	–	4

Source: CRC Reef Research Centre GBR Visitor Analysis Survey data

Table 4.3 Significant differences between senior (aged 60+) and non-senior visitors to the Great Barrier Reef in 2001

Characteristics	Non-seniors (%)	Seniors (%)
Activity participation		
▪ Swimming	56	37
▪ Snorkelling	72	48
▪ Diving	29	12
▪ Glass-bottom boat tours	27	48
▪ Semi-submersible tours	31	50
▪ Underwater observatory visit	20	35
▪ Reef talk attendance	12	22
Travel party type		
▪ Alone	8	4
▪ Couple	29	51
▪ Family	34	31
▪ Friends	23	9
▪ Other	9	6
Travel party size		
▪ 1–2 37	55	
▪ 3–10	54	31
▪ >10	9	14
Type of reef tour chosen		
▪ Large boat to reef pontoon	53	56
▪ Island trip	22	31
▪ Dive trip	8	2
▪ Independent sailing	4	2
▪ Other	13	9
Nights away from home		
▪ <8 24	18	
▪ 8–14	22	33
▪ 15–31	32	34
▪ >31	22	15
Planning approach		
▪ Take a package	16	26
▪ Arrange some/most before departure	41	44
▪ Organize on arrival	43	30
Mean importance of expected benefits from a reef trip		
(scale: 1 not at all to 5 very important)		
▪ Escape	3.5	3.2
▪ Learning/education	3.9	4.2
▪ Experience nature	4.3	4.1
▪ Physical activity	2.8	2.5
▪ Develop skills	3.6	2.9
▪ Be social	2.7	2.4

Note: All differences significant at $P < 0.01$ based on χ^2 and independent t-tests
Source: CRC Reef Research Centre GBR Visitor Analysis Survey data

Table 4.4 Senior travel motivation themes

Motivation	Specialized tourism products
Seek intellectual stimulation and learning; develop skills; have new experiences	Development of educational tours and opportunities through organizations like Elderhostel and the University of the Third Age
Maintain physical fitness; relax	Health spas and wellness centres
Meet new people and socialize	Package tours specifically for seniors, such as those offered by SAGA Holidays
Visit friends and relatives	The development of Recreational Vehicle Parks and organizations

interpreted as consistent with claims that current seniors are more active than previous generations.

The findings with regard to travel motivations reported in Table 4.3 also provide only partial support for previous descriptions of the motivations of senior travellers. The reef tourism study found that learning was the only motive rated as more important by seniors. Other reviews have suggested several motivations as being important for third-age travellers and these are summarized in Table 4.4 (Horneman *et al.*, 2002; Kim *et al.*, 2003).

Emerging issues and trends in senior travel

Constraints on senior travel

In contrast to the previous section, studies into the factors that limit or constrain travel by older people have found very similar results. Factors that limit travel for older people include (Sakai *et al.*, 2000; Fleischer and Pizam, 2002; Huang and Tsai, 2003; Kim *et al.*, 2003):

- safety/security concerns
- health issues
- available time
- cost
- family responsibilities
- poor information about suitable options.

According to Fleischer and Pizam (2002), one set of travel constraints specific to seniors is that of approval and perceived age-related limitations. Seniors can feel limited by concerns over what others will think about their behaviour and what they believe they are capable of. Long (1998) provides a discussion of seniors as general consumers in which he notes problems with ageist stereotypes held by seniors themselves and by those in service industries. Case study 4.1 highlights the issue of service provider attitudes towards senior consumers.

Case study 4.1 Recognizing seniors as a valued market

A survey conducted by the Positive Ageing Foundation in Australia found that many people aged 55 and older reported being ignored in stores and in advertising. There appears to be a wide-ranging problem with companies and customer service staff holding negative stereotypes of older consumers and not wanting to have their products associated with older groups. In this context, there are major competitive advantages for those companies that recognize and market specifically to older consumers with positive images. Some examples of companies seeking to create positive relationships with seniors include:

- SAGA Holidays (UK), which specializes in holidays for those aged 55 and over
- Target's (USA) development of a clothing line for mature customers
- Ford's development of a car for empty nesters
- Sony's advertising campaigns featuring older people engaging in adventure activities.

(Sources: Long, 1998; Canning, 2004)

Table 4.5 Summary profiles of senior Great Barrier Reef tourist market segments

Escape to nature	Nature educationalists	Active outdoor socializers
High importance for escape and relaxation as reason for visiting the GBR	High importance given to learning and experiencing nature	High importance given to being physically active, meeting others and developing skills
Lowest levels of physical activity	Highest levels of participation in educational activities	Most physically active
Highest proportion aged over 60 years	Greatest variety of travel destinations	Highest proportion aged less than 60 years
Most likely to repeat travel to the same destination	Greatest users of books for information	Highest proportion of females
Highest proportion of males		

Source: CRC Reef Research Centre GBR Visitor Analysis Survey data

Recognizing differences within senior groups

Another consistent set of findings in research into third-age travellers is that they are not a homogenous group. Numerous studies have been conducted using a variety of segmentation methods and bases. Reviews of these are provided by Kim et al. (2003) and Horneman et al. (2002). Table 4.5 provides a summary of three senior tourist market segments identified in the Great Barrier Reef study. This cluster analysis was based on reef travel motivations, and the resulting three clusters are similar in a number of ways to other benefit-based segments described for senior tourists.

In addition to these market segmentation studies, a number of authors have also suggested that gender, culture and employment status may be important factors that influence and interact with age to determine a variety of different patterns of senior travel. Sakai *et al.* (2000), for example, analysed patterns of Japanese international travel and found that gender and employment status were significant variables influencing patterns of travel across all age groups. Long (1998) argues that the best way to define third-age travellers is by employment status rather than age, and that gender and culture are key variables which interact with employment status to influence consumer behaviour.

Change over time

One of the most common predictions made about senior travellers is that they are different today from previous generations, and that they will be different in the future. Specifically, it is often argued that better health and living standards will result in more active and wealthier senior tourists. Studies of changes in seniors over time are, however, very rare, and little evidence exists to support these claims. Shoemaker (2000) provides one of the few studies comparing senior travellers over time. The results indicated that compared to a survey in 1986, seniors in 1996 were more likely to be in part-time work, to be interested in golf, to be concerned with the availability of diet meals, and to pay using credit cards. The 1996 respondents were also less interested in visiting new places, experiencing new things and seeing beautiful scenery.

Many of the predictions about third-age travellers having greater wealth and time to travel assume no change in the existing economic conditions. The Shoemaker (2000) study suggests, however, that these conditions may be changing, with a higher proportion of senior travellers reporting part-time employment. Moscardo *et al.* (2000a) list a number of issues related to predicting future travel trends. Among these is the possibility that a 'good forecast might be one that never eventuates' (Moscardo *et al.*, 2000a: xxi) – that is, governments may respond to a forecast in such a way as to avoid it actually happening. In the case of ageing populations, much government attention has focused on the problems of generating sufficient income to support growing numbers of retirees. A number of governments have now moved towards raising the retirement age and encouraging retirees to remain in some employment to support greater self-sufficiency (Walley *et al.*, 1999; Villanueva, 2000). In other words, government policies may be changing the conditions of wealth and freedom that currently underpin senior travel. In addition, the collapse of pension schemes in Europe and major investment companies in the United States and Australia may threaten the financial resources of seniors in the future.

Tourism practice

Despite the limited availability of information about the characteristics of senior travellers, and problems with the accuracy and detail of predictions regarding

Table 4.6 Examples of senior tourism services

Company/organization	Key features
Elderhostel (multinational), http://www.elderhostel.org/welcome/home.asp	Non-profit organization providing educational travel for adults 55 and over
	Offers nearly 10 000 all-inclusive programmes each year in 100 countries
	Examples of current programmes include language study programs in central America, white-water rafting, arts workshops
50Plus Expeditions (USA), http://www.50plusexpeditions.com/	Active, adventure, all-inclusive, small group tours for travellers 50 and over
	Examples of current programmes include African safaris, Antarctic cruises, mountain hiking in Europe
	Offers independent travel options
Odyssey Travel (Australia), http://www.odysseytravel.com.au/	Educational travel for over 50s
	All-inclusive packages in Australia and New Zealand
	Offers independent travel options
50+ Travel & Learn (New Zealand), http://www.newzealandseniortravel.com/	All-inclusive small group educational tours in New Zealand for adults 50 and over
Saga Holidays (UK), http://www.sagaholidays.com/	International cruises and holiday packages focused on older travellers
Valor Tours (USA), http://www.valortours.com/	All-inclusive military history tours focused on veterans
Canyon Ranch Health Resort (USA) Optimal Ageing Programs, http://www.canyonranch.com/optimal_ageing/	Specific week-long programmes offered by the resort to develop health and longevity

this tourism market, there is clearly a current high level of demand for travel within senior age groups. Table 4.6 provides some examples of the ways in which tourism businesses have responded to this demand by developing third-age tourism experiences.

The examples in Table 4.6 highlight a number of themes in the services provided for senior travellers. There is a strong emphasis on educational activities and on all-inclusive, small-group escorted tours, including cruises. Some companies, however, are beginning to offer services to assist independent travellers. These services are also available on many senior travel websites (see Table 4.6). Most of the companies set their age limit as 50 years and over. Table 4.6 also includes examples of specialist tours and the development of specific senior products as part of more general travel businesses such as accommodation. Case study 4.2 provides a summary of some US hotel chain initiatives aimed at improving service for senior guests.

Case study 4.2 Hotel initiatives for senior guests, America

Many hotel chains, especially in the United States, are beginning to recognize the business value of attracting and keeping senior guests. These senior-specific initiatives include targeted promotional activities, such as developing alliances with senior travel organizations like the Group Leaders of America (GLAMER) – for example, Howard Johnson hotels advertise in the GLAMER newsletter, and Days Inn offers specific packages and discounts for church group tours.

Other senior-specific strategies include additional services and facilities. Choice Hotels gives a minimum 10 per cent off all rooms, offers large number sizes on telephones and remote controls, and also has door handles instead of knobs for ease of opening. Cross Country Inns offers drive though check-in and check-out for seniors travelling in recreation vehicles. A resort in Palm Springs offers a gated country club community for seniors on long-distance driving tours.

(Sources: Whitford, 1998; Waters, 2002; Cross Country Inns, 2003)

A vision for the future of senior travel

The populations of many countries are ageing, resulting in high demand for travel from people aged 50 and older. There is evidence that much of this demand is focused on educational travel and opportunities for self-development. Many predictions made about growth in senior travel assume that these third-age travellers will be healthier, wealthier and more active than previous generations of the same age. Care must be taken, however, to recognize that third-age tourism is likely to change over time, and that some of the present economic conditions that support extensive third-age travel may not continue into the future.

Despite these cautions, third-age travel offers some interesting opportunities for destination development. It is likely that even with increased employment participation, senior travellers will continue to have fewer time constraints than others and thus offer an opportunity for destinations to manage seasonality issues. There is evidence that seniors are interested in cultural and educational styles of travel, and thus provide a potential market for the development of rural and peripheral destinations (Ritchie *et al.*, 2003). While individual tourism businesses, especially in the areas of group travel and accommodation, have begun to research and target this developing tourism market, few destinations appear to have seriously considered the ways in which they could become more senior oriented.

Finally, researchers and tourism practitioners need to be cautious about adopting age-based stereotypes, as an increasingly common theme in service quality studies is that of resentment of negative ageist stereotypes. However, practitioners also cannot ignore the real constraints that result from physical ageing, and operators may need to develop medical services as a part of their tourism products. A major challenge for future research in this area is to examine the facilities and services that appeal to seniors but do not create a sense of negative isolation.

5

Youth and adventure tourism

Greg Richards and Julie Wilson

Introduction

Youth tourism has been identified as one of the largest segments of global tourism, and is also seen as having considerable potential for future growth as student numbers rise and youth affluence increases. The growth of this market is particularly evident in long-haul markets, where young backpackers and other travellers often congregate in specific 'enclaves' which serve as the physical and psychological refuelling points for the modern global nomad (Richards and Wilson, 2004).

Our research shows that long-distance youth travellers are primarily experience seekers, collecting 'unique' experiences that will serve to build their self-identity narratives. Adventure and risk have a special role to play in the behaviour and attitudes of young travellers, as Elsrud (2001) has shown. The growth of the adventure travel market in destinations popular with young people underlines this link.

This chapter examines the current state of the youth and adventure travel markets, paying particular attention to the growth and development of enclaves.

The rise of youth and adventure tourism

Youth tourism

The fact that there is no widely accepted definition of 'youth' tourism highlights the shifting perception of the concept of youth in society as a whole. As Maoz (2004) shows, young people are increasingly taking a moratorium from adulthood, delaying major life decisions in order to extend the freedom of 'youth'. As a result, people in their thirties or even forties may be regarded as 'young' in spirit as well as in the activities they undertake. This is not reflected in most studies of youth tourism, which generally define youth as extending to 26 or 29 years of age.

The growing range of individuals who might be considered to fall within the bounds of the youth market is only one reason why youth travel is becoming more important. Growing travel participation by young people is being fuelled by a number of factors, including increased participation in higher education, falling levels of youth unemployment, and increased travel budgets through parental contributions, savings, and combining work and travel (Wheatcroft and Seekings, 1995; Richards and Wilson, 2003). In addition there is a range of supply-related factors that have also stimulated youth tourism, including:

- the rise of budget/low-cost airlines
- the growth of long-distance coach travel specifically targeted at young travellers
- shorter employment contracts for those working, leading to significant gaps in employment
- the growth of dedicated student and independent travel suppliers
- the global rise of the Internet culture, opening up new destinations via this new medium
- the growth of independent travel guidebooks such as the *Rough Guide* and the *Lonely Planet*.

The search for ever more exciting and unique experiences, combined with cheaper long-distance travel, has also pushed youth travel ever further towards the geographical margins of the travel industry. This process has speeded up as pioneers in a particular destination flee the arrival of their less experienced colleagues (or 'tourists'), seeking out yet more 'undiscovered' destinations (Westerhausen, 2002). Increased accessibility has arguably decreased the feeling of adventure attached to long-distance travel. Whereas in the past the act of travelling itself could be considered a sufficient 'adventure', nowadays there is an increasing need to develop specific 'adventures' or adventurous experiences to supplement what has become a less arduous travel process.

Adventure tourism

Almost 100 million Americans indicated that they had participated in some form of adventure travel in 1997 (TIA, 1998) and, according to the US-based Adventure Travel Society, adventure tourism is growing at between 10 and 15 per cent a year (Neirotti, 2003). US data indicate that 'adventure travellers' tend to be male, single, young and highly educated.

However, there has still been relatively little research on adventure tourism, and there is also no widely accepted definition. One of the key ideas underlying adventure tourism, however, is that it involves some form of physical exertion (Beedie, 2003). Most of what has been written about adventure tourism also tends to concentrate on specific places that are either wild or less easily accessible (Hudson, 2003). Ewert and Hollenhorst (1989) suggested that a sense of adventure is derived from a search for competence combined with a sense of risk and danger. A sense of adventure can therefore be obtained either from physical activities that develop competence, or from adventurous locations offering a sense of risk, or from a combination of the two. The physical demands of adventure tourism also tend to imply a high degree of youth participation.

In view of the locational and perceived risk advantages of long-haul, 'exotic' or 'wild' destinations, it is not surprising that the adventure tourism market appears to be expanding most rapidly in such regions. For example, the number of tourists to Nepal grew from 300 000 in 1994 to 464 000 in 2000. Cloutier (2003) has shown how heli-skiing in Canada has mushroomed in recent years, with a 44 per cent growth in heli-skier days between 1994 and 1999.

The growth of adventure tourism inevitably creates increasing problems of environmental and risk management (Cloutier, 2003). A sense of risk has to be managed in the context of safe experiences, or 'planned unexpectedness', as Cederholm (1999) puts it. Providing access to 'wild' nature becomes increasingly difficult as visitor numbers rise, and there is growing pressure on suppliers to manage the resource more carefully to conserve nature and to preserve the image of risk and danger.

As Elsrud (2001) shows, risk forms an important part of the narrative of backpacker and traveller culture. Risk arguably separates the real backpacker or traveller from the tourist. It is not the real degree of risk that is important, however, but the perception of risk. Elsrud argues that a bus journey in India is seen as more dangerous than a bus journey in Europe, regardless of the actual physical risk involved.

Other destinations that are perceived by most travellers as being relatively 'safe' therefore try and create a sense of risk to attract young travellers. For example, Cloke and Perkins (1998) examined the growth of adventure tourism in New Zealand, where the majority of adventure tourists are in the 20–35 age range, underlining the close link between youth and adventure travel. They point out that the degree to which adventure activities were seen as pleasant was related to the perceived, rather than actual, level of risk.

The development of adventure tourism in New Zealand is also a good example of the fact that nature alone is not enough. Specific experiences need to be added to the basic natural landscape in order to make nature more attractive. In the case of New Zealand, the added ingredient is usually adventure. Where opportunities for 'real' adventure are missing, these are created by tourism suppliers. Thus Cloke and Perkins (1998) describe how the lack of a bridge for bungee jumping at Taupo on North Island led to the construction of 'the world's first purpose-built cantilever bungee platform'.

Even at the most 'natural' of tourist places, some degree of manipulation and staging takes place, either in the method used to present nature, or in the 'rituals' established to experience nature (Markwell, 2001: 42). There is a desire among many young tourists to experience 'untouched nature', which may push them deeper into the jungle or the mountains. However, this search for untouched spaces may eventually threaten the environment. As Cooper *et al.* (2004) note in the case of Fraser Island in Australia, the promise of adventure presented to young backpackers includes the opportunity to drive four-wheel vehicles across wide expanses of sand dunes, causing significant environmental damage. The young adventurers seem to absolve themselves on the basis that it is a once in a lifetime experience for them.

Global market trends

A snapshot of the global youth tourism market has recently been provided by research undertaken by the Association for Tourism and Leisure Education (ATLAS) and the International Student Travel Confederation (ISTC; see Case study 5.1). The research programme has to date included email response surveys of 2300 young travellers from 8 origin countries (Richards and Wilson, 2003). This research concentrated in particular on the long trips taken by young tourists, not their total tourism consumption.

The role of adventure in long trips is underlined by the motivations of young tourists. The main motivation given was to explore other cultures, followed by experiencing excitement. There is a significant positive correlation between the motivations 'using physical skills', 'challenging my abilities' and 'searching for excitement'. Respondents who scored highly on all of these factors were equally likely to be male or female, underlining Elsrud's (2001) contention that the 'adventuress' is catching up with the male adventurer. Adventurers were likely to be more highly educated than other travellers, but there was no difference between the groups in terms of income.

Case study 5.1 The International Student Travel Confederation (ISTC)

The International Student Travel Confederation (ISTC) is a not-for-profit organization, founded in 1949 by the travel departments of a group of national student unions, to explore the needs of the growing numbers of student and youth travellers. Today the ISTC network includes over 5000 offices in 106 countries worldwide, which collectively serve the needs of over 10 million student and youth travellers each year.

The ISTC's mission is: 'to increase international understanding through the promotion of travel and exchange opportunities among students, young people and the academic community'. In the early years, members collaborated primarily on joint ventures – chartering planes, trains and ships, cutting the cost of travel for students. Today ISTC has a more flexible structure, providing targeted services in the areas of surface travel, air travel, insurance, ISIC identity cards and work exchanges. ISTC works closely with partner organizations such as UNESCO in order to further travel as a means for promoting cross-cultural understanding and awareness. ISTC has also branched out into general youth travel, offering the International Youth Travel Card to non-students, with the same benefits in terms of discounts on travel and cultural and leisure attractions. ISTC also offers an integrated communication package, combining phone, voicemail, SMS and email services in the ISIConnect service.

'Adventurous' respondents tended to see themselves as 'backpackers' more often than other respondents, and were more likely to use guidebooks to plan their trips. In terms of activities at the destination, adventurous travellers were more likely to have taken part in walking and trekking (83 per cent as opposed to 73 per cent), engaged in cultural activities (71 per cent *v*. 63 per cent), visited historic sites (81 per cent *v*. 75 per cent), watched nature or wildlife, watched sport and taken part in sport or adrenaline activities (41 per cent *v*. 23 per cent), and worked as volunteers (13 per cent *v*. 6 per cent), than were other respondents.

Wildlife and nature activities were most common for respondents who had travelled to Australia, New Zealand and South Africa, all of which recorded participation rates of over 85 per cent. Sports and adrenaline activities were much more common in Australia and New Zealand (62 per cent) than in other destinations (average 28 per cent). This tends to confirm the contention of Hudson (2003) that the adventure tourism industry is concentrated in countries such as Australia, New Zealand, Canada and the USA, where there is a mix of 'wilderness' and good facilities for sport and trekking.

When asked about what they had got from their travels, adventurers were much more likely to say that their confidence, self-awareness and appreciation of other cultures had increased, as well as their understanding of their own.

The feeling that adventurers had experienced more from their trips may be related not only to their motivation to experience as much as possible, but also to the fact that they spent more time travelling. The average trip for an adventurer was 82 days, compared with 58 days for other respondents.

The search for adventure also seems to be related to the development of 'travel careers' among young people. As travel experience increases, so people tend to travel further afield. The respondents in the present survey who were visiting Northern Europe had only made five major trips previously, compared with eight trips for visitors to Australia and over ten trips for those visiting India. This gives some indirect support for the idea of a travel career (Pearce, 1993) among the respondents, with Europeans (for example) tending to travel within Europe initially, and then to visit Australasia for their first big intercontinental trip before striking out for less developed Asian, African and Latin American destinations.

The 'travel career' idea is also supported by the fact that as travellers get older, they have built up more travel experience. Older, more experienced travellers tended to visit more distant regions or more 'adventurous' destinations, spending more money as their age and experience increased.

Enclaves as experience factories

One of the important spatial aspects of long-haul youth travel is the emergence of 'enclaves' that are dominated by backpackers and travellers and by the suppliers of travel services. The first backpacker enclaves began to emerge in the late 1960s, stimulated by the growth of the hippie trail to Asia. Laycock (2003) charts the development of 'Freak Street' in Kathmandu as one of the early enclaves. Khao San Road in Bangkok began to emerge as a distinct enclave in the early 1980s, and Kings Cross in Sydney later in the same decade, stimulated by the growth of long-haul air travel. Enclaves are now evident in many destinations in the developed and developing world, as well as in urban and rural areas.

Enclaves develop in new regions as backpackers move on to pioneer new locations as the wave of mass tourism catches up with existing enclaves (Westerhausen, 2002). The process is evident in South East Asia, where many travellers now avoid more long-established enclaves, such as Khao San, and head for the newer centres in Cambodia and Vietnam.

Backpacker enclaves take on a central function in the travellers' (sub)culture, becoming 'refuelling stations' where they can take a hot shower, get an imported beer, use the Internet and watch the latest movies. Most importantly, however, these are also places to meet fellow travellers. The stories and urban myths of the backpacker subculture are reproduced and exchanged in the enclave, and traveller status can be established through storytelling. Binder (2004) emphasizes the travellers' need to return to the enclave to be able to communicate their stories to other backpackers, thereby confirming their status as an 'adventurer'.

Enclaves have also become the hubs of traveller routes. Well-established trails follow the availability of work or the staging of major events, such as the Oktoberfest, the Glastonbury Festival and the running of the bulls in Pamplona. Specific events are also created by the very presence of backpackers, such as the Full Moon parties in Thailand. The enclaves therefore become a world unto themselves, in which the familiar and exotic are mixed. Lloyd (2003: 355) describes the recent development of 'traveller cafés' in Hanoi and Ho Chi Minh City to cater for a flood of young backpackers: 'Traveller cafés form a safe bubble from which travellers can gaze out at the unfamiliar, while surrounded by comforts from home'.

The young adventure-seekers therefore find neither the 'authentic' local culture they are seeking, nor a perfect copy of their home environment. Rather they are 'suspended' in the enclave, caught between the ideology of travel as an adventure in places far from home and the practice of consuming that adventure as just another westernized, commodified 'experience' (Richards and Wilson, 2004).

Future developments

Demand trends

Youth and adventure travel appear to have considerable growth potential, thanks to rising incomes in some major potential source markets, such as Central and Eastern Europe, Asia and Latin America, combined with lower travel costs. Growing student numbers around the globe, particularly in developing countries, should also fuel demand.

Rising incomes in newly industrializing countries and the globalization of youth culture are likely to drive the expansion of new source markets for youth tourism. Markets that in the past have been dominated by older, wealthier tourists will gradually develop larger proportions of youth travellers. In particular, there is considerable potential in countries such as China, India and Korea. Young Chinese, for example, are beginning to take up the Western habit of backpacking as an alternative form of travel (Richards and Wilson, 2004).

Most importantly, travel has become an essential element of global youth culture. The importance of travel experience in self-development and identity creation means that not having travelled will increasingly be equated with lack of experience, or having missed out. The more young people travel, the more they also realize how much more there is to see. The most frequently quoted benefit of travel is 'a thirst for more travel', according to the respondents to the ATLAS/ISTC survey (Richards and Wilson, 2003).

There is evidence that as the youth market develops and social pressures to grow up diminish in many countries, so more older 'youth travellers' are emerging. Research in New Zealand (Newlands, 2004) indicates the presence of a significant proportion of over 30 travellers who have similar travel patterns to their younger counterparts. These travellers will probably demand a greater degree of comfort as well as less time-consuming ways of travelling, while continuing to maintain the ideology (if not the reality) of adventurous travel.

It is also likely that youth and adventure tourism will become less male-dominated in future. The shift from the adventurer to the adventuress noted by Elsrud is mirrored in the growing proportion of female long-haul travellers. This may be one aspect of change to which the youth and adventure travel suppliers will find it harder to adapt.

Supply trends

A wide range of commercial suppliers is discovering the youth and adventure travel markets, and the original small-scale producers are gradually being joined by larger players. Accor has entered the backpacker market with their Base Backpackers brand, which now has seven hostels in Australia and New Zealand (see Case study 5.2). Transport is also being increasingly packaged, with operators such as Oz Experience and Contiki offering complete experiences and comprehensive routings. Stray Travel, for example, runs 'travel networks' around Europe, Australia and New Zealand, which get you 'further off the beaten track, closer to the locals, outstanding attractions and exploring; better value for money'. The development of such networks has a particularly strong influence on

Case study 5.2 Base Backpackers: a new concept in youth travel?

The Base Backpackers brand has been launched by Accor Hotels, one of the world's largest hotel chains, in an effort to tap the growing youth market. Base Backpackers is directed by Graeme Warring, a veteran backpacker operator who previously worked for Oz Experience and Backpackers World. The Base website sets out the concept: 'base is all about offering a premium service at value prices with quality facilities and packaged up with an abundance of fun', with key values of quality, service, value and fun. Not surprisingly, this sounds like an application of basic business principles to the backpacker market – but there are some differences. For example, Base has developed 'Sanctuary – an upmarket girls only zone' in which customers will be offered a gift pack including skincare products and a 'fluffy white towel'. Base is also packaging its services to backpackers, providing them with accommodation, travel products, information, work and even a reality TV series about the backpacker life. The Base hostels tend to be relatively large, with almost 400 beds in the Auckland hostel, and provide a mix of facilities, from shared dorms to twin rooms with private facilities.

youth travel patterns in countries such as New Zealand, where public transport alternatives are limited.

Even areas such as voluntary work abroad are gradually becoming more professionalized 'products' offered on the youth and adventure travel markets. For example, i-to-i is a volunteer travel company that offers products aimed mainly at young people on a gap year (a long trip usually taken between school and higher education). Volunteer travel, which includes experiences such as language teaching, conservation projects and healthcare, gives young people the opportunity to 'support meaningful projects and to develop {yourself} as an independent traveller' (2003 brochure, p. 3). The gap-year market is growing rapidly in the UK and elsewhere, although the impacts and actual benefits of this form of 'tourism' have recently been the subject of some debate.

A coherent niche?

The increase in long-haul travel by young people will soon lead to a blurring between niche and mass tourism. We only have to look at the numbers of backpackers heading for Australia, where they account for almost 25 per cent of all international visitor nights (Cooper *et al.*, 2004), to see that this is already a big 'niche'. There is also a growing concentration of young people in particularly popular enclaves, which is giving these destinations the feel of 'mass tourism'. The development of resorts such as Queenstown in New Zealand and former rural backpacker enclaves such as Ubud in Bali underline this process.

The developing travel career of young people also has implications for the tourism industry. For example, destinations need to recognize the importance of attracting young travellers who may not generate such a rapid return for local hotels or high-class restaurants, but who may return later in their travel careers if treated well now. It is also important to recognize that the rising travel frequency of young people means that their return visit may not be delayed for decades, but may happen within a few years. A surprisingly high proportion of young travellers are already on a return trip to a long-haul destination (up to 50 per cent in the case of Australia), and their average spending tends to rise with each visit.

In the adventure tourism market there is a specific challenge emerging for the industry in providing sufficient challenge and perceived risk for the consumer. Not only is physical development beginning to reduce the number of places that can be considered to be 'wild' or 'natural', but the pressure on suppliers to ensure that their 'danger' is really 'safe' also looks likely to grow. Every time safe danger becomes real danger, and an adventure traveller doesn't make it home in one piece, there is more pressure to adopt safety measures that remove real danger and force suppliers to manufacture it instead. This suggests that youth and adventure travel products will need to be increasingly innovative and creative in future.

6

Domestic and visiting friends and relatives tourism

Philip L Pearce and
Gianna Moscardo

Introduction

Visiting friends and relatives (VFR) as a topic in tourism research is now an active area of analysis. Studies began during the 1990s, and consolidation of this research effort is continuing (Jackson, 1990; Seaton, 1994; Lehto *et al.*, 2001; Pennington-Gray, 2003). It can be argued that this research area has grown because the findings have consistently revealed the substantial scale and socio-economic importance of the VFR markets in diverse domestic and international settings. Both industry voices and academic analyses now view VFR travel as an integral part of the broad definition of tourism, bringing its own important commercial outcomes and opportunities.

Defining visiting friends and relatives

One measure of the growing sophistication of studies in the VFR arena lies in the effort directed towards understanding the complexities and parameters of the phenomenon. There are now clear answers to the question: what does VFR mean in contemporary tourism study? For example, a typology of VFR travel was proposed by Moscardo *et al.* (2000b) which acts as an extended definition of the phenomenon. It suggests that there are five defining features of VFR tourism; sector, scope, effort, accommodation used, and the focus of the visit. The first VFR feature (that of sector) identifies that VFR tourism may function as the major motive for a trip, or alternatively it may be one of a number of holiday motives. These sector types may be subdivided by the next level of analysis (that of scope), which specifies whether the travel is domestic or international. The difference between short-haul and long-haul travel is labelled as effort. For countries with a small physical area most domestic travel will be of the short-haul type (defined as less than four hours' travel time), but in larger nations some domestic VFR might involve substantial interstate or regional travel effort and cost. One of the earliest and most basic descriptions used to portray VFR travel was that of accommodation use, but the simple proposition that VFR travel always involves staying with friends and relatives is not sound because the research has revealed more varied arrangements. The distinction employed in the VFR typology is to note the difference between AFR (accommodated solely with friends and relatives) and NAFR (not accommodated solely with friends and relatives), where the latter term refers to travellers who spend at least one night in commercial accommodation as a part of their travel structure. It can be noted that NAFR may be due to restrictions on house space, or the size of the visiting party, as well as motivational considerations. Nevertheless, while travellers with VFR motives or who have VFR as an activity may choose not to be accommodated with the visited personnel, they may maintain a suite of VFR links and behavioural patterns. A final factor in the typology, labelled the 'focus of the visit', notes the differences among visiting friends, visiting relatives, and visiting both. The socio-economic and behavioural considerations contingent upon this final factor can be considerable, such as the contrast between a quiet weekend with the grandparents or an enthusiastic reunion with school friends.

An important implication of the typology is that these factors need to be taken into account when considering the kinds of VFR market under study. The typology results in 48 possible VFR types, since there are four factors each of which is at two levels, and one factor of three levels ($2 \times 2 \times 2 \times 2 \times 3 = 48$ possible types). In addition to defining VFR tourism, the typology helps categorize the concentration of existing VFR research and reveals potential markets for more specific industry promotional efforts (*cf.* Pennington-Gray, 2003). Figure 6.1 provides a summary of the typology with its different factors and potential combinations.

State of the art – VFR research

Market size and distribution

The overall statistics describing VFR travel in its multiple phases are impressive. Mostly these statistics relate to VFR as the main purpose of travel, so they can be seen as underestimating some of the VFR as an activity segment. When the VFR market is conceived as the main reason for travelling and applied to domestic visitors, figures from the United States indicate that it may constitute over 40 per cent

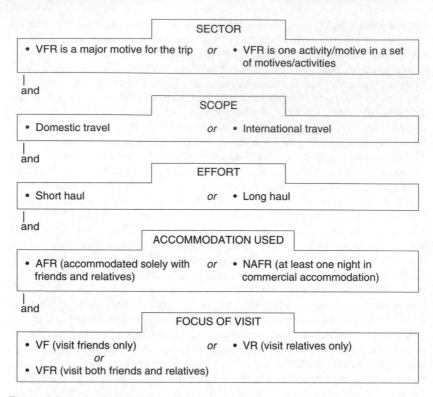

Figure 6.1 A typology of VFR travellers

of all domestic visitors (Hawkins, 1986). Further data reveal that VFR travel provides a similar proportion of all domestic trips – *circa* 40 per cent – within the United Kingdom (Denman, 1988).

It is also valuable to report a broader international perspective on domestic VFR tourism. Many citizens in developing countries not only have less money available for travel purposes, but socio-cultural norms also effectively require them to stay with family and friends when visiting. Taken together, these forces promote VFR tourism as a dominant form of travel in poorer countries. It is not surprising, therefore, that studies in Indonesia (Gunawan, 1996), Mexico (Barkin, 2001), India (Rao and Suresh, 2001) and China (Ghimire and Li, 2001) have all attested to the significance of VFR tourism.

In Table 6.1, some of the key studies outlining the scale of VFR tourism internationally are reported. An examination of this table highlights the importance of migration and ethnic links connecting international source markets and destinations. There is a strong vein of demographic and geographic analysis in VFR tourism research that can be characterized in at least two ways. One approach is to view current VFR tourism as reflecting the historical trends and migration links that have been established in previous decades. Thus in Table 6.1 Chadwick's (1984) work in Canada reflects the British ties to that country, while King and Gamage (1994) observe the return-visit behaviour of Australian-based Sri-Lankans to their country of birth. Lehto *et al.* (2001) produce an array of VFR

Table 6.1 Illustrations of research on the international VFR market

Researchers	Region/country	Study findings
Chadwick, 1984	Canada	VFR is the main reason for travel for over 50 per cent of UK visitors to Canada
Devas, 1986	South America	VFR and business travel together lead international visitation statistics in South America
Gillmor and Kockel, 1994	Ireland	41 per cent of international visitors to Ireland gave VFR as their reason for visiting
Huang et al., 1996	Taiwan	Outbound Taiwanese travel is dominated by VFR travel to Hong Kong and mainland China
Theuns, 1995	Western Samoa	Expatriate Samoan VFRs form a large proportion of all Samoan travellers
Meis et al., 1995	Canada	VFR underlies multiple repeat visit behaviour for many US visitors to Canada
Lehto et al., 2001	United States	Analysis of multiple international VFR markets to the USA confirmed differences based on the Moscardo et al. typology

figures from international destinations to the United States, but leading the VFR visit list is, not surprisingly, Mexican VFR tourism.

The studies by Theuns (1995) and Huang et al. (1996) reinforce the same links in different parts of the world. These historical ties and migration and re-visit affiliations can also be seen in a second and more contemporary framework. Boyne (2001) notes that travel in general, especially for older age groups, may identify desirable locations for retirement. When such retirement takes place – for example, UK residents and Northern Europeans relocating to Southern Europe – a new wave of contemporary VFR tourism is set in train as the grandparents, children and grandchildren flow between the newly established destinations.

The historic and contemporary influences on VFR tourism proposed here constitute one part of an argument that VFR travel will exist wherever people have their friends and relatives. Such an argument is, however, not entirely straightforward. Boyne (2001) sees a synergy between the high-quality environmental factors that encourage retirement or out-migration, and the appeal of the destination to would-be VFR visitors. Seaton and Palmer (1997) offer a contrasting view and argue that the intensity of VFR tourism is directly related to the size of the population in a destination region. The contrast is clear; in one view VFR tourism simply reflects population density and the opportunity for visits, while in the other view VFR tourism is heightened by attractive locations of friends and relatives. This debate represents one research direction in an array of such new possibilities in the analysis of VFR.

Differences in VFR markets

There are two cautionary points that must be specified before reporting differences in VFR markets. First, as has already been established, VFR is a complex, multifaceted phenomenon, but one that is likely to differ between countries – particularly in terms of traditions of expenditure and host behaviours. Second, quite a number of existing VFR studies have been conducted on small-scale convenience samples, so the broader validity of the information may be questionable. The focus of the discussion in this section is therefore largely drawn from one of the largest studies of international VFR tourism, that of Lehto *et al.* (2001), although it must be noted that their work applies to the ten most important VFR markets to just one destination – the United States.

Lehto *et al.* (2001) reported that VFR travellers spent less if VFR was their main purpose for visiting, rather than simply being an activity. This was also linked to the use of commercial accommodation, and hence higher expenditure. That is, those travellers for whom VFR travel was linked to multiple trip purposes and activities were more likely to pay for their accommodation in a range of establishments. Nearly half of the international VFRs to the United States used commercial accommodation, and this finding signals that international VFRs are worthy of promotional attention for regional marketers. The commercial accommodation user group (NAFRs) also tended to spend more on food, beverages, transportation, golf, souvenir shopping and entertainment.

These United States findings on expenditure are in accord with the research efforts of Moscardo *et al.* (2000b), also using large-scale samples, who established that there were Australian VFR groups who differed markedly in their activity participation. Moscardo *et al.* (2000b) identified four VFR activity groups:

1. A beach relaxation group, characterized by those seeking warm sunny weather, the coastal destinations, beaches and shopping
2. An inaction group, where people appeared to do a small amount of touring but were largely short-haul visitors focusing on being with their hosts
3. Active nature lovers, who, by way of contrast, used airlines to reach their destinations, were strongly attracted by the weather, and were the highest users of outdoor settings such as reef and rainforest natural environments
4. Those actively involved in theme parks, family activities and accessing local attractions; this group was younger, accompanied by children, and used suites and apartments as well as staying with friends and relatives.

This kind of study begins to construct a richer picture of the multiple realities of VFR tourism. The diversity of activities described in the research is a reminder that VFR tourists are ubiquitous in many different sectors of tourism, including attractions, shopping malls and restaurants.

Social considerations

The relationships associated with relatives and friends provide a powerful stimulus to repeat travel. Meis *et al.* (1995) observed the critical importance of relationship links in multiple visits to Canada, and found dozens or more contacts over extended periods of time. VFR tourism may also involve reciprocity – that is, families and friends moving between two locations on a cyclical or turn-about basis. There are untapped research issues here, such as whether or not multiple VFR traffic is only sustained if there is reciprocity or return travel, and also whether the processes work differently for friends and for family relationships.

Seasonality has also been discussed in relation to VFR tourism, with the common observation that this kind of travel is beneficial to regions because it provides visitors in low- and shoulder-season periods (Boyne, 2001). A study by Seaton and Palmer (1997) observed that VFR tourism peaked in non-traditional or low-season months of the year. They note that the month of December is particularly important in the United Kingdom VFR market, and suggest that such peaks of activity may represent a form of seasonal compensation for more general tourism markets. As highlighted earlier, generalizations about VFR markets need to be considered within the local cultural and regional contexts. Massive VFR activity exists in China and Japan at quite different times of the year – notably the Golden Weeks, which influence the holiday calendar in Asia. The implication of these diverse seasonality perspectives is that close attention to local holiday-taking patterns must be a part of any specific appraisal of VFR seasonality. Case study 6.1 provides an example of VFR and seasonal travel.

There are further social and quality of life dimensions associated with VFR travel. When an individual or family group has moved away from an original base or is relatively new to a setting, the arrival of friends and relatives may provide an opportunity to justify and assess the new location through the eyes of others. For longer-term residents, the opportunity to show visitors around their local environment may engender some civic pride and foster a sense of belonging to a developing and changing community.

As other topics elaborating the complexity of VFR tourism are explored there is increasingly less research evidence, and more questions waiting to be answered. The issue of who makes decisions regarding the on-site behaviour of VFR guests, for example, is not well established. Cross-cultural differences in VFR analysis have been mentioned indirectly in the preceding discussion. Certainly the differences

Case study 6.1 Christmas travel in Australia

Unlike in the northern hemisphere, where much of VFR research data is based, the Christmas season in Australia coincides with the summer holidays, suggesting that VFR travel may not always be concentrated in low tourist seasons. According to the Bureau of Tourism Research (BTR), in Australia domestic overnight travel associated with visiting family and friends to celebrate Christmas accounts for more than 12 per cent of all visitor nights each year.

The data on these travel patterns also suggest that this type of travel is associated with younger generations visiting parents and grandparents. This reinforces the connection between retirement location and VFR travel. The BTR also reports that while average daily expenditure for these VFR Christmas trips is lower than that of other domestic travel types, Christmas trips are often longer. This means that the average expenditure per trip is much higher for a Christmas VFR trip (AUS$438) than for other VFR travel (AUS$273). Finally, the statistics available on this phenomenon suggest that one aspect of VFR travel that may have been neglected is that of joint travel by different family groups to a tourist destination to share a holiday experience.

Source: Robertson (2002)

between Western countries have been noted, and the importance of understanding the context for any specific VFR analysis has been highlighted.

Business dimensions

Many analyses of VFR markets stress the value of the studies for promotional and marketing purposes, describing initiatives to aid VFR travel such as promoting local awareness of commercial offerings, discounts for locals who bring a visitor or friend to an attraction, and seasonal campaigns to stimulate off-peak travel (see Case study 6.2). These suggestions reflect some of the ways in which businesses and economic returns can be traced to VFR influences. First, there is the additional expenditure incurred by locals who host their friends and relatives. This may be simply additional food items, but can extend to furnishing additional bedrooms and bathrooms. The stimulus of having visitors may also prompt greater use of local restaurants, and additional car travel and entertainment options.

Another source of income for businesses created by VFR travel is generated by visitors purchasing gifts and thank-you mementos for their hosts. Further, since some guests stay for considerable periods of time in the hosting accommodation, there may also be multiple occasions where the visitors buy meals for both themselves and their host group.

Case study 6.2 Developing a VFR marketing campaign in Canada

Lighthouses are important historical sites in Bruce County, Ontario, in the Great Lakes area of Canada. Like many other types of historic building, finding the funding to support the preservation and maintenance of the lighthouses is an ongoing challenge for those responsible for their management. Also like many other historic sites, tourism is often one of the few options available to meet these challenges. The Bruce County development commission decided to focus on developing and promoting lighthouse tours to the very large VFR market that the area already attracted. For the marketers, the VFR segment appealed due to its size, stability and likely interest in the local product. The promotional campaign consisted of:

- the creation of a lighthouse tour map printed on placemats and distributed to restaurants throughout the region
- the creation of a lighthouse website with a virtual lighthouse tour
- media editorial provided to regional media outlets.

The campaign was very effective, with an average increase in visitation to the lighthouses of 21 per cent and reports of extended visitor stays from local businesses. The campaign was recognized for its creativity and success with a number of awards and additional funding from the provincial government.

(Source: Lighthouse Destination in Great Lakes Canada; http://www.ontcfdc.com/success.asp?Code5=277 (accessed August 2004))

Future directions

The consolidation of VFR travel into the mainstream of tourism business thinking and its incorporation into tourism promotional practices is one element in the shift towards newer hybrid forms of tourism. There is an argument that a simple unidimensional assessment of travel types is limited because there are intersections between, for example, business travel and pleasure travel, and, of interest to the present chapter, some new hybrid links between VFR travel, pleasure travel, business travel, and conference and events attendance.

One particular feature of contemporary global business has important implications for VFR travel. Increasingly, there is enhanced mobility of labour both within and between developing and developed nations. Such mobility may generate more VFR travel in at least two ways: first, many individuals who have relocated due to work opportunities may wish to return to their source countries or regions for VFR linked vacations; and secondly, the presence of known contacts in a new location may stimulate those who do not usually travel to undertake trips to appealing and even marginal tourist destinations. Deregulated airlines and budget travel carriers, particularly in Europe, are also powerful forces in permitting friends and relatives to reconnect. These newer forms of mixed motive, multipurpose trips suggest that destinations should endeavour to identify themselves as VFR-friendly, since a multitude of links and benefits can progress from the VFR core. An important part of this development is the extent to which local citizens feel they are supported by regional tourism bodies and businesses when their friends and relatives come to stay.

7

Conference tourism – MICE market and business tourism

Adele Ladkin

Introduction

The Meetings, Incentives, Conferences (or Conventions) and Exhibitions (MICE) industry is extensive and rapidly growing, and is largely associated with travel for businesses purposes. MICE-related events include meetings, conferences, conventions, congresses, exhibitions, expositions, and incentive travel (Ladkin and Spiller, 2000: 1). Each of the different subsections of MICE has quite different characteristics, and although the industry often refers to MICE in the holistic way, the four sectors are quite distinct. However, despite the varying characteristics, there are overlaps between the sectors. For example, hotel accommodation may be the same for conference events, incentive trips or attending exhibitions. Conferences may be organized in association with a major exhibition, or as part of an incentive travel reward. The sectors may use the same facilities at venues or destinations, and they may have similar information technology (IT) requirements. Increasingly, convention bureaus serve the needs of meetings, incentives and exhibition organizers, and service providers supply each of the sectors. Therefore, despite the distinct nature of each sector there are commonalties between them that result in the blurring of boundaries. The multidimensional nature of the sectors is likely to be increasingly apparent in the future.

Each of the sectors is important within its own right, but due to the size and complexity of the industry it is impossible to discuss them all. Therefore, the approach taken in this chapter is to focus on the conference and meetings sectors, and refer to incentives and exhibitions where appropriate. Within the MICE industry, conference tourism is one of the main sectors, and it refers to all those activities associated with planning, travel to and participation in conferences and meetings, both domestic and international. It has the additional benefit of also including an element of leisure tourism, in the form of delegates extending their stay after the event for leisure purposes, in social programmes, and in persons accompanying delegates, blurring the distinction between business and leisure tourism and contributing to the benefits of conference tourism to destinations (Davidson, 1998).

Although assessments of the value of the sector vary, in the UK the British Conference Market Trends Survey (2001) estimated that conferences contributed £7.3 billion to business tourism revenues (Rogers, 2003:65). In Australia, it is recognized that the MICE sector provides about US$7 billion annually in direct expenditure to the Australian economy (McCabe *et al.*, 2000:21). Due to the diversity of activities and the international nature of the industry, figures that demonstrate the volume and value of the industry are not easy to collate; however, both the Union of International Associations (UIA) and the International Congress and Convention Association (ICCA) provide statistics on the market share of meetings held, by a region, country and city. Both organizations also collect information on conferences relating to their nature and characteristics. Table 7.1 shows the market share of meetings organized in 2002, based on UIA statistics, and from these figures it is evident that Europe holds the dominant market share.

Table 7. 2 lists the top five countries and cities for meetings held in 2002, using ICCA statistics.

Whilst the USA dominated in terms of the country that held the most meetings, the top five cities were again in Europe.

According to Rogers (2003: 15), one explanation for the limited statistics regarding the size and value of the conference sector is the lack of accepted and properly defined terminology for the industry. This debate on definitions has been reviewed by Rogers (2003) and Ladkin (2002). However, the *International Meetings Industry Glossary 1993* (cited in Rogers, 2003: 15) provides the following definition that is useful to assist in an understanding of the conference industry. A Conference is defined as:

An event used by any organization to meet and exchange views, convey a message, open a debate or give publicity to some area of opinion on a specific issue. No tradition, continuity or periodicity is required to convene a conference. Although not generally limited in time, conferences are usually of short duration with specific objectives. Conferences are generally on a smaller scale than congresses.

Table 7.1 Regional breakdown of meetings in 2002

Continent	Percentage share
Europe	56.7
North America	16.5
Asia	13.7
South America	4.7
Australasia	3.8
Africa	4.6

Source: www.UIA.org

Table 7.2 Top five countries and cities for meeting, 2002

Ranking	Country	Meetings held	City	Meetings held
1	USA	225	Barcelona	79
2	Spain	177	Copenhagen	73
3	UK	149	Stockholm	64
4	Japan	148	Vienna	58
5	Germany	144	Lisbon	52

Source: www.ICCA.nl

The debate on definitions is likely to continue in the future, with new ideas and the changing nature of the business resulting in different concepts and definitions.

A complex industry

The MICE industry is a complex and fragmented one, which is comprised of a number of different elements. These are summarized in Table 7.3.

Whilst Table 7.3 gives a simplified view, it serves to indicate the variety within the MICE sector. Rogers (2003) and McCabe *et al.* (2000) provide a detailed examination of the different elements specifically in relation to conferences and conventions.

In terms of the consumers who will shape the future of the industry, the buyers, suppliers, and agencies and intermediaries are important elements. The buyers are the purchasers of the MICE products and are those people who, for a variety of reasons, wish to hire a conference or exhibition venue, together with a range of services in order to hold a particular event. The suppliers in the industry are those elements that provide the destinations, venues and services to fulfil the demand. Agencies and intermediaries may provide a buying role on behalf of clients, or act as the 'middle man' for a range of activities including the running and planning of an event. The three elements of buyers, suppliers and intermediaries interact to form the total product, and changes in any of these areas will impact on the nature of the MICE sector in terms of their future development.

Table 7.3 The different elements of the MICE industry

Element	Divisions
Sector	Meetings, incentives, conferences, exhibitions
Buyers	Corporate, association, public sector
Suppliers	Destinations (the facilities at the location), venues (hotels, purpose-built convention centres, unusual venues) and service providers, destination management companies
Agencies and intermediaries	Professional conference organizers and venue-finding agencies
Others	Trade associations, national tourist associations, industry consultants, educational institutions, catering services, translators, photographers, video services, and merchandizing

Emerging consumer trends

Several changing consumer traits are evident that are shaping the future of the industry, and these include:

- market demand
- venue selection, satisfaction and organizing conferences
- information technology
- marketing and branding.

Market demand

The growth of the industry can be attributed to a number of factors which are closely related to the demand for tourism in general. However, some factors have driven demand specifically in the conference sector:

1. An increase in commerce and global corporations, with globalization fuelling the rise in undertaking business overseas and creating the need for more meetings and exhibitions
2. The increased need for training and knowledge transfer, skills sharing and working on multinational teams (this is related to the first point, above)
3. The formation of new societies and associations that have regular meeting requirements
4. The constant need for sales and product launches that require face-to-face meetings
5. Incentive travel trips increasingly being offered as a reward to employees in corporate environments.

The buyers of the above products often have different needs, and this demand creates a range of different suppliers in terms of location, venue types, service providers and organizers. The different types of demand are fuelling variety and diversity in the supply and new products are emerging, with the appeal of long-haul and exotic destinations attracting delegates further afield. A current trend is the

Table 7.4 Important elements in venue selection and satisfaction

Venue selection	Venue satisfaction
Cost	Value for money
Location and access	Good service quality
Time and duration of conference	High-quality food and beverages
Technical requirements	Audiovisual capabilities
The size of the conference	Availability of breakout rooms
Configuration of rooms	A high ratio of space to participants
Destination image	Control of lighting, ventilation and temperature
Leisure opportunities	Social programme and sightseeing opportunities

diversity in the types of venues used. Although city centre and airport hotels are still favoured locations for many corporate buyers, there is a growth in 'unusual venues'. These include sporting venues, museums and tourist attractions, historic houses, etc., and are designed to provide a different type of conference experience. Responses to changing consumer tastes and new demands will continue to influence the supply to the MICE sectors. The future will consist of greater diversity in the range of venues for events.

Venue selection, satisfaction and organizing conferences

Given the variety in the supply of facilities, an understanding of how venues are selected by consumers, whether they are satisfied with the experience, and who is responsible for organizing conferences and meetings offers an insight into future trends in demand. Beginning with venue selection, there is a wealth of research that explores how venues are selected, with each study providing similar findings (Oppermann, 1996; Crouch and Ritchie, 1998; Upchurch *et al.*, 1999). Aspects that are important in venue selection and satisfaction are identified in Table 7.4.

Poor service quality along with an inadequate standard of furnishings and facilities are cited as some of the most common causes of dissatisfaction with the event. With the new consumers as discerning conference attendees, the importance of creating the right environment and providing good facilities and service quality is paramount. Future events will have to satisfy higher consumer demands and expectations.

Organizing conferences falls to a range of different people, depending on the size and nature of the buyer and the event. For the larger events, the services of a professional conference organizer (PCO) are often employed. These carry out a range of services in the planning and running of the activities. Large organizations may also employ a dedicated organizer if conferences are a regular activity with the corporate environment. However, for smaller conferences and for regular corporate meetings, the organization often falls to a manager in the company or, more commonly, a PA or secretary. This variation in the person responsible for organizing events causes problems for the industry, as it is not easy to target marketing and promotions to the relevant person. However, the people responsible for organizing conferences are the contact point for the conference providers, and are clearly influential in the venue selection process. It is likely that as products diversity and the number of events increases, the role of PCOs will be expanded in the future.

Information technology

A combination of new technology, the availability of IT services and increasing consumer competence in using IT could reduce the need for conferences. Indeed, face-to-face meetings are cost-ineffective compared to communication by technological means (Munro, 1994: 200). However, rather than being detrimental to the growth of the conference industry, developments in IT and consumer willingness to use them have a positive effect on the industry as IT encourages communication between people who are separated by long distances, which may result in a physical meeting.

One of the factors that has had a major impact is the development of the Internet (Buhalis, 2003). The information needs of the industry have benefited from IT developments, particularly in terms of destination and venue selection and conference management systems. Destination and venue selection is improved by the variety and range of information available online that can assist in the decision-making process. Management systems, information and programmes, booking forms, abstracts and papers, attendance confirmation, hotel reservations and payment details can be posted, downloaded and completed via the Internet. Event management software reduces administration, time and financial costs (Ladkin and Spiller, 2000). McCabe *et al.* (2000: 291) offers a useful categorization for analysing the IT developments that currently are used in the industry: technology in convention operations and technology for the client. Technology in operations includes the software available for meeting planners, all aspects of marketing, online reservations and registration, food and beverage services, management systems, and desktop publishing for the range of printed conference materials. The technology for the client includes audiovisual equipment, and tele- and video-conferencing. In terms of IT benefits for delegates, a whole range of information from hotel details to electronic maps can be produced via the Internet. At the event delegates can access a host of IT facilities, including personal programming smart cards, and CD-Roms (Ladkin and Spiller, 2000: 74). Delegates also often have access to a range of business facilities that include IT services such as e-mail and fax. Finally, the use of IT after the event should also be remembered. This includes evaluation on a range of issues, from food and beverages to the technology used during the conference.

These technological advances have two distinct implications for the industry in the future. The first is in relation to staff in the industry at conference venues, who will be required to be competent in IT skills in order to provide an effective service to the clients and delegates. The second relates to competitive advantage. If venues are to be competitive and wish to attract clients, they need to offer the latest IT services. Venues will have to respond to the consumer demand for up-to-date technology.

Marketing and branding

With increasingly sophisticated marketing strategies used by all elements of the tourism industry to attract consumers, branding and relationship marketing are being employed by suppliers to attract custom. In terms of branding, the importance of destination marketing organizations has been highlighted by Rogers

(2003), whereby DMOs are responsible for the creation of a destination image and in the selling of a destination. Effective branding facilitates a positive action in customers by influencing the decision-making process, thereby encouraging them to choose a brand that they recognize and identify with. Effective destination branding is therefore vital for the attraction and sustainable development of conference tourism (Morgan *et al.*, 2002).

Relationship marketing is a further integral part of the marketing activities of suppliers. One of the key features of venue and destination marketing is the forging of relationships between the suppliers and buyers – the building of trust between those offering the facilities and services and those looking to make use of them to stage events (Rogers, 2003: 104). It is in the interests of the suppliers and the buyers to work together and to forge relationships that are beneficial to both parties. Therefore, the focus on marketing to the new consumers is on building good relationships that will in turn generate profitable transactions (McCabe *et al.*, 2000). Future marketing efforts will focus on the development of relationships and creating a strong brand identity.

Future trends

As with most businesses, the MICE industry is not static. As demand for certain elements alters, changes in supply will inevitably follow. As supply changes in order to meet perceived or new demand, it is the consumer who is often at the forefront of any changes in the industry. For the MICE industry, in recent years a number of issues have occurred:

- increased demand for conferences
- changes in the business environment
- increased competition
- service quality issues
- safety and security
- disabled travellers' needs.

These are the drivers of future trends.

Increased demand for conferences

The conference industry operates within the same economic and political environment as the rest of the tourism business and, despite recent economic difficulties, the outlook for conference tourism is optimistic. Research by Weber and Ladkin (2003) indicates that companies and associations predict they will hold at least the same, and probably more, conferences over the next five years. Evidence from the ICCA and the UIA supports this growth trend. Despite advancements in information technology that have altered the nature of international communication, there is still a perceived need for face-to-face meetings. The range of meetings is varied and has been identified earlier, and the conference industry forms a major component of business tourism. Alford (2002) suggests that despite the developments in video-conferencing, face-to-face meetings will still be popular as conferences are active and participatory in style, with the emphasis on dialogue and networking. Furthermore, conferences are often located in cities of tourist interest which offer good opportunities for social activities.

Changes in the business environment

Set against the background of increased demand, changes in the business environment also impact on the demand for MICE activities. Although the need for personal meetings is recognized, in reality employees are facing increasing time pressures and workloads. This results in shorter meetings, often with fewer delegates. Meetings may also be undertaken with less notice, resulting in shorter lead times for meeting organizers. The desire to meet has to be viewed in balance with the economic realities that businesses face. However, the development of international businesses and worldwide markets ensures that the need to meet continues. Furthermore, incentive travel opportunities are frequently used as rewards to hardworking executives as a means of reducing employee burnout.

Increased competition

Given the encouraging trend amongst venues for continued demand for conferences, competition amongst venues and organizers for business is increasing. The increase in the number of venues, the improvement of existing facilities, more competitive prices from new and emerging destinations and higher consumer expectations are fuelling competition in conference industry supply. The favourable pricing and high service quality of many Asian destinations is drawing business away from some of the European destinations. Therefore it is essential, if venues are to remain in business, that they stay one step ahead of consumer demand.

Service quality issues

As with other elements of the tourism industry, service quality is an important component of the MICE product. It is the service quality that often gives a venue the competitive edge, yet service quality is one of the main causes of dissatisfaction with conference venues and events. With an increasingly demanding consumer to satisfy, venues and destinations have to ensure high service quality in all aspects of the business, from recognizing client needs to the food and beverages at an event. Poor service quality is no longer acceptable to the buyers of event facilities and services. Venues will have to ensure high service quality in order to remain competitive. In the incentives sector, it is increasingly high-quality and luxury products that are most often used as a travel reward.

Safety and security

Increasingly, issues of safety and security are on the agenda when organizing major events, and in the selection of destinations and venues. Events such as the

11 September 2001 terrorist attacks on the USA, and associated media coverage, have heightened safety issues in the minds of international travellers, and have become a serious concern for many modes of transport and accommodation venues. Although terrorist activity may be seen as one extreme, the security of delegates at destinations and venues is a real concern for the MICE industry. Buildings have to be designed that comply with health and safety issues, and destinations have to work hard to combat any negative images caused by security concerns. A further factor is financial security and the limitations of the Internet. Concern about security of credit card details, lost e-mails, inaccuracies on databases that recur, and lost data due to systems failures are all issues that the conference industry must address in order to provide a secure environment for conference and exhibition delegates.

Disabled travellers' needs

A recent consumer trend that will have an impact on the MICE sector relates to the Disability Discrimination Act (DDA), which took effect from October 2004 in the UK. This Act gives disabled people a full range of access rights, including to buildings, transport, and cultural, commercial and social activities. The impact of this on venues is that both new and existing facilities will have to be designed to allow for disabled access. This includes access for those with visual and hearing disabilities, for wheelchair users, and for people with learning disabilities. Venues will have to adapt physical space, catering facilities and means of communication so that they are accessible to less able delegates.

The future MICE industry

The MICE industry in the future is likely to be similar in structure to the industry we see today, with the main changes in demand being those that have been reviewed here. In terms of supply, convention centres with state-of-the-art facilities and infrastructure represent one way forward (see Case studies 7.1, 7.2). These combine a one-stop service for the organization of events, and have a huge variety of meeting spaces for both exhibitions and conferences. For smaller gatherings, unusual venues are meeting the needs of consumers looking for a new experience, although location factors will always ensure the success of airport and city centre hotels. Companies will also increasingly provide meeting rooms within their own buildings, thus saving on travelling times and cost. Improved service quality at all venues is a further likely future trend, to cater for more discerning consumers, and PCOs will be expected to provide tailor-made packages to suit the specific requirements of their clients. New destinations that can offer a competitive edge regarding value for money and service quality will also be successful in the future. In terms of the incentive travel market, again consumers are seeking new experiences and destinations, with novelty, luxury and convenience being key areas that determine future trends. Improvements in service, facilities, the design of venues, IT developments and competitive destinations in terms of value for money are the drivers of change in the future of the MICE industry.

Case study 7.1 BEXCO – The Busan Exhibition and Convention Centre, Korea

The BEXCO Exhibition and Convention Centre, located in the port of Busan, Korea, opened in 2001 and offers a state-of-the-art location for exhibitions and conferences. Occupying an area of $92\,761\,m^2$, it features a large and a small exhibition hall, an outdoor exhibition hall, and a permanent exhibition hall for small businesses. The Centre also has a range of conference rooms, all equipped with high-tech communication services. The BEXCO also features auxiliary facilities, such as shopping malls and restaurants, and it has the customized services of the Busan Convention Bureau. The Centre also has fast and efficient transport links by air, rail, bus and car. The BEXCO website offers a virtual tour facility, along with detailed information about the services and facilities provided. Offering a self-contained and easily accessible facility, the Busan Exhibition and Convention Centre is an example of a modern and successful convention facility.

(Website address: www.bexco.co.kr)

Case study 7.2 The New Orleans Convention and Visitor Bureau, USA

Of primary importance in the marketing and promotion of a conference destination is the role of the CVB (Conference and Visitor Bureau). The CVB serves to act as a one-stop place for information relating to all aspects of the destination and the conference facilities, dealing with a whole range of aspects such as accommodation, transport, maps and venue facilities information. Increasingly, CVBs have developed websites as the main contact point, and these can provide the user with up-to-date information on the various aspects. One such CVB with a well-developed website is the New Orleans Convention and Visitor Bureau. This CVB provides all the information that might be required for somebody wishing to find out about the various characteristics and facilities of the destination and venue. The aim of the New Orleans CVB is to offer convention services and information for visitors to New Orleans, and the site is conveniently divided into different market sectors. This enables the site-user to go directly to the relevant information for their particular inquiry.

(Website address: www.neworleanscvb.com)

Conclusions

The MICE industry is a complex and dynamic one, and its future is inevitably linked to global trends in business tourism. The future of the industry will be influenced by changes in demand, as consumer choices are the driving force behind such issues as venue selection, satisfaction with the product, expectations of venues and service quality, IT requirements, and the desire to participate in face-to-face meetings. Currently the future for the MICE industry looks positive, with emerging trends resulting in more choice, better service quality, and a diversification of products and markets. It is anticipated that the industry in the future will continue to mature and develop, benefiting all those concerned with this important business tourism sector.

8

The moralisation of tourism, and the ethical alternatives

Jim Butcher

Introduction

In recent decades, mass tourism has increasingly become a fraught affair in the view of many critics. It is often presented as culturally problematic – a typical sentiment is that tourists 'seem to be the incarnation of the materialism, philistinism and cultural homogenization that is sweeping all before it in a converging world' (McNaught, 1982: 360). According to this view tourists are carriers of the modern disease of materialism, and there is an imminent danger that they may infect others on their travels. In similar vein, tourism is viewed as essentially environmentally destructive by many critics. For example, the *Guardian* newspaper environment editor, in an article entitled 'Tourism is bad for our health', asserts that mass tourism 'wreak{s} havoc on the environment' and that despite attempts to clean up the industry, 'tourism is essentially and inescapably, environmentally destructive' (Griffiths, 2001).

The Moralisation of Tourism (Butcher, 2003) offered a polemical response to the tendency to talk up the problems and talk down the advantages associated with modern mass tourism. It argued that this tendency to exaggerate problems and dismiss the progress of which mass tourism is exemplary is a reflection of a deep-seated disillusionment with modern development in Western societies – those societies generating the large majority of tourists.

New tourism types – most notably ecotourism – have been presented as being potentially more ethical, focusing as they do on conservation and the support for traditional ways of life in host communities (see, for example, Acott *et al.*, 1998; Neale, 1999; Goodwin, 2000; Mann, 2000). Yet the moral high ground adopted by mass tourism's critics is phoney. Its contribution to the tourism experience is often guilt and angst, and it can feed into a stultifying lack of vision for economic development in impoverished host societies. This chapter discusses, and criticizes, this moralisation of tourism, and explores future implications.

Mass tourism – the problem

It is estimated that by 2020 there will be some 1.6 billion international tourists. Tourism directly employs 74 million people, with tourism-related activities estimated to provide some 200 million jobs worldwide. It provides the largest source of export earnings for countries as diverse as Spain and Barbados. By 2020, it is predicted that tourism expenditure will top US$2 trillion, or US$5 billion per day. The industry's contribution to global wealth, measured from Gross National Products, is estimated to be 4 per cent directly and 11 per cent including indirect effects (UNEP, 2001). In economic terms, mass tourism seems self-evidently vitally important.

However, it is increasingly discussed less as an economic phenomenon linked to jobs and investment, or indeed simply as enjoyment, adventure and innocent fun. Rather, tourism has progressively become discussed as a cultural and environmental phenomenon, and more often than not as fraught and destructive. It is this emphasis on mass tourism as a cultural and environmental problem that informs the moralisation of tourism.

What is the moralisation of tourism?

The moralisation of tourism involves two mutually reinforcing notions. First, mass tourism is deemed to have wrought damage to the environment and to the cultures exposed to it, and hence new types of tourism are proposed that are deemed benign to the environment and benevolent towards other cultures. Secondly, this ethical tourism is deemed to be better for tourists, too – more enlightening, encouraging respect for other ways of life and a critical reflection on the tourist's own developed society. There is a plethora of terms that academics and those in the industry have applied to this more 'moral' version of tourism, such as alternative tourism, ecotourism and responsible tourism.

Perhaps the term that covers them all, and helps to identify what is distinctive about them taken together, is that coined by industry specialist Auliana Poon – 'new tourism' (Poon, 1993). She argues that new tourism is both an appeal to a certain sense of enlightenment about one's effect on others, and also an environmental imperative. Poon outlined the marketing aspects of new tourism thus:

- holidays must be flexible and able to be purchased at prices that are competitive with mass-produced holidays
- holidays are not simply aiming at economies of scale, but will be tailored to individual wants
- unlike mass tourism, production will be driven by the wants of consumers
- mass marketing is no longer the dominant ethos – holidays will be marketed differentially to different needs, incomes, time constraints and travel interests
- holidays are consumed on a large scale by more experienced, more educated, more destination-oriented, more independent, more flexible and more 'green' travellers
- consumers of new tourism consider the environment and culture of the destinations they visit to be a key part of the holiday experience.

Poon clearly considers the new tourist to be the 'thinking tourist' – more educated, independent of mind and aware. Also, from this definition new tourism could be regarded as post-Fordist tourism – tourism that moves away from a standard, mass-produced product towards a flexible, individually tailored one, led by individual demands rather than a homogenous mass market.

For Poon, and for many other advocates of new tourism, it is far more than dry marketing for 'thinking tourists' – it is an ethical imperative; it is ethical tourism. As such it is not simply suggested as an option for prospective tourists, but is also advocated as a solution to problems caused by mass tourism. Advocacy, by NGOs (non-government organizations), campaigns and 'new tourism'-oriented tour operators, and also by many academics, is a key feature of Poon's new tourism. The charge that mass tourism has had a generally destructive impact on host societies is widely asserted in the context of this advocacy. For Poon (1993: 3):

> The tourism industry is in crisis ... a crisis of mass tourism that has brought social, cultural, economic and environmental havoc in its wake, and it is mass tourism practices that must be radically changed to bring in the new.

However, advocates of new tourism argue that there is a growing market of more ethical tourists who are rejecting mass-produced, homogenous tourism products in favour of tailored holidays that are kinder to the environment and benign to the host culture. These people perhaps constitute a new school of 'ethical' tourism, referred to here as the *new moral tourism*. The key features of their conception of leisure travel are a search for enlightenment in other places, and a desire to preserve these places in the name of cultural diversity and environmental conservation.

New moral tourism – a pervasive agenda

New moral tourism is far more than a whim of the chattering classes. It finds expression across the commercial and NGO sectors, and also, as Poon argues, is in demand from the holiday-buying public. Many academics have also pioneered the advocacy

of ecotourism, community tourism and other brands associated with the moralisation of tourism on ethical grounds, and with reference to the perceived destructive tendencies of mass tourism (e.g. Acott *et al.*, 1998; Honey, 1999; Goodwin,
2000; Scheyvens, 2002; Fennell, 2003).

There is also a diverse range of NGOs involved in the promotion of what they
perceive to be ethical tourism. Global conservation NGOs such as the World Wide
Fund for Nature (WWF), the Audubon Society and Conservation International
(CI) increasingly view ecotourism as a means of winning support, both amongst
local populations and more widely, for conservation aims. Ecotourism is at the
cutting edge of conservation initiatives, as it seems to offer opportunities for people
to benefit from preserving their natural environments rather than changing them
(Goodwin, 2000). Its ethical credentials, then, reside in its ability to combine conservation with limited development goals. More traditional forms of tourism are
regarded as less ethical as, although they generally yield more in the way of economic development, they are deemed to be environmentally destructive and culturally problematic.

More specific projects aimed at particular destinations or types of tourism
include Alp Action, the Proyecto Ambiental Tenerife, the Save Goa Campaign, and
numerous others. In general, they highlight the impacts of tourism and lobby against
developments they perceive as unethical. The range of goals of these organizations
makes any categorization problematic. However, they often express a disdain for
package tourists. For example, the Proyecto Ambiental Tenerife, a project seeking
to sustain rural traditions and traditional agriculture on this Spanish island, makes
the following comment on mass tourism:

> Mass tourism was introduced to the island of Tenerife in the 1960s. It made
> a few local people and many foreigners very rich. It also devastated the
> rural communities resulting in abandoned terraced farms; beautiful but
> dilapidated buildings; an age old culture on the edge of extinction; youth
> unemployment of 43%.
>
> (Proyecto Ambientale Tenerife, undated)

So whilst the Tenerife and Spanish economies have benefited greatly from
tourism, this NGO damns the developments as destructive of tradition. This rev-
erence for tradition over change is characteristic of the moralisation of tourism.

The International Ecotourism Society is influential in marketing and promoting the ethical credentials of 'green' holidays. Their role is not just to network
with like-minded tourists with a love of the natural world, but also to advocate
the superiority of eco-holidays for both parties concerned – tourists and hosts.
The Society claims that:

> ecotravel offers an alternative to many of the negative effects of mass
> tourism by helping conserve fragile ecosystems, support endangered
> species and habitats, preserve indigenous cultures and develop sustainable
> local economies.
>
> (TIES, undated)

It encourages prospective tourists to 'travel with a purpose – a personal
purpose and a global one'.

The International Ecotourism Society also works with various development agencies, such as the InterAmerican Development Bank, to advocate ecotourism as an environmentally benign development option – as indeed do other development and conservation NGOs such as the WWF, CI and SNV. This trajectory looks likely to develop further – it is an aim of the Society to develop this, and it also fits in with the trend towards the 'greening of development aid' (Adams, 2001) through nature-based tourism.

Calls for ethical tourism feature ever more prominently in the media, too. Journalist Libby Purves argues that 'tourists should not travel light on morals', and paints a grim picture of the effects of the industry (Purves, 2001). Green campaigner and journalist George Monbiot sums up the dim view taken of tourism by media advocates of ethical tourism when he asserts that 'tourism is, by and large, an unethical activity, which allows us to have fun at everyone else's expense' (Monbiot, 1999).

Television holiday programmes have come in for criticism over their supposed lack of ethical credentials. A recent report castigates British ITV's *Wish You Were Here* for not taking sufficient care to encourage thoughtful behaviour on the part of prospective tourists. The compiler of the report argues that: 'editorial content that meets the growing thirst for a rounded insight into a destination will enable viewers to understand the impact their visit may have on the host country' (cited in Wells, 2001). In this vein, it is not simply tourism itself that is subject to the critical eye of the new moral tourist, but also representations of places. These are deemed to appeal to our hedonistic streak, which may preclude ethical consideration. Similar points are frequently made with regard to tourist brochures, and even travel guides have been castigated for failing to present what ethical tourism campaigners consider to be an enlightened view.

These examples are illustrative of the moralisation of tourism. The holiday is represented as an arena for ethical behaviour to the benefit of other peoples and the environment, leading to a holiday experience deemed to be far superior. Many of the above assertions implicitly present mass tourism as an environmentally destructive cultural imposition. That mass tourism development has a creative side, with regard to new opportunities arising from economic development, is rarely alluded to.

The commercial sector

Advocacy of new moral tourism is also evident in the commercial sector. A host of companies, spurning the four Ss (sun, sea, sand and sex) in favour of the three Ts (travelling, trekking and trucking), have set out to appeal to the new moral tourist. Their advocacy of ethical tourism is often met with scepticism by the NGOs and campaigners, who question whether their concern to be ethical is genuine or merely a marketing ploy. Nonetheless, many such companies echo the criticisms of package tourism made by the NGOs and express a similar commitment to the environment and the host's culture. They also display a similar disdain for package tourists. Explore, a trekking holiday company, has advertised its holidays as being for 'people who want more out of their holiday than buckets of cheap wine and a suntan'. Dragoman views its trucking holidays as visiting places that have been 'shunned by the masses who prefer resorts and beaches'. Other brochures set out the important role of their clientele in relation to supporting the culture and environment of their hosts in the Third World. Encounter Overland, for example, regards its customers as 'today's custodians of the ancient relationship between traveller and the native which throughout the world has been the historic basis for peaceful contact'.

Preserving the environment is an important motif of most tours of this type – most donate a small portion of the price paid to organizations engaged in wildlife and environmental preservation. Indeed, the dividing line between private tour operator and conservationist NGO can be a fine one. Discovery Initiatives, for example, works with a number of conservation charities including WWF, whose Director, Julian Matthews, argues that 'tourism should guarantee that things which draw us now should be the same in 100 years' (cited in Coward, 2001). Discovery Initiatives donates money to help fund wardens and other resources to help bring about this vision. In similar vein CI, one of the richest of the international conservation NGOs, utilizes ecotourism as a way to win over local stakeholders to the cause of conservation. It operates its own ecotours to this end. In northwest Bolivia, ecotourists pay large sums to canoe down the Rio Tuichi to stay in stilted cabins on the edge of a lake in the rainforest. Revenue helps to train local inhabitants as guides, cooks and lodge managers, and contributes to Conservation International's goal of rainforest preservation (CI, undated). Such projects clearly involve an orientation towards the eco-consumer, and hence marketing of ecotourism-for-conservation projects is a growing issue for NGOs.

The growing gap-year phenomenon is also influenced by the ethical travel imperative. One gap-year company, Trekforce, organizes 'adventure with a purpose' for prospective customers (Trekforce, undated). The projects are focused on rainforest conservation, the construction of a jaguar research centre, work preserving coral reefs in Belize, and orang-utan conservation in Borneo. Raleigh International made the news in the UK in 2000 when Prince William took part in a typical project, which included helping in the building of a wooden cabin in rural Peru.

This much-publicized gap year, and the experience of many others, suggests that gap years can be an exciting and unique experience for those inclined to such work. However, the claims to be contributing to these poor societies may be more circumspect. Projects based on preserving the environment are, in truth, unlikely to help in liberating people from poverty. Their ethical credentials seem to come from the personal (but very limited) role an individual can play in development, and from a sense of personal mission accompanying such pursuits.

What all the pronouncements from this variety of organizations and individuals point towards is a profoundly negative view of the development of mass tourism, and also an appeal, implicit or explicit, for tourists to change their lifestyle and regard their holidays in a different way – as vehicles for environmental and cultural conservation. It is held that host communities, their environment and culture – and indeed the tourists too – will be the losers if this does not happen. It is suggested that the tourist also benefits from the new moral tourism approach by being engaged in something more meaningful and enlightening than typical package holidays. The influence of these sentiments constitutes the moralisation of tourism.

Demand for new moral tourism?

There is some evidence of a growth in market segments that might be associated with the moralisation of tourism. According to the World Resources Institute, whilst tourism grew by 4 per cent in the early 1990s, 'nature travel' grew at a rate of 10–30 per cent. World Tourism Organization estimates show global spending on the more narrowly defined ecotourism market increasing at a rate of 20 per cent per year – about five times the rate for tourism generally (UNEP, 2001).

However, leaving aside the newness of new moral tourism in terms of practice, it is evident that there is much that is new and changing in terms of the debates regarding tourism. Whilst we may not all be new moral tourists, the moralisation of tourism profoundly colours the debates about the future of the industry, and how tourists see themselves. The rise in codes of conduct (Mason and Mowforth, 1995) and critical guides promoting ethical tourism (titles such as *The Good Tourist*, *The Green Tourist Guide*, *Community Tourism Directory* etc.), and the increase in campaign and NGO activity around the issues (Mowforth and Munt, 1998), illustrate that the new moral tourism is a prominent moral agenda. The weight given to ecotourism in the burgeoning number of college and university courses featuring tourism, and the talking up of ethical tourism in the media, also point in the same direction.

The breadth of deference to the ethical agenda gives it an air of moral authority – it is often simply assumed that we must all agree. For example, in *The Green Travel Guide*, Greg Neale, the *Sunday Telegraph* environment correspondent, informs us that:

> surely we know the damage that modern day mass transport and tourism docs: polluted beachlines, once undisturbed hillsides now scarred by the paths of numberless walkers, package holiday jet planes churning out more pollution into the atmosphere, formerly tranquil fishing villages now concrete canyons that reverberate every summer's evening to the beery brayings of tee shirted tourists.
>
> (Neale, 1999)

Presumably resorts such as Torremolinos come into this category – a place that 50 years ago was a poor fishing village ('picturesque') and now hosts affordable fun for many foreign and Spanish sunseekers (written off as 'a monstrosity' in the words of this Guide).

A key aspect of new moral tourism, then, is *advocacy* – new forms of tourist behaviour (or 'tourism practice') are advocated from the commercial and public sectors, and from civil society. Hence whilst much tourism continues as before, there is a certain etiquette that many are prepared to buy into. Few take issue with the assumption implicit in new moral tourism – that tourism is essentially a destructive feature of modern society, in relation to the environment and the cultures it impinges upon.

Far from being ethical, the new moral tourism's assumptions can be restrictive in the field of development. The notion that environments can be inherently fragile should in general be viewed with caution. Economically developed societies have progressively transformed aspects of their environment in pursuit of development. One of the benefits of modern development thus defined is the ability, for many, to travel widely.

Further, the desire to preserve other cultures in the face of mass tourism and modern society ignores the truism that culture embodies aspirations for change. It is easy for tourists to see an iconic 'culture' and pristine environment as fragile, as a welcome respite from the modern world. It is also unproblematic. However, when NGOs and other influential bodies and individuals present this romantic caricature as part of an 'ethical' strategy to clean up mass tourism, then it deserves greater scrutiny than it currently gets. It is an outlook that overlooks the pressing need for development and the demand for equality in the name of environmental and cultural conservation. Should we not have the aspiration that the host should have the same opportunities, including to travel, as the tourist?

Conclusion

Tourism is becoming increasingly moralised. On the one hand, certain types of tourism, and tourist, are considered unethical, as they fail to recognize a particular notion of environmental and cultural risk. On the other, the new, ethical alternatives are seen as not only better from the perspective of the host societies, but also better for the tourists themselves. Consumer choices over what kind of holiday one prefers are transformed into moral choices, seen as having significant consequences for one's host, and also for oneself.

Whilst it is the case that distinct 'new tourism' markets remain relatively small, the moralisation of tourism is a pervasive, fluid agenda, colouring the way we see contemporary leisure travel. It casts a shadow over the growth of leisure travel – a growth that one may have assumed would be viewed in more upbeat fashion. It also questions the notion of innocent fun, traditionally associated with holidays. Simply pleasing oneself has become moral terrain … but with dubious benefits for either host or tourist.

Part Two: New Products

9

Re-engineering established products and destinations

Dimitri Ioannides

Introduction

More than two decades ago Richard Butler (1980) presented his tourist area lifecycle (TALC), which has become the 'theoretical benchmark' (Johnston, 2001a: 2) illustrating the evolutionary nature of tourist areas. Despite receiving much criticism, the TALC has proven its worth as a 'hypothetical development path' (Priestley and Mundet, 1998: 86) highlighting the forces dictating the growth, consolidation, decline and, occasionally, rejuvenation of destinations (Johnston, 2001a, b; Butler, 2004).

The single most important contribution the TALC has made to the field of tourism studies is its demonstration of destinations' dynamic character. The model portrays how a destination matures, eventually reaching a stage where it starts losing its appeal. During this phase the growth rate of arrivals stagnates and, without a major intervention by policymakers and businesses, arrivals and/or earnings are likely to decline. While some destinations do not recover from their decline, others introduce – albeit to varying degrees of success – measures to re-engineer their product and image (see Case study 9.1).

In recent years there has been growing alarm worldwide that many so-called 'mature' destinations are stagnating or declining, finding it increasingly difficult to maintain their competitive advantage. Given this phenomenon, it is perhaps surprising that few researchers have examined the latter stages of the TALC – especially regarding the manner in which a destination's revival may occur. It is evident, however, that in any destination where the TALC is experiencing stagnation, decline is inevitable if corrective measures are not implemented.

Nowhere has the impact of growing competition been felt more acutely than in the Mediterranean, where numerous coastal resorts and islands have suffered a decline in arrivals as their traditional northern European markets are drawn to emerging destinations in more 'exotic' parts of the world (e.g. the Indian and Pacific Oceans). Thus, the question on the minds of policy-makers and industry representatives is: what measures can be taken to ensure that well-established mature destinations (such as the ones located in the Mediterranean) can enhance their competitive edge *vis à vis* new entrants?

The primary aim of this chapter, then, is to focus on available measures taken by existing tourist localities to enhance their appeal to tourists. Moreover, it offers a discussion of tourist destinations that have made significant steps towards

Case study 9.1 Branson, Missouri, USA

In the early 1990s, the CBS television documentary *60 Minutes* catapulted Branson, Missouri, to instant fame as one of America's leading tourist hotspots. Half a decade later, based on its reputation as a country and western music hotspot, this tiny town was drawing more than 6 million tourists per year. However, authorities and industry representatives became alarmed that the phenomenal growth of the previous years had already peaked as Branson exhibited symptoms of stagnation, including declining occupancy rates and high business turnover rates. Reasons for this stagnation included the appearance of similar destinations in other parts of the US. Since development in Branson had taken place rapidly and uncontrollably, serious problems had emerged – including severe traffic congestion and declining overall environmental quality.

These negative factors reduced Branson's draw, leading authorities to adopt steps for diversifying the product to enhance the town's competitiveness. Among the new measures implemented were the development of discount shopping malls and the construction of luxury lodging facilities, while recently a proposal for initiating an urban redevelopment project encompassing convention facilities and upscale shops along Branson's lakefront has been examined. Retroactively, attempts have been made to alleviate the serious environmental problems associated with rapid tourism development by implementing a comprehensive land-use plan and expanding the infrastructure. Overall, authorities wish to project an image of quality as they increase their efforts to attract high-spending tourists.

reinventing their product as they strive to re-emerge as genuine contenders in the international tourism scene.

The story in Case study 9.1 is hardly unique. Like Branson, numerous places now traverse the stages of their evolutionary cycle much more rapidly than ever before (Butler, 2004). While it took places like Kona, Hawaii, decades to progress through their lifecycle (Johnston, 2001b), in other cases stagnation of the resort arrives soon after it was first explored. Various factors explain this rapid rise and fall in destinations' popularity, including changes in consumer behaviour and supply-side forces affecting the global tourist industry. In turn, because today many destinations reach the latter stages of their lifecycle more rapidly than ever before, this has dramatic implications for public authorities and private businesses in receiving areas. Specifically, both sets of actors realize that to avoid stagnation in their TALC and to boost the area's competitive advantage *vis à vis* other destinations, they must not be complacent but must instead proactively take steps to strengthen the quality and image of the products on offer.

Changing patterns of consumption

Butler (2004: 161) argues that tourism adapts and innovates frequently:

> Tourism, much more than leisure and recreation perhaps, is a fashion industry, subject to whims, fancies, and promotions. While individual forms of leisure such as music and entertainment change in popularity more frequently than most things in life, it is mostly the superficial elements which change, the activities (e.g., listening to music) themselves remaining constant. In tourism, not only such elements but also the patterns of activities change, as do the places in which they take place. Few destinations remain constant and unchanging, and those that do are most likely to be perceived as out of date and unattractive. While there may be fascination and appeal in staying at a century-old hotel, if the interior and accommodations are not up to contemporary standards, the appeal quickly disappears.

His premise is that destinations must adapt, not simply because they must modernize but also because they have to retain and enhance their competitiveness over other localities.

From the demand perspective, consumers situated in the traditional tourist markets of Western Europe and North America have become increasingly discerning and no longer are satisfied with inflexible, all-inclusive travel packages to traditional destinations such as Mediterranean seaside resorts. Instead, the so-called 'post-tourists' desire independent holidays catering to their special interest needs. They are unlikely to demonstrate loyalty to any one particular destination, choosing each year to add to their 'collection' of places visited (Butler, 2004). Consequently, each destination finds itself in a situation where it must constantly reinvent itself to edge out the competition. The problem is that while a few places, like Las Vegas, remain strongly poised to keep substituting or adding attractions, other destinations lack the diversified resources for retaining their competitiveness and may be forced to contemplate a future without tourism.

79

External and internal forces

Beyond the changing tastes of consumers, the interaction of several external with internal forces undoubtedly influences a destination's lifecycle (Agarwal, 2002). External 'macro-structural conditions' (Johnston, 2001a: 17) include happenings on the geopolitical stage, such as war and international terrorism, but also major catastrophic natural disasters like earthquakes or hurricanes. Changes in transportation systems can also create macro-structural shifts from either positive or negative perspectives – for example, the introduction of long-haul aircraft on trans-Pacific routes had a devastating impact on Fiji's tourist industry, since the island nation had originally benefited as a stopover destination for flights between North America and Australia (Ioannides, 1994).

Globalization has caused more localities, many of which were once inaccessible and undeveloped, to embrace tourism in order to amass capital. Thus, numerous 'rural and urban areas have become increasingly popular destinations, and substitutes for the touristic experience have been created' (Agarwal, 2002: 33). These offer more choices than ever before to holidaymakers.

The internal forces affecting the lifecycle of any given destination include its base resources (e.g. cultural and environmental), services (e.g. accommodation) and government (Johnston, 2001a). Thus, severe damage to the natural and/or cultural environment of a destination resulting from heavy numbers of arrivals could reduce its popularity, leading to stagnation or perhaps decline. Similarly, the decision of private developers to limit further investment in accommodation, the implementation of a new land-use plan, or a government-led action to either expand or halt infrastructural works may change the internal frame conditions for further tourism development, in turn influencing the destination's TALC.

Vulnerability enhanced through powerful intermediaries

An obvious outcome of the proliferation of new tourist destinations throughout the world is that numerous traditional localities face an increasing threat of being supplanted, by less environmentally spoiled places offering similar attractions. This threat is especially intense for undifferentiated mass-market destinations depending heavily on package tourists as their principal market, since they are highly susceptible to the decisions of major tour operators who are in a strong bargaining position *vis à vis* key players at the destination (e.g. hoteliers). Because as a consequence of risk minimization large-scale tour operators market product type rather than specific places, when a destination falls out of favour it can easily be substituted by a competitor (Bastakis *et al.*, 2004).

Vulnerability to the whims of external tour operators makes authorities in certain stagnating destinations think twice before implementing drastic changes (new land-use laws or tourist policies) to revive their tourist product. This has happened in Cyprus, which for years sought to replace its image as a mass tourist destination for budget travellers with one as attracting high-spending individuals. Despite substantial investments on luxury facilities and infrastructural improvements, it has been difficult to achieve this goal – and consequently the island finds it hard to shake its downmarket reputation (Ioannides and Holcomb, 2003). This is largely because major European tour operators dictate extremely low rates with hoteliers, given the existing overcapacity of hotel beds, and in turn this means that low-spending mass tourists continue to be attracted to this destination (Bastakis *et al.*, 2004).

Fighting stagnation and/or decline

If destinations begin experiencing telltale signs of stagnation or decline, what can policy-makers and industry representatives do to fight this problem? When a destination has trouble maintaining its competitive advantage, despite having up-to-date facilities meeting the expectations of modern travellers, it may simply have to market itself more aggressively in order to be revitalized (Weber and Tomljenović, 2004). In more serious situations, where facilities and infrastructure give an outdated image, strategies must aim at product reorganization and transformation. According to Agarwal (2002: 36–37):

> Specific product reorganisation strategies include investment and technical change, centralisation and product specialisation. Product transformation strategies include service quality enhancement (improving the quality of service delivery), environmental quality enhancement (improving key areas of the resort), repositioning, diversification, collaboration, and adaptation.

It is usual for stagnating destinations to introduce new facilities, such as casinos or conference centres, to diversify their product and draw visitors from new markets. Improving the physical infrastructure is also vital for localities to regain their competitive advantage. Additionally, places in the latter stages of their TALC commonly encourage the adoption of legislation to better protect their natural or built environments – steps which in turn serve to improve their image as quality destinations.

Emphasis on quality enhancement as a mechanism for appeal improvement has become a popular strategy in many destinations throughout the world. This approach has been spurred on by the rhetoric on sustainable development, and calls for softer-impact alternatives to mass tourism. Documents by international organizations such as UNESCO and national tourism development plans advocate increasing emphasis on quality-oriented tourism products, in the hope of enhancing the competitive position of destinations (Ioannides and Holcomb, 2003). Authorities in receiving areas believe that by emphasizing quality they will be able to target upmarket tourists and, hopefully, improve *per capita* spending.

Cyprus, Malta, Mauritius and Greece are destinations where policy-makers have repeatedly tried to achieve quality enhancement, specifically with an aim of attracting upmarket visitors. However, the jury is still out as to whether quality enhancement alone in the hope of replacing masses of low-spending tourists with higher-spending individuals is a realistic long-term option for the sustainable development of tourist destinations.

Upmarket tourism may prove counterproductive from an environmental and economic standpoint. Luxury hotels and facilities, like golf courses, can be environmentally taxing, not to mention that they are often foreign-controlled, given the large amount of capital necessary for establishing and operating them. Additionally, it is unrealistic for every place to target upscale tourists, given that this market is quite small. It is more prudent for destinations to improve their planning/growth management framework so that tourism is not treated in isolation, but as an integral part of the entire development process. Such an approach may help mature mass-tourism destinations to evolve more sustainably. A handful of mature mass-tourism destinations, such as the Balearics, some of which were facing serious decline, have now embraced a comprehensive strategy following the tenets of sustainability.

Best practice scenarios

'[Rarely] and perhaps Atlantic City is the flagship, have destinations that appear to have reached the end of their cycle been able to be rejuvenated in a complete manner' (Butler, 2004: 163–164). Some destinations have changed their function altogether as they enter a post-tourism era. For example, lodging establishments may be transformed into language schools or care facilities for the elderly. Nevertheless, a handful of places around the world have adopted drastic steps to rejuvenate their product, offering a cause of optimism for other destinations in the latter stages of their TALC. Taking advantage of its art deco heritage, Miami Beach, which only fifteen years ago exhibited all the symptoms of a glorious resort in decline, has undergone drastic transformation to emerge as a key tourist destination in Florida (Liebman, 1997).

The Balearics offer one of the most celebrated success stories of a destination's revival. Two decades ago they were the black sheep of Mediterranean destinations. By the mid-1980s a 'moment of truth' had emerged, when the regional government realized that heavy numbers of visitors threatened the resources that made the islands attractive in the first place (Bruce and Cantallops, 1996: 247). Bardolet (2001) explains that since the Balearics are part of a free market economy, the sole realistic way to implement revival was through combining spatial planning with a push for quality improvement. It was recognized that strict capacity limits should be set, while accommodation facilities had to meet minimum standards. Demonstrating a commitment to follow a sustainable development path, authorities originally adopted development moratoria to halt further construction of accommodation facilities until firm land-use and other regulations could be implemented.

Included in the implemented legislation were the CLADERA Acts, recommending environmental protection for approximately one-third of the islands' area. Further legislation ensures that almost 40 per cent of the Balearics is now protected (Bardolet, 2001). Measures to improve the islands' quality include the demolition of obsolete buildings and their replacement with green areas, the modernization of hotels, and infrastructural improvements (including the construction of a comprehensive sewerage system). To curb further urban sprawl, green belts have been implemented around each resort. Authorities have also emphasized product diversification by promoting alternatives to traditional sun, sea and sand oriented attractions, such as rural-based and heritage tourism.

On Mallorca, the most touristified island in the region, an ambitious programme adopted under the auspices of Local Agenda 21 was the Building Clearance Plan for revitalizing Calvia's town centre (Calvia, 2004). This aimed to transform the town's image, which after years of unchecked mass-tourism development suffered from widespread architectural pollution. After 1993, many coastal establishments deemed to be damaging to the environment were demolished through building clearance plan actions. The land where these facilities originally stood (about 13 500 square metres), plus a further 50 780 square metres of undeveloped urban land, was bought by authorities and saved from further construction. These lots are now designated as green spaces and a maritime esplanade.

The experience of the Balearics demonstrates the ability of certain mature tourist destinations facing crisis to reposition themselves as superior quality environments and regain their popularity. For this to be achieved a series of drastic steps must be implemented – something that may not always be popular with all of the industry's principal stakeholders. Happily, in the Balearics it appears that, despite considerable initial opposition, 'established hoteliers, European tour operators (especially German), local ecological associations, and ordinary citizens have welcomed the strategy', although 'developers have been reluctant to accept the idea of limiting growth in new construction' (Bardolet, 2001: 211).

On the downside, certain measures designed to enhance the Balearics' sustainability have been frostily received by some stakeholders, even though these steps were designed to diversify the tourist product and improve the overall quality. In particular, the proposed ecotax by the Regional Government of the Balearics, amounting to 1 euro per visitor per night, was vigorously opposed by hoteliers and British-based tour operators worried that holidaymakers might choose other destinations (*Daily Telegraph*, 2002). The International Federation of Tour Operators warned that a drop in visitor numbers arising from this extra charge could result in lost revenue for the destination. The ecotax was implemented after a lot of debate, only to be repealed in 2003 after a change of the regional government. Even though the money gathered from the ecotax had been used to purchase land earmarked to be the largest natural park on the Balearics, many observers have blamed this additional charge for causing a downturn in arrivals.

Conclusions: constantly revitalizing destinations

As more and more localities throughout the world are adopting tourism to boost their flagging economies, and since a growing number of out-of-the way places are being discovered as exotic alternatives for increasingly demanding holiday-makers, mature destinations are struggling to maintain their competitive advantage. This has led authorities in numerous destinations to embark on a search for ways to revive their products and reinvent their image (Weber and Tomljenović, 2004).

This chapter has sought to reinforce Butler's (1980) original argument that destinations facing stagnation or decline must adopt corrective steps to help shed their tired image and strengthen their competitive advantage. While it is impossible for every place to avoid the post-tourism stage in its lifecycle, the good news is there are situations where mature mass destinations have rid themselves of their most serious problems and managed to re-establish or even strengthen their competitiveness. The Balearic Islands demonstrate that such repositioning occurs only after all stakeholders realize that quality of existing resources and products must be upgraded, and that product diversification is essential. As more destinations go through the stages of their TALC much more rapidly than ever before (Butler, 2004), consequently facing the possibility of a rapid decline, the challenge for policy-makers is to heed the lessons from other areas before it is too late.

As a final note, it is imperative to stress that confusing quality-oriented tourism with upmarket tourism is a short-sighted strategy, especially as there are simply not enough high-spending tourists for every destination. Instead, a destination's focus on quality must be far broader, meaning that policy-makers should adopt a comprehensive approach recognizing tourism's links to all other sectors. If a locality's quality is improved not just in terms of tourism but also in terms of all aspects (built environment, infrastructure, traffic management etc.), and if strict limits to all growth are imposed through the recognition of capacity constraints, then surely the place will have a bright future as a popular attraction.

10

Urbanization and second-home tourism

Aurora Pedro

Introduction

Over the last few years second-home tourism has become more popular, emerging as an important part of the tourism sector in a number of countries. In most cases second homes are located near attractive locations, such as the sea, lakes, mountains or rural areas, whilst often they have a connection to their owners' origins and may be inherited properties. They offer a peaceful and environmentally friendly holiday home for city dwellers. The USA is considered to be the country in the world with the largest proportion of tourism second homes (Varela *et al.*, 2003). In the European Union the demand for second homes is increasing, notably in southern European countries, and such homes are very often purchased by northern Europeans.

Although initially the demand for second homes was driven predominantly by nationals seeking regions with better climatic conditions, recently there has been an important growth in the sector from foreigners. In Spain the foreign investment in second homes reached 5.7 billion Euros in 2002, which represents a total of 90 000 houses and an average growth rate of 10 per cent. Studies conducted demonstrate that the highest levels of demand come from Great Britain (35 per cent), Germany (31 per cent), France (7 per cent), Italy (5 per cent) and The Netherlands (3.1 per cent). A number of factors have contributed in the growth of second-home demand in Europe, namely:

- greater confidence in the European Union
- experience of destinations through frequent visitation
- the internationalization of the building industry
- the low profitability of other investments
- differences in the cost of living
- the development of no-frills airlines
- a preference for better climatic conditions often associated with the health benefits of living in milder climates
- an improvement in health services across Europe, and better collaboration between health systems
- the internationalization of products and retail chains
- the need for experiencing different places with different cultures.

Definitions of second-home tourism and residential tourism, and key stakeholders

Second-home tourism deserves special attention from researchers, in revealing what sort of reasons lead someone from elsewhere to decide to spend long periods of time in a particular place, and to constantly return to that place. There are also issues related to the impacts of second-home tourism, and planning implications. The definition of second-home tourism is based on two main aspects:

1. The type of tourist dwelling where tourists stay, which may be privately owned, rented or cost-free (visiting relatives or friends)
2. Frequent return to the same holiday place.

Generally, second-home tourists live in privately owned or rented dwellings, and have particular characteristics. They return to the same place for leisure time, and thus demonstrate great knowledge of, loyalty towards and appreciation of the destination (Hall and Muller; 1993; Dasse and Aubert, 2000). They often make friends or have relatives in the location, establish close links with the destination and are committed to the sustainability of the place. Second-home tourists spend long periods of time at the destination where they purchase their house. Such periods of time are long compared to the other forms of tourism, but are obviously less than a year at a time – otherwise the individuals concerned would not be considered tourists.

It is useful here to highlight the difference between second-home tourism and residential tourism, which is based on the period of time travellers stay at the destination. In the case of residential tourism, the length of stay may be longer than a year – that is, people change their place of residence and in some cases can even get a job at the destination. According to the WTO definition, if that happens the travellers cannot be classified as tourists. This can be the case with aged people living in rest homes. There is, however, an important difference between such travellers and local residents, since the former consume income at the destination whilst their money is generated at their usual place of residence. Distinction between second-home tourism and residential tourism involves consideration of the reasons why second-home tourists become residential tourists. There are certain socio-economic determinants or jobs that might facilitate the change of place of residence. According to recent research (IECX, APCE; 2002), climatic conditions, price, political and social stability, cultural factors, etc. are amongst the factors that influence the demand for second homes.

Timesharing is another form of second-home tourism, but in this case tourists do not spend long periods of time at the same destination. It could be considered a particular form of second-home tourism, depending on the way the participants use their tourism dwelling.

The final consideration demonstrates the third characteristic of second-home tourism, which is related to the relationship established between the tourist dwelling and the visitor. Often tourists stay in private dwellings that can be owned, rented, owned just for a period of time (timesharing), or free (the visiting friends and relatives (VFR) market).

Second-home tourism has a considerable impact on the local economy through the economics of the building industry. However, the impact is different from that of the 'classic' tourism industry, as these tourists tend to cook their own meals and often organize their own trips and entertainment. Hence hotels, restaurants, travel agencies and tour operators may not be used, whilst the building industry, agriculture and retail may gain more benefits from second-home tourism demand.

When researching second-home tourism, four main aspects should be considered:

1. The second-home tourists, who are very often characterized by a strong affiliation with and loyalty to the destination.
2. Businesses that provide products and services to this market, including the building industry, which is responsible for the construction of private tourist dwellings and a wide range of decorative and household services.
3. The government and local authorities, whose responsibility is geared towards the provision of adequate levels of services and infrastructure. If second-home tourism is a dominant sector at the destination, there are special needs and services that must be provided by the planning and governmental services. For example, the process of urbanization, generally depending on local government, requires planning and the provision of land and infrastructure.
4. The host community, which often looks on the sector as being responsible for creating employment. It is also important to consider the social and cultural consequences of the interaction between the local communities and second-home owners.

As second-home tourism implies long-term commitment from visitors, it is only when all the stakeholders have compatible aims and objectives that coexistence can be peaceful and mutually beneficial. The local authorities therefore need to provide a planning framework that ensures coordination of the activities and the optimization of impacts.

Analysing second-home tourism

It is difficult to gather statistics regarding second-home tourism, and as a result there are very few specific statistics available. Most of the dwellings (owned and rented) are private, and such tourism is often a non-declared activity. Hence there are only estimates of the number of units owed or rented, which makes it impossible to calculate the number of rooms or beds occupied. In some countries there are surveys that include some questions regarding the types of dwelling where tourists stay. For example, in Spain two main surveys are regularly conducted:

1. The Spanish Inbound Tourism Survey (*Frontur*) offers information about the number of inbound tourists and the characteristics of their trip, including the place where they stay and for how many nights.
2. The Spanish Domestic and Outbound Tourism Survey (*Familitur*) provides information about internal tourists and the characteristics of their trips, including where they stay and for how many nights.

The situations and definitions of dwellings in each country are an additional problem. Although some efforts have been made by international organizations to create and standardize some concepts and definitions, the current situation worldwide makes comparative analysis and forecasts difficult owing to the many different ways in which this form of tourism is measured (Rodríguez-Salmones *et al.*, 2003). Some progress has been made in this area by the World Tourism Organization and by the European Union (Decision of the Commission 9 December 1998 on application of the Directive 95/97CE), to try to improve this situation in the future. In Spain, for example, the demand and supply statistics for second-home tourism are estimated from surveys conducted by the Spanish Government.

The demand for second homes

The demand for second homes is estimated from data available in the *Frontur* and *Familitur* statistics. Table 10.1 provides evidence of the importance of private dwellings in tourism. In the case of Spain, 63 per cent of total trips are short breaks that usually take place at weekends. The average stay of inbound tourists (15.6 nights) is higher than that of internal tourists (4.3 nights). Other studies reveal that the regions of Valencia (especially Alicante) and Andalucia (Malaga in particular) each attract 28 per cent of the total inbound tourists. Surveys also demonstrate that about 75 per cent of second-home tourists show an inclination to move permanently to the destination areas when they retire (ICEX, APCE; 2002).

In spite of the quality and interesting nature of these data, it would be useful in the future to conduct further research regarding the following areas:

- the origin of the demand
- the socio-economic characteristics of residential tourists (age, type of family, income, educational level, etc.)
- the main factors affecting the demand

Table 10.1 Contribution of second-home tourists to Spanish tourism

Tourism (2002)	Millions	Percentage	Conventional tourism accommodation (%)*	Private tourism accommodation (%)**
Inbound international tourism	51.4	30	69.4	30.6
Internal domestic tourism	120.4	70	11.8	88.2
Total	172.2	100	12.3	87.7

*Conventional tourism accommodation includes hotels, rural houses, camping
**Private tourism accommodation includes owned, rented and free houses, etc.

- how tourists get information about the destination area
- the kind of accommodation preferred
- the relationship between tourism and specific activities (golf, watersports etc.)
- the expenditure and services used.

The supply of second homes

Most second homes are not registered, as they are privately owned. Estimates of the numbers of second homes in Spain can be made using the information from the 2001 Census of Population and Housing, which distinguishes between main homes, second homes and empty homes. In 2001, the total housing units amounted to some 21 million. Second homes represented 16 per cent of these, the number having increased by 15 per cent between 1991 and 2001. The number of families owning a second home was 1.9 million, which represented 13.4 per cent of Spanish households. Fifteen per cent were empty homes, which reached the impressive figure of 3.1 million. It should be noted that some of these may since then have been, or may yet be, acquired or used as second homes. Hence the total number of second-home beds available in Spain would amount to about 12.6 million (Varela *et al.*, 2003).

A wide range of accommodation is therefore available, including tourist apartments, villas, hotels with apartments (aparthotels), and timeshares. There are no specific studies on the kind of product the building industry is offering as second homes, or on their characteristics and evolution over time. Considering the supply side, future research must focus on:

- the product offered
- the distribution channels
- the pricing policy
- the different legislation affecting the development
- the effect of the second-home tourism on the local economy, housing prices, and the integrated impact of the expenditure on all economic activity and sectors at the destination

- the services and products that contribute to this market, and the value chains developed within the local economy.

New products for second-home tourism

Naturally, second-home tourism is evolving rapidly to reflect customer needs and preferences. The new tourism residential developments are often linked to some specific activity – usually a form of sport. Golf tourism is becoming one of the most important segments for the development of second homes as a result of several factors:

- golfers tend to belong to affluent socio-economic segments and spend considerable time near golf courses
- golf tourism is related to high-expenditure tourism, as the average spend is greater than that in conventional tourism
- this type of tourism demands a high-quality environment, which means integral treatment of sewage, recuperation of secondary landscapes, etc.
- golf is primarily a social activity, with players forming social networks.

There has been an enormous expansion of this market segment in Europe. The number of golf courses has increased from 2914 in 1995 to 6000 in 1999. The number of players is estimated to be 5 million in Europe and 26.5 million in the USA (www.turismoresidencial.com). Golf provides an important contribution to the local and regional economy. Its impact on employment, investment, recreational facilities, foreign currency, improvement in the infrastructures, etc. is very significant.

In the USA, a recent study has shown that the second-home attributes most sought by respondents are low maintenance, proximity to shops and restaurants, walking routes and outdoor activities such as hiking and bicycling. Surprisingly, the same study reveals that in the USA, second-home tourists show very limited interest in private golf courses, tennis courts or nearby ski slopes. Distance, relaxing conditions and pleasant climatic conditions are amongst the most important reasons that determine the demand for second homes (ir.centex.com).

Some experts include other kinds of innovations in this market – especially the use of real estate leasing. Here, the family uses the house for a specific number of years and then decides whether or not to purchase it (Torres, 2003).

The development of residential tourism has to take into account the needs of the aged population, in particular in terms of special services such as rest homes, medical support and health services. Recently, in Spain, the firms promoting these types of products have proposed the creation of a new quality certification scheme. This may be the first step towards better coordination of this market, with the objective of improving its quality and serving all the stakeholders better.

Product development and the public sector require much more detailed statistics and information in order to support innovation. It is critical therefore that research is undertaken to establish demand and supply gaps, product development, impact optimization and carrying capacity levels in order to help politicians and developers to achieve rational decisions.

Implications for tourism destination management

The impacts of second-home tourism on destinations must be considered. There is a wide range of economic, socio-economic and environmental impacts for destinations, and destination management organizations need to be able to analyse these before developing suitable policies (Strapp, 1988; Klemm, 1996; Bourrat, 2000).

The second-home tourism has a number of economic impacts, including the following:

1. This type of tourism is labour-*un*intensive, and hence fewer economic resources are spread throughout the region. The employment generated by this kind of tourism is mainly related to the building, decorating and household maintenance industries.
2. Visitors have a lower expenditure in general, as second-home tourists spend less money in accommodation and catering. They are primarily self-catering, and thus their expenditure is primarily on agricultural products and retail. They also spend little on excursions and sightseeing, as they have visited local attractions before. Their primary expenditure is on the building and decorating industries, and hence they have a similar spending schema to the local community. However, they inject money into the economy from their region of origin, contributing to the local economy.
3. Traditional accommodation companies regard this activity as direct competition. Second homes are more affordable, owing to lower levels of services, and are also seen as being an investment for the future.
4. Second-home tourists do not pay tourism taxes, and are not subject to the legislation often associated with tourism accommodation.
5. There is a considerable need for land to develop dwellings and infrastructure. The pressure on prices can result in increased cost of houses and land, contributing to inflation in the house and consumer good markets.

The social and cultural impacts of second-home tourism include the relationship between local communities and second-home tourists (Girard and Gartner, 1993). Often, second-home owners have local origins but have migrated to cities for career purposes. However, there is a major trend for northerners to purchase second homes in the south for recreational purposes. Often one of the most evident consequences of second-home tourism is the segregation of communities by nationalities and conflict of interests. Enclaves of foreigners often enjoy luxurious properties, and may thus create envy in local residents. In addition, they bring their customs and way of living. In certain parts of Mallorca, for example, the main language used is German, and most of the tourists cannot speak Spanish; the German lifestyle is just adopted in a sunny environment. If the communities are not compatible and there is little integration, there is a greater likelihood of conflicts arising. Hence the relationships between local communities and second-home tourists need to be managed by the tourist and local authorities in a way that encourages mutual understanding and respect, as well as a certain degree of integration.

Environmental impacts also have to be considered. Second-home tourism demands large quantities of land, water and infrastructure, so environmental impacts may be significant. The demand on environmental resources depends on the type of development. Different kinds of urban developments related to tourism can be identified:

1. *Extensive development* is dominated by villas or houses. In this case, the need for land and other basic resources – such as water – is high.
2. *Intensive development* is dominated by multi-storey buildings. This model reduces the extent of resource consumption and requires concentration of infrastructure in a limited space. However, negative environmental impacts include violation and visual deterioration of the landscape, as well as the concentration of a large number of people in a small area.

Case study 10.1 Second-homes tourism in Valencia, Spain

The region of Valencia hosts most of the second homes in Spain (Juan *et al.*, 2003). The 2001 Census of Population and Housing showed that second homes made up 22.1 per cent of the total homes (558 000). Between 1991 and 2001 the number of second homes had increased by 7.8 per cent, whilst the Alicante region experienced an increase of 12.5 per cent. Estimation of the number of beds indicates that the Valencian region has about 2.6 million beds, or 20.9 per cent of the total Spanish bed capacity in second homes. Empty homes represent 16.5 per cent of the total homes (416 000). Between 1991 and 2001, their numbers increased by 32.6 per cent, especially in Castellón (61.4 per cent) and in Alicante (33.6 per cent). Although a distinction is made in the Census, some of the empty homes may be used as second homes. About 17.8 per cent of the families living in the Valencia region own a second home. The Census shows that 1.9 per cent of second-home residents were born in other European countries, whilst the Spanish average is 0.88 per cent.

These data demonstrate that second-home tourism is a very important tourism typology in the Valencia region, leading to a number of planning and policy implications. The Tourism Law in the region aims to resolve one of the most important problems of tourist municipalities: the local fiscal gap generated by the need to provide services for second-home tourists. The local population in most of the coastal tourism destinations pays the majority of the local taxes that local authorities use to provide services. The taxes associated with the building activity are almost the only way to increase fiscal resources for the local government (Pedro, 2000).

In order to improve the process of generation of land to urbanize, during the 1990s the Law on Urban Activity was passed. This Law has one important difference compared to the rest of Spain: it has created a new figure, the urban agent, as an intermediary between the owner of the land and the municipality proposing special plans to develop. The Law has been effective in the way it has facilitated the supply of land to urbanize; however, it has also been criticized because it forces landowners to participate in the development or to sell the land. Although the municipality has the responsibility of passing the special programmes of urbanization, there are few urban experts working for them. As second-home tourism is vital for Valencia, a comprehensive review is required to ensure the quality of service and the equitable sharing of responsibilities and costs.

As in all tourism, a maximum capacity needs to be applied to second-home tourism and planning should ameliorate environmental impacts. To establish the capacity, the availability of natural resources (land, water, beaches, etc.) and the geographical characteristics of the region must be examined and the best type of development defined. However, controlling the process and the establishment of limits is not always easy, as there is pressure from local developers, tour operators and other stakeholders for the expansion of the industry (Gallent *et al.*, 2003). In tourism destinations where there is a predominance of private second homes, the quality dimension is very difficult to control because private properties and developments are often excluded from policies and actions taken by tourism boards. The improvement of quality requires special action, with the involvement of a range of different stakeholders.

Case study 10.1 describes the case of second-home tourism in Valencia.

Conclusions and policy implications

Second-home tourism is increasing in importance in several regions. As this type of tourism has specific requirements and different impacts from those of mainstream tourism, it necessitates specific policy and planning actions. Each region must assess its resources and decide what kind of development is preferred in order to optimize its tourism impacts through developing specific products and services. If second-home tourism is selected, there needs to be a comprehensive assessment of the resources required, the capacity of the region and the impacts anticipated, as well as an extensive impacts analysis which should inform the policy formulation and planning process. The pressure on neighbouring areas close to second-home honeypots, such as coastal or alpine areas, and local rural communities also needs to be examined. The planning system should provide an adequate instrument for influencing the tourism and the housing markets, although it has limitations regarding managing wider growth pressures. The role of local and national governments will therefore be crucial in managing the interests of all stakeholders, and in outlining an adequate course of action to maximize the benefits of the second-home tourism expansion.

The influence of fashion and accessibility on destination consumption

Richard Butler and C. Michael Hall

Introduction

Destinations are geographic locations to which tourists travel (Leiper, 2000; Framke, 2002). They are therefore determined both by the motivations of the tourist and by the provision of tourism resources and infrastructure that may satisfy tourism demand. Destinations are, therefore, specific locations of tourist consumption separate from travel routes to and from the tourist's home environment. However, in some cases (as, for example, cruise ships, touring yachts, canal- or steam-boats and tourist trains) the means of transport itself constitutes a mobile destination.

In designating tourism destinations, however, we are not simply interested in the travel patterns of individual tourists, significant as these might be for some locals. Instead we are interested in the locations in which tourists are concentrated, particularly in terms of overnight stays – which, along with numbers of visitors, is often a key measurement criterion of the relative attractiveness of destinations. Nevertheless, it is important to recognize that the number and variety of destinations have increased markedly as the world's population has grown and the capacity and desire to travel have increased, and, barring a major change in economic, socio-political or environmental conditions, this trend will continue. Yet while there is widespread agreement that the number of tourists will continue to increase over time, the distribution of destinations to which they will travel is likely to change.

Despite a substantial body of literature on destination management, and planning and forecasting arrivals at specific destinations (e.g. Davidson and Maitland, 1997; Ritchie and Crouch, 2003), there is no specific body of literature within tourism studies as to the identification of new and emerging destinations. One specific example is that of Plog (1974), who produced a listing of global tourist destinations at various stages in their development cycle and predicted the general process of destination acceptance and rejection at that scale. Literature does exist on the changing fashions and tastes in tourist consumption, as well as the importance of accessibility for destinations (see, for example, Shaw and Williams, 1997), and it is these factors that will primarily determine the emergence and relative competitiveness of new destinations.

Fashion as a key factor in the consumption of destinations

Fashion influences not only how we present ourselves to others in terms of matters such as clothing or what we eat and drink, but also affects where and how people travel. The media as well as peer groups can have enormous influence on travel tastes and the selection of tourism destinations and activities. Most significantly, we know that fashions change. For example, the attractiveness of destinations such as the Lake District in England and the Highlands in Scotland was substantially influenced by the writings of poets such as Wordsworth and Coleridge and novelists such as Walter Scott, and even the visits of the British Royal Family. Indeed, European taste at the end of the eighteenth century witnessed a wholesale shift in the landscape preferences of the aristocracy and the emerging educated middle classes, in which wild romantic landscapes became to be looked at favourably. Without such a perceptual shift, the legacy of which is still being felt today in terms of travel patterns, many places would not be seen favourably as potential destinations (Shaw and Williams, 1997; Bergoff et al., 2002).

Another example of how shifts in taste can impact on destination choice is the fashion of suntans among Caucasians. Up until the late 1920s it was fashionable in European and North American society for skin to be as pale as possible, as this indicated that one did not have to work outside and therefore was relatively wealthy. However, in the summer of 1929 *Vogue* magazine featured models with suntans for the first time, as many of the pictures were taken in the South of France – which had just started to become a destination for American film stars and models, and for members of the American elite (Feifer, 1985). The demonstration effect of the *Vogue* magazine was that gaining a suntan was a sign of wealth (because one had the capacity to travel) as well as health.

The idealized bodies of the fashion models had much the same influence regarding the desirability of skin colour as the present-day fashion industry has on the supposed ideal body shape. Both of the above examples emphasize the capacity of fashions to change, often within a very short period. In fact it is remarkable that, regardless of warnings of skin cancer from too much exposure to the sun, the desirability of a suntan is still so strong for many holidaymakers, and hence extremely important for many destinations that have been developed to take advantage of such fashion. However, fashion is only one component of the destination selection equation.

Accessibility as a key factor in the consumption of destinations

Destinations have to be accessible. 'Accessible' in this sense not only refers to the existence of transport infrastructure to and at destination locations, but also to consideration of the mobility of the traveller. Mobility is determined by both the economic budget of the traveller (on which many analyses of the market for destinations have been made) and, just as importantly, the time-budget of the traveller.

People need access to both temporal and economic resources in order to be able to travel. Access to greater amounts of disposable income for travel is typically related to increases in the speed of travel involved in order to be able to reach certain destinations within the given amount of time available for tourist activities. Such considerations are vital for assessing the potential of destination success and emergence into the marketplace. Relative accessibility in comparison with other destinations (the potential market reach) is as significant as the various amenities and products offered to meet tourist preferences. Indeed, the implications of globalization for tourism, and therefore for destination choice, are as much related to the effect of transport and media technology on time–space convergence (Janelle, 1968) as they are to trends in cultural convergence and governance.

Time–space convergence occurs through both 'space–time distantiation' and 'space–time compression'. The former refers to the stretching of social and economic relations over time and space, for example through the utilization of communications technology such as the Internet and by advances in transport technology, so that they can be controlled or coordinated over longer periods of time, greater distances, larger areas, and on more scales of activity. The latter involves the intensification of 'discrete' events in real time and/or increased velocity of material and non-material flows over a given distance. Again this is related to technological change, including communications, transport and social technologies (Jessop, 1999). The demise of Concorde in 2004 was the first time that mankind had stepped backwards in terms of speed of travel. Previous rejections of other methods of transportation, such as airships, were mostly related to safety aspects (as with Concorde); however, they did not result in a loss of speed, rather a form of travel. Although the use of rockets or scram jets for commercial travel may materialize in the future, particularly with respect to space tourism, for the short term at least supersonic travel for tourists has ceased to exist, and this will have minor effects on some destinations.

Reductions in the cost and time of movements over space have long been the foci of innovations in transport technology, and are a feature of the increasing connection between different parts of the globe and growth in mobility (Hall, 2005a). For example, Forer (1978) referred to 'plastic space', noting the manner in which time–space compression had shrunk the United States in relative travel time with each advance in transport technology. In the case of Germany, Lanzendorf (2000) reports that the average distance travelled per person per year for leisure and vacation increased from 600 km in 1976 to just under 1000 km in 1996. For work-related travel, it increased 300 km to 500 km in the same period. Such shifts in the capacities of people to travel are extremely significant for assessing the future prospects for locations in terms of the extent to which they may then become considered as potential travel destinations.

Moreover, such accounts of human mobility also indicate that there are definite limits to tourism in terms of the cost and/or time available to travel. Indeed, potential travel destinations such as space, the deep ocean or even some polar regions will remain limited in terms of the numbers of visitors they can attract simply because of the substantial economic and time budgets required to get to those locations. For existing and emerging destinations, the market situation will become increasingly competitive in terms of ensuring accessibility.

The significance of accessibility is witnessed in contemporary destination competition for access to transport routes, whether through achieving hub status or being a secondary destination through low-cost and budget air carriers. In many ways contemporary destination competition for air transport is reminiscent of competition between places to receive the railway line in the nineteenth century, or the motorway in the twentieth century (Hall, 2005a). As Stansfield (1978: 242) noted with respect to Atlantic City:

> Connecting customers with the resort is the basis of all resort development; all recreation and tourism patterns take place within a time and space frame. Atlantic City's time-distance and cost-distance relative to Philadelphia were a successful blend of shortest straight line distance and the efficiency of the railroad.

Therefore, in terms of attracting tourists, transport accessibility is critical as the transportation system dictates the velocities at which individuals can travel and the time available for activity participation at dispersed locations which are themselves transport points or nodes (Miller, 1999).

The role of accessibility as a key factor in the determination of the emergence of locations as destinations has been significant in the transport literature for many years (see, for example, Moseley, 1979). However, it has not received the same prominence in the tourism studies literature (Smith, 1995; Hall, 2005a), although the role of distance effects in the relative attractiveness of attractions has recently been highlighted (Hanink and White, 1999).

Hall (2005a, 2005b) has argued that accessibility models can be generated that provide a more detailed understanding of the spatial interaction between a tourist-generating origin and a destination area. This approach highlights the importance of accessibility as a key factor in the development of tourist areas (Butler, 1980, 2005). If destinations are defined in terms of locations of overnight stay, then key factors affecting their location will include:

- means of transport and the velocity of the transport system (economic budget)
- availability of time to travel (travel-time budget) and engage in tourist-related activities (activity-time budget)

- limitations related to the need for rest while travelling (e.g. tourists cannot continue to drive continuously without sleep)
- time/distance trade-offs between the time budget and the economic budget.

Such factors are accounted for by Miller's (1999) notion of Potential Path Space (PPS), defined in terms of the space–time prism that delimits all locations in space–time that can be reached by an individual based on the locations and duration of mandatory activities (e.g. home, work) and the travel velocities allowed by the transportation system. For example, assume an individual is located at time t_1 at the point of origin (X_0, Y_0). Again, assume that at time t_2 the individual has to be back at the origin. Then the available time for all activities is given by:

$$t = t_2 - t_1$$

The projection of PPS onto two-dimensional XY space represents the potential path area that an individual can move within, given the available time budget. However, changes in time accessibility caused either by new or improved transport technology and/or by transport infrastructure will lead to changes in relative accessibility of locations in space. These changes can be represented as a wave analogue in which changes in time/distance from a central point of origin will lead to different densities d of overnight stay at a specific destination location L over times $t_1, t_2, \ldots$ in relation to the overall distribution of overnight stays as a function of distance from origin (Figure 11.1). In terms of destination product life courses, some comparisons can also be drawn between ideas of destination product life-cycles (Butler, 2005) and Hägerstrand's (1967) pioneering work in Sweden on innovation diffusion as a spatial process that likened the innovation diffusion process to a wave-like pattern which loses its strength as it moves away from the initial point of origin (Hall, 2005a).

Such parallels are significant, as transport accessibility also requires communication accessibility so as to be aware that a destination exists within the particular set of destinations that may be under consideration by consumers. In the case of innovation diffusion, the logistic curve may be expressed as:

$$p_t = (1 + e^{a-bt})^{-1}$$

where p_t = the proportion of adopters at time t, a = the intercept, and b = the slope coefficient. Similarly,

$$y_t = k(1 + e^{a-bt})^{-1}$$

where y_t = the number of adopters and k = the maximum possible number of adopters – that is, the saturation level.

In a parallel with some accounts of changing markets, as destinations develop, work on innovation diffusion has suggested that the people among the first to adopt innovations (initiators) tend to be young, better educated, more widely travelled, more willing to take risks and more likely to have closer contact with high-quality information sources. The late adopters and laggards tend to be older and to have more traditional views, similar to the behaviour of allocentrics and pyschocentrics in Plog's (1974) classification of tourists.

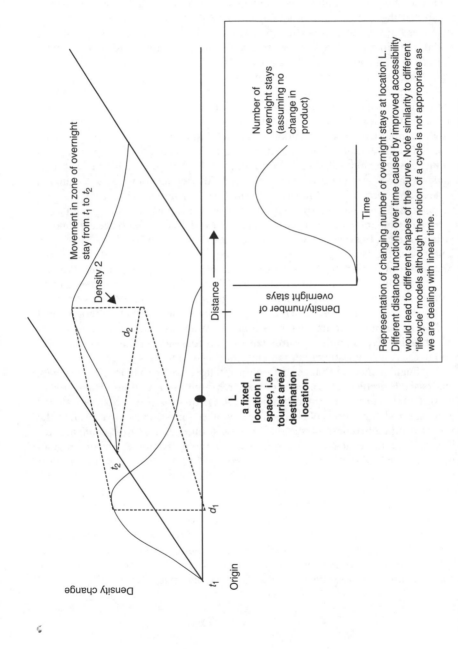

Figure 11.1 A wave analogue model of the implication of changed accessibility for a fixed location in space (after Hall, 2003)

99

Vision for the future

Although space may be the next prominent destination for tourism, the reality is that, at least in terms of substantial numbers of people, individual economic budgets mean that the vast amount of holidaymaking will stay down to earth. However, this does not suggest that destinations will stay the same. Some will lose favour and decline in popularity as expressed in visitation numbers, and perhaps cease their tourist function, while others will alter their marketing strategies and aim to rejuvenate themselves in a variety of ways.

Although the amenity factors of destinations are spatially fixed, destinations seek to change their product offerings so as to entice new markets or improve their promotional capacities in an already competitive market. For example, in the 1960s destinations such as Benidorm and the Costa Brava grew primarily as the result of relatively cheap direct airline access in relation to other competitors with similar environmental attributes. More recently, the Isle of Skye has had substantially changed user patterns because of a bridge connection to the mainland instead of a ferry that did not run on Sundays. Yet importantly, it is only very recently that there has been a renewed focus on the importance of accessibility as a key determinant in destination growth and development. The success of budget airlines such as Easyjet and Ryanair have not only increased tourism numbers in Europe despite the effect of 11 September 2001, they have also 'created' new destinations and reinforced the position of existing ones (e.g. Dublin and Prague) through the introduction of low-cost air travel combined with easy accessibility to secondary airports. This serves to make competition more severe for established destinations, particularly those in relative proximity to their markets, as most budget airlines fly short to medium distances. Some existing destinations have needed to adapt their offerings more towards leisure and recreation rather than tourism, and to focus on domestic rather than international tourists.

Although qualitative changes in fashion and taste are open to longitudinal data analysis, the predictive capacities of such research are not great (Hand, 1996). Nevertheless, substantial opportunities exist for quantitative analysis of spatial and temporal dimensions of changed accessibility for destinations, as well as the relative competitiveness of such destinations. Indeed, a central challenge for investigation of destination competitiveness is the utilization of existing mathematical models of spatial interaction and competing destinations from transport and retail studies, and the geography of industrial location within tourism (Hall, 2005a). Indeed, such considerations of time and space studies and destinations as specific locations in space that compete for visitors with other destinations are likely to provide a stronger predictive basis for destination change (Butler, 1980, 2005; Hall, 2005b). The improved mobility of individuals will provide many opportunities for the development of new destinations. Improving the understanding of the space–time characteristics of such locations will greatly improve the potential contribution of tourism studies to predict which ones will succeed.

12

Experience design in tourism

Antti Haahti and Raija Komppula

Introduction

Within theoretical discourses on value creation, the experience theory (Pine and Gilmore, 1999; Gilmore and Pine, 2002) spearheads new ways to model economic and sociocultural discovery in order to understand reality. Experience design is an approach and a method for discovery of value creation in all spheres of society.

Within the tourism marketing literature, there is limited reference to experience theory. Conventional product planning models still prevail. In tourism practice it is evident that commoditization and 'productization of services' dominate, and product orientation is often strongly adhered to. Consequently, in conventional product development and itinerary planning, there is little evidence of analysis of the customer experience. This chapter integrates experience design with product development models to enhance value creation for actors within the tourism system. It includes a conceptual model to bridge recent views introduced by Pine and Gilmore, which are epitomized in the phrase 'Experience is Marketing', and the more conventional approaches to tourism product development.

Consumer behaviour and product attributes towards utility

Lancaster's (1966) economic theory of consumer behaviour formalized the connection between consumer utility derived from objective and subjective product attributes. An attribute may be defined as a quality or characteristic ascribed to a person or thing. Different levels or a particular characteristic will distinguish it from competing products or services. It is these characteristics of 'different levels of attributes' that underlie much of the present-day marketing thinking. The theory precipitated multi-attribute choice theories and established a theoretical economic base for differentiation between utility, and derivation of benefits, not from the good itself but from the product attributes.

Product attributes, as sources for value creation, may be:

- *objective* and concrete attributes – for example (in relation to tourism attractions), hours of sunshine, availability of swimming pools, number of stars in the hotel classification
- *subjective* attributes – attributes that refer to appeals chosen by marketers to construct the image of a destination in advertising
- *perceived* attributes – attributes that are important personally and are formative for customer satisfaction or dissatisfaction, such as the perceived friendliness of hosts.

The theory contributed to several streams of marketing discourses in the late 1960s, 1970s and 1980s. It influenced applications of marketing thinking to service and relationship marketing.

Experiences defined

The context of experience economy, as discussed by Pine and Gilmore (1999; Gilmore and Pine, 2002), proposed an interesting model for the evolution of economy. They suggested a method of value creation that challenged mainstream views, traditional product development models and conventional marketing. Experience theory posits the realms of an experience in terms of two conceptual dimensions:

1. The extent of participation by the customer/guest (which may vary from active to passive)
2. The emotional mode and extent of involvement in the experience (which varies from immersion to absorption).

The second dimension anchors the experiences deeply in the realm of emotions and feelings.

An experience may be just an instantaneous emotional or intellectual revelation that can have lasting influence for the person. It may be a short event or a stream of connected events, or it may be revealed over a long duration – such as an expensive or much anticipated holiday trip planned with family members. The viewpoint Gilmore and Pine (2002) put forward for planning is posited already in the subtitle of their book, 'work is theatre'.

Tourism dramaturgy

An application of experience design

Much of travel and tourism is mass marketed, planned through conventional approaches to product development and itinerary planning. This results in a low-contact and low-involvement experience. Application of the model of theatre to tourism opens new perspectives regarding the possibility of replacing the 'productization philosophy'. It also challenges the conventional, mainstream marketing thinking, and remodels value creation to generate more satisfying experiences. Moreover, it generates strong pressure to create design teams where all stakeholders, from architects to users, may have an early input to stage designs.

Dramaturgy principles can assist the design of process of value creation in experiences. Dramaturgy is a field of science that analyses the rules of composing dramas and representing them on stage. For tourism purposes, there is an interesting example. The Finnish Theatre Academy developed a process application called '*Tourism Drama*' for local tourism experience design. The dramaturgic approach consists of idea generation, creative writing sessions, studying the manuscript of the play, designs of and for the stage, plans for acts and roles, rehearsing the play, planning the staging of the play, role playing and involvement of the audience. To manage the participating guests, tourists may be guided to the stage(s) and actively take the roles of the 'play'. Thus, in high-contact, high-involvement tourism, active tourists co-create this experience with professional stagers (i.e. facilitators). Therefore the consumers together with their hosts co-create value for themselves and others. This is often the case in holiday camps and clubs such as Club Med, where consumers actively participate in and co-organize sports, shows and cocktail parties. Similarly, 'murder she wrote' weekends are staged in several hotels, where guests are charged with a role to play.

The ideas for the manuscript and for the staged experience are created to fit the needs and expectations of the guest. Often the idea generation uses the available sources in the myths, stories, anecdotes and social or cultural history of the place or event. This enables the creation of a place and a space for being together and the development of a group identity in experiencing. A central aspect in experience design is the staging. Too wide a gap between intended stages and intended experiences, and realized stages and realized experiences, distorts the total ambience by non-fitting signals or other mismatches. Consequently, it is important to evaluate whether the realized stage (e.g. hotel, restaurant, airport interior) matches the intended design. The tool for the critical evaluation of the stage is the human senses: what we see, smell, taste, hear and feel gives us an understanding of the quality of the sensed physical reality, and whether the offering is experienced as it was designed to be. Perceived experience versus expectation determines levels of satisfaction.

There is a plethora of recent cases where themes of the historic past have been recreated for stage and role-play. Such opportunities were often further developed with tourists co-creating 'time-travelling' experiences. Another example of staged, co-created experiences is the televised series on 'paradise' islands and representations of televised 'sexperiences', depicting hedonistic and erotic tourist experiences.

Dramaturgy introduces powerful possibilities for experience design. It provides a methodology for integrated management of the tourism experience, from design to service delivery. This integration not only concerns products sold to the tourist, services provided to them and experiences during the tour, but also an integrated approach to value creation, addressing every event and occasion as a 'theatre play'. This starts from the architect designs and continues all the way to the memories carried from the place by a tourist.

The high contact and involvement encounters between guest and hosts, as well as the quality of such encounters, determine the quality of the experience. This is a typical advantage of small and medium-sized tourism enterprises which have very little market power but direct contact between guests and hosts. Clearly, there must be synergies between the guest personal experience, the substance of the encounter and the business processes in order to delight the guest. The strategic processes of the firm determine much of the value creation capability, and their ability to create competitive advantage.

Methodology for experience design processes for value creation

There are several design processes used for developing experiences, and these processes should be part of the core strategy and value creation of the firm. These processes are listed below.

1. *Understanding the needs, wishes and choice behaviour of guests and potential customers.* This is essential in order to create sustainable relations. This includes targeting, segmentation and positioning, as well as adopting and customizing. It is also critical to recognize differences in desire from time to time, as well as between heterogeneous groups.
2. *Meeting the guest.* This is the most critical encounter between the buyer and seller in high-contact encounters. Experienced hosts can read the requirements of guests and customize their experience accordingly. Especially in small businesses, personal relationships often develop that lead to product customization to the desires of regular customers. In low-contact services, customers are left to their own devices to create a self-service experience. In no-contact encounters, such as in the virtual world, the representations of artificial bonds through Customer Relationship Management become important.

    The moment of truth. The customer may regard the early stage of the relationship as the main source of satisfaction, delight or stress, irritation, ambivalence and feelings of uncertainty. This is before getting to know a new destination or a new place as the stage for holidaying. It is the first impressions that often fully determine the evaluation of the quality of the stage, the staging, and the hosts' competence in staging. The first encounters also mean meeting and keeping the promise to the customer.

3. *The stages and staging the experience*. This is dependent on the spirit of the place, its location and the super- and infrastructure available. The hospitality culture supports information-handling structures, and work processes are used to create and enable the experience formation. The stage offers important possibilities for delighting and building trust in the relationship between hosts and guests.

4. *The enabling management structure*. This includes communications, information technology, accounting and finance, leadership and management processes. These create the internal-to-the-firm structure that is essential for supporting the successful experience whilst encouraging profitability.

5. *The quality management*. The total quality management philosophy, ideology and instruments permeate the above core processes, and are critical in forming the experience values and the profit chain (Parasuraman *et al.*, 1991).

The dedication and competence of the personnel and the management in staging memorable experiences make the difference between success or failure in building a satisfied clientele. Understanding these core processes, in order to create experiences that meet the dynamic needs of customers and guests, should explain much of the variance regarding the degree of guest satisfaction and a firm's profitability.

From experience design to product development

The tourism and service marketing literature emphasizes the creation of added value for the tourist and the firm (Grönroos, 2000; Murphy *et al.*, 2000; Middleton and Clarke, 2001). The focus is often on subjective experience and on the factors that determine the destination competitiveness (Ritchie and Crouch, 2003).

On the level of individual travel services and products, detailed itinerary planning and product development are the instruments to create marketable experiences. Herein lies the bridge between experience design, product development and itinerary planning. When the components of such an itinerary are planned, the distinct modules are amalgamated as individual stages. A tourism experience emerges by interconnecting those stages and ensuring that the whole experience exceeds consumer expectations.

Proposed tourism product development model

Practical service development planning models should have three basic components, namely service concept, service process and the service system (Edvardsson and Olsson, 1999). The core of the tourist product, the service concept, consists of the elaborated service mission that specifies the values to be created and plans for the prerequisite designs. The service concept is represented and expressed in a way that evokes mental images of the potential guest's ability to gain the very experiences and values expected from the chosen trip. The description of the service process defines the formal components of value creation (Kotler *et al.*,

1999; Komppula and Boxberg, 2002). For the customer, these components are represented through the communications instruments. The location, place, and spirit of the place are central representations supported by communication and advertising vehicles. The formal product determines and defines the chain of activities forming the customer and production process, whereby the high-quality service production is implemented. The chain can be illustrated as a service blue-print, charting those activities and processes which customers go through at different stages of the service (Zeithaml and Bitner, 1996: 206–207). The value chain framework helps in identifying the attributes of service situations and describing the episodes in a chain of travel experiences for quality control and development purposes. For example, SAS uses such descriptive detailed consumption flow analyses to find out the specific attributes related to all stages in their airline flights' product development and quality planning in order to fit the work flows with the customers' needs (Gustafsson and Johnson, 2003).

The service system includes those resources available to enable the creation of the process and to implement the service concept. The underlying prerequisite for successful tourist product development is a functioning service system, driven by the company strategy (Edvardsson et al., 2000). The augmented tourist product (Lumsdon, 1997; Kotler et al., 1999; Middleton and Clarke, 2001) includes the company itself, its reputation and its image. The corporate image refers to the perceptions, impressions and preferences people have about the organization in general. The corporate identity consists of the perceptions formed by external audiences of everything a company is seen to do. Branding does, at the level of the product, what corporate identity does at the level of the firm (Seaton, 1996).

Adding together the service concept, the service process and the service system creates the prerequisites for the designed experience, which can synchronize with the experiences of the customer. For the customer, the tourist product is a personal experience, at a given moment in time and at a given price. It is the outcome of a process where the customer co-creates the experience designed for either high-contact staging or self-service, and enjoys or dislikes the experience. Figure 12.1 illustrates the nature of the customer-oriented tourist product.

The tourist product, created through the processes described above, forms a service package that consists of several fragments that form distinct parts (modules) of the product and together create the total experience. The core of the product is the service concept, which should be based on the dynamic needs of the customer. The service concept is the essence of the expected customer value. It is the reason for which the enterprise creates the different activities that form the service process in which the customer takes part. The activities are implemented within the service system: in the service environment with the resources available. The service modules are often produced by several tourist businesses and actors in the destination network, frequently operating in collaboration as a cluster.

A second integrative element between conventional product development and experience design is that every one of the service modules depicted in Figure 12.2 creates a need for a distinct stage, stagers and product designs throughout the destination experience. The customer experiences are thus intimately linked with the suppliers' superstructures, the hospitality provision and the local cultures. The tourist experience may be illustrated as an amalgam of product modules, as depicted in Figure 12.2.

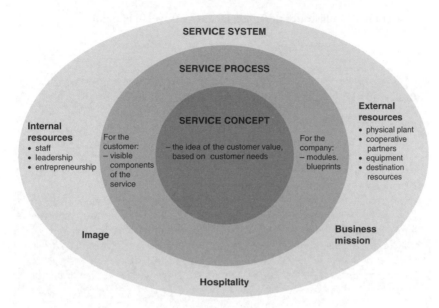

Figure 12.1 Customer-oriented tourist product development
Source: Komppula and Boxberg, 2002

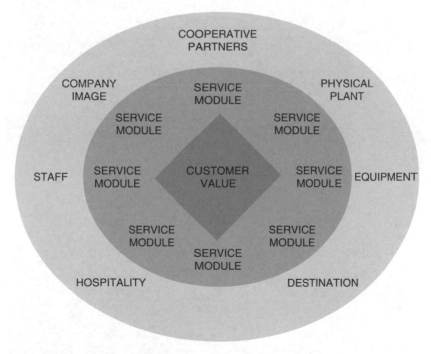

Figure 12.2 Packaged tourist product
Source: Komppula and Boxberg, 2002

Case study 12.1 illustrates designing incentive travel in Finland.

Case study 12.1 Designing incentive travel in Finland

Finland offers unique opportunities for experience product design. A typical Finnish B2B tourism product, such as an incentive-product for foreign customers, is often designed in a similar way. The service concept is elaborated according to the clients' need to offer their staff an exclusive nature adventure experience. Experiencing the cold climate, with temperatures reaching as low as −40°C, rewards participants mentally by allowing them the feeling of exceeding their limits, and they are then indulged with luxurious hospitality. Each of the activities forms its own module, for which a specific production plan and blueprint is drafted. The modules form an integrated entity, which is implemented in an appropriate environment. Figure 12.3 illustrates an example, describing an incentive tour for a group of salesmen. In order to illustrate the usability of the dramaturgic approach in the product development process, the stages of experience design

Figure 12.3 An example of a typical Finnish incentive product
Source: Komppula and Boxberg, 2002

Table 12.1 Stages of experience design

	Stage	What happens in experience design
Stage 1	Idea generation	Analysis of the customer needs and expectations, definition of expected customer values
Stage 2	Creative writing sessions	Content writing for chosen programme, alternatives for value creation (service concept design)
Stage 3	Manuscript of the play	Manuscript to create the intended experience and itinerary (service process design)
Stage 4	Designs of and for the stage	Using all the senses to think through, evaluate and design the site and the stages (continuous service system development)
Stage 5	Plans for acts and roles	Manning and scheduling contact personnel tasks, control for timing and behaviour patterns and contact content with guests (= blueprinting)
Stage 6	Rehearsing the play	Pilot trials of the experience
Stage 7	Planning the staging of the play	Master plan and the corrected blueprint
Stage 8	Role-playing	Implementation of the service, moments of truth
Stage 9	Involvement of the audience	Involvement of all concerned with realized experience

are adopted as demonstrated in Table 12.1. One well-known Finnish activity-operator expresses the idea of service concept development as follows:

> Very often the clients are looking for a product which is short, sharp and attractive. Sharp means that the idea has to appeal. The presentation of the core product, the idea of the product, has to appeal. One can almost sell an old activity with a new presentation and a new aim, the same activity for a different reason, which then comes as a new activity.

The modularized design of combinations allows for dynamic change of the basic design to variations that meet each individual's or segment's specified expectations. An experienced master stager can skilfully integrate the various experience stages to produce a satisfying total experience. This needs to be both a proactive (planned in advance) and a reactive (adapted according to the needs, abilities and preferences of customers) process. The service process for the same service concept would be quite different if the target group was, for example, a senior club consisting of former female managers of a large bank. The service system and concept could be the same, but the activity service models would probably incorporate softer adventures, such as beauty treatments and wellness, which may have enhanced the emotional experience.

Conclusions

Current attention in tourism product development focuses on the technical properties of the product rather than on the total experiences of the customer. Nevertheless, tourism businesses should aim to develop service processes and systems where it is possible for customers to combine products and services according to their personal expectations. This will enable them to build their customized experience and to devise unique value according to their preferences. Product development in a tourism business can be seen as a process with three stages: service concept development, service process development and service system development. The task of the company is to provide the best possible prerequisites for the experience – an attractive idea and description of the product (service concept), a successful process, and a reliable and well-functioning system. That can include complementary products offered by other companies within a cluster of collaboration.

Service process development comprises developing the functional and technical dimensions of the service quality. The underlying prerequisite for a successful product is a dynamic system that evolves continuously to reflect market conditions, and instigates company strategy adaptation. Service concept development inevitably leads to customer orientation as well as to the establishment of a marketing communication strategy that emphasizes the value of the product. Service concepts should therefore reflect customer expectations and ensure that they deliver a comprehensive and delightful experience.

13

Nature-based products, ecotourism and adventure tourism

Tanja Mihalič

Introduction

In the search for new tourism products, travellers and suppliers are today seeking to reshape the meaning of nature as a tourism attraction. Genuine, non-urbanized nature – not just the whispering of the sea heard from a swimming-pool restaurant in the Costa del Sol, or skiing on well-maintained ski runs in the European Alps – has emerged as a new attraction in the tourism market, a new business opportunity and a challenge to researchers. Indeed, over the last two decades much attention has been devoted to the complex field of these new forms of nature-related tourism. New concepts and paradigms have been developed in order to guarantee the quality of a nature experience and to protect the natural and cultural bases for future businesses and generations of visitors. Of these, the present chapter studies the following: nature-based tourism, which focuses on experiencing flora and fauna in natural settings; ecotourism, which is a broader, environmentally friendly theoretical concept; and adventure tourism based on the involvement of natural resources. Although they differ in their meaning, all of these forms share some common points that can be discussed and extrapolated for the future.

The environmental movement has boosted awareness of the importance of natural resources for tourism development and business. Indeed, natural attractions (and cultural and social ones) are some of the main reasons for travelling. Most tourism is somehow connected to natural features like water, beaches, snow, forests, landscapes, caves, and flora and fauna, as well as to socio-cultural attractions such as ancient civilizations, and endogenous people. At the same time, the rapid growth of tourism has resulted in significant negative natural and socio-cultural impacts.

First, environmental quality itself (in the form of an undisturbed, uncontaminated and unpolluted virgin or wild natural environment) is important for all forms of nature tourism. Environmental quality management of a tourist destination involves protection and environmental information, and logos pointing to environmental quality (such as the Blue Flag campaign for bathing water quality). Second, environmentally friendly tourism tries to minimize the negative impacts of tourism activities (Mihalič and Kaspar, 1996) through environmental management, by limiting impacts which may or may not be part of nature-based tourism products, and by adopting eco-labels and certification for tourism products/destinations (Honey, 2002). In addition it attempts to maximize the positive impacts and to incorporate environmental education and ethics, and long-run social and economic benefits, for the local population. Such concepts, like the ecotourism concept, may also be certified.

Concepts of nature-based tourism

Nature itself had already become the subject of interest in the eighteenth century, when the new 'back to nature' movement appeared in European art and society. The former fear of wild, unknown and unpredictable nature was replaced by knowledge of natural phenomena, while technological development enabled people to master nature. At the beginning of the nineteenth century, Leslie Stephen predicted that Europe's greatest natural area – the Alps – would become the playground of Europe, being divided into pedestrian zones for sightseeing tourists, and would thus lose its wilderness (Mueller and Fluegel, 1999: 13).

The accelerated growth seen in international tourism has brought some novel diversification in tourism forms and nominations. Mainstream mass tourism, largely being either urbanized summer sun–sea–sand tourism or technically-supported concentrated winter ski tourism, gradually becomes ethically, politically and ideologically intolerable. Concentrated, large-scale industrial travel is labelled 'mass' or 'hard' tourism, and is blamed for all kinds of damage to the natural environment, and for socio-cultural ignorance and destruction. The search for a substitute to the traditional mass-market tourism model culminated in the 1980s in the alternative tourism concept. This was demand-driven by travellers wishing to travel away from and differently to the masses, towards new, virgin yet attractive places still largely undiscovered by tourists – places where they could interact with the local environment. Unfortunately, these new alternative travellers turned out to be pioneers of mass tourism. First, their numbers grew over time and they thus formed a mass market; secondly, they discovered new attractive places and turned them into (mass) tourism destinations. Krippendorf (1999: 38) illustrated the fall of alternative tourism through a story of a lovely distant Greek island where alternative travellers spent a wonderful summer, returned the following summer with some friends, and once more the next summer with some more friends and so on. Local supply started to develop: fishermen started to rent out rooms, cook for visitors and import Coca Cola®. In a few years tourism supply and demand had grown, and the fishing village had become a destination. Obviously, alternative tourism and, most importantly, planning regulations failed to beat traditional (mass) tourism, and consequently it lost most of its popularity as both a concept and a commercial product.

The search for a substitute for the traditional tourism model continued. New idealists with a concept of soft tourism learned from the decline in demand-driven alternative tourism, and sought a better model on the side of tourism supply. Thus, soft tourism, as developed in Europe (mainly in the Alpine area) was small-scale, based on small businesses, and aimed to integrate locals and visitors. For a little while it even became a promising alternative to mass tourism. Once again, it emerged that soft tourism could present a development opportunity for under-developed regions and for places with tourism attractions that still had not developed infrastructure. Yet soon the story of Krippendorf's Greek island was repeated, except that this time it was supply-driven. Stakeholders tried to attract more visitors, and as soon as they started arriving the appetite increased for more growth and development in order to attract even greater numbers of visitors and more (economic) benefits for the area. In many Alpine destinations, tourism development started out as 'soft' but ultimately emerged as 'hard', large-scale and highly technically supported tourism.

The ecotourism concept was developed in the late 1970s and, unlike alternative and soft tourism, it remains popular. It was based on pretty much the same criticism of mainstream tourism as that of alternative tourism, and more persistently recognized the environmental quality of unspoiled natural places as the main motive for some travel segments. Nature-based tourism and adventure tourism are newer expressions, although the trend towards adventure travel was already identifiable more than twenty years ago (Krippendorf, 1999: 38).

Nature-based tourism and ecotourism

Modern nature-based tourism focuses on experiencing flora and fauna in natural settings, and occurs in such forms as whale watching, trips to rainforests and the habitats of large mammals, and viewing scenery in natural parks or virgin areas. It has become popular as a result of growing environmental awareness and an increasing interest in natural tourism attractions. Technological and economic developments have made remote and preserved areas more easily accessible.

Today the term 'nature tourism' is often used synonymously with 'ecotourism', although it shares only some of ecotourism's requirements. While nature-based tourism relates to nature, its attractiveness, and the visitor experience in natural settings, ecotourism takes unspoiled natural and socio-cultural attractiveness into account. Further, ecotourism is closer to sustainable tourism since it also takes care of environmental (natural and socio-cultural) impacts. Thus, the concept of ecotourism refers to environmentally responsible travel and visits to relatively undisturbed natural (including cultural) areas that promote environmental education, management and conservation, while providing for the beneficially active socio-economic involvement of the local population (Buckley, 1994; Ceballos-Lascurain, 1998; Page and Dowling, 2002: 63).

Adventure tourism

Adventure tourism also falls into the category of nature-based tourism, as it involves the use of natural resources. Its purpose is to explore a 'new experience, often involving perceived risk or controlled danger associated with personal challenges, in a natural environment or exotic settings' (Morrison and Sung, 2000: 11). It is usually connected to sports tourism, and is exercised in forms of hiking, walking, mountain climbing, white-water rafting or black-water paddling, canyoning or kayaking. Adventure experiences vary from hard to soft – i.e. from extreme to mild (Hudson, 2003: xv–xvi) – and so do their impacts on the environment.

Growth of the adventure tourism market has been accompanied by enhanced commercialization of outdoor recreation and the development of specialized high-tech sports equipment. New social trends and specialized magazines and journals promoting active and adventurous lifestyles and holidays create a specific sport, active, adventure and nature-based tourism segment. The growth of adventure tourism is also a reaction to sun and beach mass tourism. Modern travellers are fed up with holidays 'spent lazing away between deck chair, swimming pool and hotel bar, and want to go after quite different holiday experiences: physical exertion, nerve tingling excitement, team spirit and camaraderie' (Krippendorf, 1999: 38).

Comparing nature-based, eco- and adventure tourism

Regarding tourism ethics, true ecotourism is the strongest concept that takes environmental and socio-cultural standards into account. Nature-based tourism is weaker, and may not take care of environmental impacts, while high-tech sport and adventure tourism is the most dangerous in terms of environmental impacts. Although commercial ecotourism is a vague term and is used to market anything related to nature, true ecotourism can also be developed by meeting several criteria. To illustrate these criteria, we refer to two cases known in the ecotourism literature (Shepherd, 2003): SeaCanoe and Siam Safari (see Case study 13.1). SeaCanoe ran kayaking trips in Phang Nga Bay, whereas Siam Safari organized nature tours in Phuket and South Thailand. Both operators received international awards and recognition for their work and implementation of the total concept of ecotourism, yet both businesses were destroyed by the growth of tourism demand and supply.

Today, in some countries, the majority of tourism may be considered nature-based yet not necessarily true ecotourism. Only 1–2 per cent of Canada's or Australia's tourism may be classified as true ecotourism (McKercher, 1998), although the commercial term 'eco' is used much more often than that. Some

Case study 13.1 SeaCanoe and Siam Safari, Thailand

In the late 1980s, the founder of SeaCanoe, John Gray, discovered Phang Nga Bay (Shepherd, 2003: 137) – an area of 150 limestone islands, cliffs and caves that was home to many species of tropical wild fauna and flora, was only known to local fishermen and was not yet used for tourism. In the broader area of Phuket, alternative backpackers had already consumed the area as an alternative in the late 1970s and were leaving it in the search for new, 'more alternative' ones. Mainstream tourism started to develop in the mid-1980s, and saw meteoric growth in the 1990s. John Gray created an eco-kayaking business that was based on cooperation with the local people, promoted environmental conservation, provided high-quality recreational adventures, and specialized in natural history and cross-cultural education. The company involved locals in its share structure, limited the number of tourists per day, and enforced a no-drinking, no-smoking, no-eating, no-talking and no-souvenir-taking policy in order to minimize the impact on the environment. As tourist visits to the area grew, the market potential for selling kayaking trips also grew – as did opportunities in this new lucrative tourism business. The number of imitators increased, and by the middle of the 1990s more and more companies were selling sea-kayaking tours in Phang Nga Bay. Unfortunately, they did not follow the ecotourism standards and expanded the number of visitors to unacceptable limits, thereby damaging the environment. Although the need to limit visitor numbers in order to protect the true eco-business was obvious, the authorities showed no interest in stopping the imitators and the excessive growth of nature-based kayaking tourism. Creating jobs for the local population was a higher policy priority that outweighed environmental protection of these natural resources from and for visitors.

A similar story is that of Robert Griefenberg. His company, Siam Safari, specialized in elephant treks in the area of Phuket. By 1999, his business idea had been imitated by seventeen elephant-trekking companies in Pukhet and mass tourism had driven the prices down.

Both cases show the destruction of ecotourism by tourism growth led by market forces. Environmental impacts increased alongside ever-expanding visitor numbers, with environmental operating standards being eroded by the presence of too many suppliers. This is an experience observed in many destinations around the world with destinations that do not know when to stop (Buhalis, 1999: 184).

operators are already avoiding the term because it has been overused and misused so many times. However, some stakeholders see enough coalescence in markets and even concepts between nature-based, eco- and adventure tourism to speak about the NEAT (nature, eco-, adventure tourism) industry sector (Buckley, 2000: 437).

Critical issues in NEAT tourism and trends

The future of nature-based, eco- and adventure tourism involves many issues. Most tourism products are still nature-based, but not many of them can be labelled true ecotourism. Some may promote environmental education or take visitors to wild, unspoiled areas, but often fail to bring benefits to the local community, protect the environment or minimize negative impacts of visitors. From the marketing perspective of a tourism operator, what can be sold in the tourism market is important. Commercial, nature-based tourism products are in great demand, but does environmental management or protection as part of a tourism product sell? How much are customers willing to pay for it? How much does 'friendly to the local community' influence the buying decisions of travellers?

Indeed, ecotourism may be supply-driven but the final judgement is on the demand side. Thus, from the perspective of a market supplier the question of how many ecotourism criteria to incorporate into a commercial ecotourism product may be easy to answer. Research shows that tourists select a tourism product not primarily for its environmental management practices, but for the environmental quality of the destination as a whole. Tourists are therefore more likely to make holiday choices on the basis of the environmental quality of beaches, national parks and rural landscapes than on the basis of energy or water savings in an eco-lodge. And even if the ecotourism buyer market is strong enough, as in the case of SeaCanoe, how can growth towards a larger-scale business be stopped when all the other tourists who arrive in large numbers want to visit the same places as the earlier true ecotourists? In the SeaCanoe case, the authorities were unwilling to protect the eco-business from being destroyed by too many suppliers and customers since, owing to their other priorities, they were unwilling to intervene with efficient, protective, economic policy measures.

Critical issues in ecotourism development are the scale involved, and the willingness to regulate, legislate and implement policy. Without the implementation of exclusive business rights, concessions and other administrative instruments, ecotourism products are 'part of the cyclic process of destination development' (Burton, 1997: 370); they are not immune from the commercial forces that drive that cycle, and will be squeezed out as the destination and type of visitors change. Thus, the new nature-oriented tourists are just the modern version of yesterday's alternative travellers. They avoid overdeveloped urbanized destinations just like the previous backpackers and individuals tired of civilization did, and, although unwillingly, prepare the 'new' places for a tourism development take-off. What happened to alternative and soft tourism twenty years ago is being repeated with today's ecotourism. Indeed, the great enthusiasm for the new ecotourism concept has turned into slight scepticism, based on present experience and future extrapolations of such tourism development, and has raised the question of whether there is actually something like 'eco mass tourism' (Kirstegs, 2003: 1).

While the search for true eco mass tourism may be an impossible quest, ecotourism practice seems to be slowly extending at least some principles of environmental management and protection into all tourism forms. Thus, ecotourism may become a benchmark (Fennell and Dowling, 2003: 343) influencing the development of other tourism forms in the direction of more ecologically, culturally and socially responsible forms. There is a new recognizable trend in the traditional mass tourism market whereby suppliers tend to implement environmental management and protection together with the environmental education of all stakeholders. Many tour operators have developed certain activities and environmental criteria for destinations, hotels and carriers (Lueck, 2003: 189). The shift to more environmentally-friendly mass tourism is driven by mass-tourism operators who desert mass destinations and demand environmental improvements.

Commercially, nature-based tourism is an attractive product. The NEAT sector is growing faster than the tourism sector overall, as it also includes parts of the leisure, outdoor recreation and sports equipment industries. In the search for a critical mass, some stakeholders see enough similarities in the markets of nature-based, eco- and adventure tourism to discuss the economic importance of the NEAT sector, where part of that attractiveness involves nature – i.e. the attractive quality of the natural environment. However, NEAT has failed to incorporate traditional mass nature-based tourism, mainly in the form of sun and beach tourism, as it is often too urbanized to be recognized as nature-based. NEAT tourism represents newer forms developed as a reaction to the negative image of urbanized, passive and polluted old traditional mass tourism. However, the question remains open as to whether the NEAT sector will follow the same development path as the old one, once also recognized as including nature-based traditional tourism forms.

Further, many forms of hard adventure tourism are extremely environmentally demanding. Adventure tourists aim to master and take new wilderness areas by storm. Compared to the good old low-budget and slow-travelling alternative travellers of the late 1970s, they attempt to use their scarce time more efficiently, are financially stronger, much more frequently equipped with jet boats, four-wheel vehicles, and modern and sophisticated high-tech equipment, and are supported by helicopters and other modern transport means. Even the traditional urbanized sun–sea–sand tourism looks soft compared with the hard technical equipment of adventure tourists. Perhaps these new adventurers will turn into masses in the near future, and will burden the environment more than alternative and traditional tourism ever did.

Conclusions and future trends

Tourism authorities should learn from mistakes, and environmental damage should not be repeated. Growing environmental awareness, requirements for safe and healthy surroundings, the implementation of a sustainable development concept, aversion to hard and damaging tourism forms, and other environmental initiatives such as eco-certification programmes and other changes in our society will influence our relationship with environments in the future. Even future mass tourism should be friendlier to the natural environment if strong incentives are provided for cleaning up the overall environment through the control of water and littering, and for improving environmental aesthetics through landscaping programmes, urban planning, and better building maintenance. It should take the local benefit more into account and continue to educate customers on environmental issues. Although demand-driven and small-scale, some true ecotourism suppliers will continue to satisfy a specific market niche, and some may even stay truly 'eco' in the longer run and influence other tourism forms with their good practices. Hopefully, the tourism of tomorrow will be more environmentally friendly than the old tourism types of yesterday.

14

Sport and events tourism

P. De Knop

Introduction

Nowadays vast numbers of people are interested in sport, and almost everyone aspires to a holiday. Though the connections between sport and tourism have always been well established, this association is gaining global significance. Media attention has increased, and people are becoming more aware of the health and recreational benefits that sport and tourism can provide.

Furthermore, the growing number of travel companies that now produce specialist brochures to advertise their sports and adventure holidays demonstrates the increasing interest in sport tourism. Amongst travel and tourism magazines, resort advertising continues to emphasize the availability of sport facilities and opportunities (Redmond, 1990). Spectator vacations are also increasingly popular, with huge numbers of visitors attracted to sports events. The Olympics and the Football Euro and World Cups provide good examples.

Sport and tourism are now very strongly linked. As globalization progresses, new and exciting possibilities are opening up to enrich tourism experiences through sport, and to enhance sport development through tourism.

Definition

Although there is no universally accepted definition of sport tourism, the terms 'sport tourism' and 'sport tourist' are very often found in recent literature. Hall (1992: 147) argues that:

> Sport tourism falls into two categories, travel to participate in sport and travel to observe sport. Therefore, sport tourism may be defined as travel for non-commercial reasons, to participate or observe sporting activities away from the home range.

It also should be outlined that, in spite of not being expressly mentioned in the above definition, business/commercial tourism must also be included. This means that for the purposes of this chapter, the definition of sport tourism should be considered as follows:

> Sport tourism includes all forms of active and passive involvement in sport, casually or in an organized way, for non-commercial or business/commercial reasons, that imply travelling away from home and work locally.
>
> (Standeven and De Knop, 1999)

Forms of sport tourism

A two-part division of tourism is used where sport tourists can be on holiday (e.g. skiing holidays), or they can travel and participate in sport for business (non-holiday) reasons (e.g. fitness in the hotel after business meetings). According to our model (see Figure 14.1), sport tourists may be active or passive.

Active sport tourists may engage in 'sports activity holidays' in which sport is a main intention of the trip, or in 'holiday sport activities', where sport is incidental and not the main intention. There are two types of sport activity holidays: the single-sport activity holiday, where a specific sport is the overriding objective of the holiday; and the multiple-sport activity holiday, where several sport forms provide the holiday experience (e.g. the club/camp formula). Two types of holiday sport activities are identified: incidental participation in organized sport, provided during holidays (usually in groups such as competitive beach games); and private or independent sports activity on holiday (e.g. taking a walk or playing a round of golf).

Passive sport tourists can also be grouped according to how important sport is to the purpose of their trip. Connoisseur observers are those who have extensive passive involvement, and are discriminating in the sports activities they watch and venues they visit as spectators or officiators (see Case study 14.1). Casual observers are those who simply enjoy watching an event and who usually happen to be present rather than plan their visit.

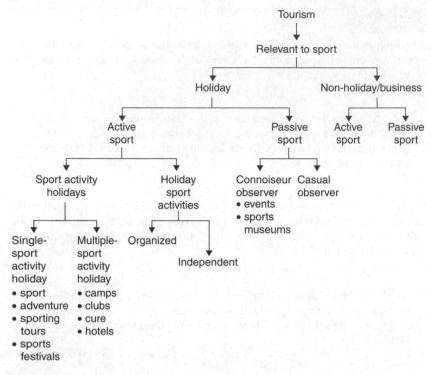

Figure 14.1 A typology of sport tourism (Standeven and De Knop, 1999)

Case study 14.1 The Olympic Museum, Lausanne, Switzerland

The Olympic Museum is probably the best-known sport museum in the world. It was built on the shores of Lake Geneva, close to the place where, for a time, Pierre de Coubertin dreamed of building a modern Olympia. In his opinion, the true secret of Greek beauty lay in a virtually perfect and indisputable harmony between landscape and architecture, and between architecture and man. Today we would probably say it has a respect for proportions and the environment. It was with this spirit in mind that the architects – Pedro Ramirez Vazquez of Mexico and Jean-Pierre Cahen of Lausanne – did everything in their power to ensure that the museum was harmoniously integrated within the landscape.

The aim of the museum managers was to make visitors aware of the breadth and the importance of the Olympic movement – to show, by means of images and symbols, that this is not purely a matter of sports competitions, but rather a philosophy of life whose roots are deeply embedded in our history.

The museum managers also wanted visitors to rediscover the emotions experienced during the Olympic Games, to relive the beauty of effort and physical movement, the strength of will and joy of victory, and the pleasures of celebration and ceremony.

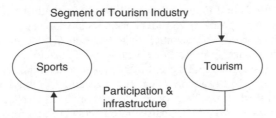

Figure 14.2 Basic model of sport tourism (Standeven and De Knop, 1999)

Tourism and sport: a symbiotic relationship

The relationship between sport and tourism in our modern world is symbiotic. It is not simply that sport acts on tourism, producing an ever-increasing range of valued visitor experiences; tourism also acts on sport. This is illustrated in Figure 14.2.

Impact of tourism on sport

Tourism provides the opportunity for people to exercise and undertake participation in sports. Most people have learnt how to swim in swimming pools or during their holidays. In contrast, and with the exception of the Alpine countries, skiing is learnt during holidays. Skiing is the classic example of sport tourism, and the most popular of all winter-sport activities. Every year it introduces 40–50 million visitors to the European Alps, with 40 000 ski runs and around 12 000 cables and lifts to support this popular holiday industry capable of handling 1.5 million skiers an hour (Mader, 1988). The ski market is now said to account for around 20 per cent of the total European holiday market.

However, tourism not only influences sport participation; sport infrastructures have also followed the example put forward by the tourism industry. To complement the beach and to provide an inclement weather attraction that will extend the length of the holiday season, resorts have constructed indoor leisure swimming pool complexes. Beach volleyball is probably the only sport that started as a holiday activity and became an Olympic sport.

Impact of sport on tourism

Sport also generates tourism as people travel to participate as athletes, as members of the organization team or as spectators. The BTA (British Tourist Authority) claims that in 1992, 26 per cent of its respondents affirmed that 'sport' was the main purpose of their trip. Gibson and Yiannakis (1995) also found that 22 per cent of all respondents considered the opportunity to participate in sports to be important when planning a holiday.

In Belgium, 27 per cent of tourists participate in sports during domestic holiday trips, and this figure increases to 30.4 per cent when including holidays spent abroad. Similar figures may be found in countries such as New Zealand (Kleskey and Kearsley, 1993) and France (Burton, 1995). If instead of holidays in which sport is the main purpose one considers holidays in which sport is an incidental aspect, participation rates rise significantly to between 25 per cent and 80 per cent.

The Tour de France, France's three-week prestigious cycle race, claims to be the world's largest annual sports event, attracting several million spectators along its 2500-mile route. In Britain it is alleged that around 2.5 million watch outdoor sports, while a further 1 million view indoor sport events (NOP, 1989). In the Athens Olympics, 11 000 athletes participated and were accompanied by 10 000 coaches and members of national teams. The event attracted 20 000 journalists, 50 000 volunteers and 50 000 members of the organizing committee, whilst 5 400 000 tickets were sold to spectators.

Sport also generates post-event interest for the destination. A report on the televised production of England's cricket tour to the West Indies was shown to have increased ongoing package tourism by as much as 60 per cent after the event (Elliott, 1995). This feature was also noted by Ritchie and Lyons (1990) in their post-event study of the 1988 Calgary Winter Olympics, where holiday visits increased dramatically due to Calgary being featured during the Games. Research indicates that 88 per cent of the 110 000 international visitors who went to Australia to attend the Sydney Olympics returned there as tourists. Furthermore, between 1997 and 2004 the event was responsible for attracting an additional 1.7 million visitors, and generating an A$ 6.1 billion economic boost. As a result of the Olympics, the brand Australia remained strong in the market over the following ten years (ATC, 2001).

Changes in the international travel market are leading to an increasing variety of tourist types, needs and patterns. Adventure and active holidays are recognized as growing segments, and sports training is acknowledged as an important and potentially health-enhancing process for which tourism can be the catalyst.

Wellness healthcare and training of the body have boosted an important industry. Sport as therapy is another growing segment of the tourism industry, with an estimated 15 million annual visits to spas in Europe alone – a figure that is comparable to similar markets in the USA and Asia (Benton, 1995).

It should be emphasized that the history of tourism is very much associated with health reasons. In its early days, people used to travel to seaside resorts because of the 'presumed health-giving properties of sea bathing' (Urry, 1990: 37). Nowadays such a situation has been fuelled on account of the importance given by people to fitness and other health activities.

Sport as part of business hospitality is also big, profitable and growing, with most of the clients watching events miles away from where they live. Active sport associated with business tours is also booming, thanks to teambuilding and incentive trips.

It has also become almost impossible for professional sports men and women to embrace their careers without travelling abroad. International travelling has become very important even for amateur sportspeople.

Travel agents look for new markets as a way of broadening their range of clientele. Jolley and Curphey (1994) give the example of 6000 agents who attended the American Society of Travel Agents World Travel Congress in Portugal in 1994. A major conclusion of this event was that sporting activities will become one of the world's major tourism markets – 'whatever the special interest, a company somewhere will organize a holiday around it' (Jolley and Curphey, 1994: 35).

Case study 14.2 Club Med, France

Club Med is one of the biggest tour operators in the world, with 2 million clients a year served by 9000 GOs (gentil organisateurs) and 12 500 staff members of 68 different nationalities. The Club Med business results in more than US$2 million. These clients, or GMs (gentil membres), stay in one of the 98 Club Med villages all over the world, in a cabin, a luxurious bungalow, a hotel, or onboard one of two luxury ships (Direction des Ressources Humaines Club Med, 1994).

The Club Med concept differs from that offered by other tour operators. Club Med wants to give people a relaxing journey to an unforgettable place, far away from the stress of everyday life. In these magical places, social differences disappear and people can feel totally free. They can choose from a broad range of activities, drinks and food, and everything is included in the price apart from some extras, for which they pay separately. The GOs are staff (i.e. activity leaders) who spend a lot of time with the clients, making sure they are comfortable and offering them a wide variety of services.

The importance of sport tourism

Standeven and De Knop (1999) encountered wide evidence to support the claim that sport tourism has increased significantly over recent years. The evidence provided by them is as follows:

- large numbers of people participate in sport tourism or are involved with it
- demand for active sport holidays is still increasing
- more and more people have seized upon its potential – commercial entrepreneurs, public providers and consumers themselves (participants and spectators), and authorities (e.g. community, country) organize sport promotional campaigns during holiday periods or use sport to promote tourism to the country (e.g. the Tourism Authority of Thailand promoted the year 1993 as the 'Visit Thai Golf Year' for the purpose of increasing the number of foreign tourists in Thailand)
- the number of organizations offering club holidays is increasing very fast – for example, Club Méditerranée, Club Aldiana, Club Robinson, Club Escolette and Holiday Club (see Case study 14.2)
- mass sport and tourism events produce large numbers of travellers – a first tourism-flow is generated by the event itself (e.g. 12 000 of 28 000 participants in the New York marathon come from outside the US), but a second source of travellers emerges from the publicity generated by the media about the destination itself
- sport tourism has become big business – for example, the size of UK consumers' expenditure on skiing holidays in 1987 was almost the same as that on newspapers (Rigg and Lewney, 1987), and the total market value of sport tourism in the UK is estimated to amount to US$ 4.5 million.

The future of sport tourism

It is likely that tourism, sport and sport tourism will continue to expand. Nonetheless, one of the major challenges in the future will be to launch closer links between sport and governmental (tourism) organizations, so that better coordination, more profits and sustained policies may be achieved.

Indeed, there is a clear lack of coordination between tourism and sport organizations in most Western European states. The separation of sport and tourism functions in most governments is very common. Tourism surveys rarely provide detailed information about the purpose of the trip, which means that accurate sport tourism statistics are not available. Similarly, sport participation statistics rarely identify non-resident activity, except occasionally in surveys of individual centres. Domestic sport tourism generally goes unnoticed in the system too. Some recent surveys do at least allow identification of the proportion of trips of a generally sporting nature (planning or spectating), and increasingly permit their separation from broader outdoor interests such as sightseeing or swimming.

Weiler and Hall's (1992) discussion on special-interest tourism (which includes sport, adventure and health tourism) provides a broad and brief forecast. Following on from the demographic, economic and technological changes in society, they expect special-interest travellers to become increasingly more sophisticated. Special-interest tourism:

> will be driven by the demands of these tourists and by the opportunities and limitations of the cultural and natural environments on which special interest tourism depends ... special interest tourism has an exciting and dynamic future.
>
> (Weiler and Hall, 1992: 204)

In the future, the nature of sport tourism will largely remain the same. It will continue to be a two-dimensional cultural experience of physical activity tied to a cultural experience of place. New sport forms will emerge as long as new physical challenges can be devised, but these will most likely be hybrids of present sport forms – in the same way as snowboarding developed from a combination of surfing and skiing, and sky surfing from sky diving and surfing. Sport tourism will expand geographically to include emerging destinations in Eastern Europe, Latin America, Africa, and Asia.

The future participant in sport tourism

Sport tourists will increase in number, and there will be an increasing diversity in their profile and participation. Sport participation will be one of the differentiators of tourism. As the tourist market itself broadens with the addition of new travellers generated in countries such as China, India, Russia, Africa and Latin America (albeit only the most wealthy in the short term), the market for sport tourism will continue to expand. However, the addition of new travellers from countries barely represented in present statistics is not the only growth that can be expected.

As Europeans, Japanese and other Asians, South Africans and many others pursue leisure travel in increasing numbers, sport tourism, as a special segment, will also expand. Moreover, their profile will become more diversified as new groups of people start to travel.

The boom observed in fitness activities has fuelled people's consciousness of the links between physical activity and health. Apart from enjoyment, this will be the strongest reason, especially among the ageing population, for getting actively involved in sporting events – both as participants and as spectators.

More middle-aged and older tourists will participate in sport tourism as this age group enlarges and finds it has both the time and the financial means to travel. Earlier retirement and more active generations will benefit and diversify the sport tourism market.

New and enlarging markets will display new tastes and make new demands. Individualization has accelerated in recent years, and has led to what Roberts (1994) calls the do-it-yourself sport movement. Robinett (1993), reporting on trends in the US leisure market, notes that customers wish to be seen as individuals in a custom-made world, and that economic concerns, related to value and intrinsic worth, are assuming centre stage. Generally, better-educated, more discerning participants will demand more tailor-made and specialized opportunities.

The traditional two-week or one-month holiday will change. Flexible-duration sports holidays will be enjoyed by those with the most time at their disposal. These will range from budget hiking and cycling safaris to more expensive long-haul tours with sporting experiences included. Short duration trips of a weekend or five days will also increase. Weekend ski trips from Britain to mainland Europe are becoming more popular, and now one-day trips are on offer to Slovenia including two-hour flights each way. The Japanese market is also known for its preference for international golfing weekends.

While specialization will characterize some sport tourists, others will choose multi-activity opportunities in club locations such as Center Parcs. The latter will be favoured by many for their budget-conscious provision and for the chance they provide to try out a number of new activities. Individuals with larger disposable incomes, however, will gain access to increasingly wide opportunities.

'Organized' groups will continue to be popular, though the level of organization will vary. Groups of friends and families will participate in sports together, making their own private travel arrangements. Package tours are by definition more highly organized, and will add sport opportunities both as novelty day-trip options (such as white-water rafting during a visit to Nepal) and as more of a sport development programme, such as Kuoni's bowling holidays to South Africa, New Zealand, the Far East and America. Sports clubs will continue to travel domestically and also internationally to test their skills and combine social and tourist opportunities with their game; professional teams will of course do likewise. Professional players from all over the world will also become increasingly visible as more of them sign contracts abroad, and, in turn, they will encourage their fans to travel. There will be a growth in the range of sports played in different countries with, for example, American and Australian codes of football becoming increasingly popular internationally. Thus, sport tourism spectating will continue to be popular, encouraged by the addition of new sports, new teams, new stars and new places to visit.

Conclusion

Sport activities are gaining increased importance all around the world as a result of growing disposable time and income, and also on account of the increasing importance given by people to health concerns. Such a situation is prompting the expansion of a new and very dynamic market.

Sport and tourism activities are closely linked to each other, so a symbiotic relationship may be established between them. Sport activities demand an efficient tourism industry to support their expansion. Tourism demands new and diversified forms of travelling in order to ensure forms of sustained travelling in the future.

15

Shopping and tourism

Yvette Reisinger

Introduction

Shopping represents an important travel motivator, destination attraction and tourist activity. Tourists often travel to take advantage of lower prices, brand names, duty-free shops and product uniqueness. Shops such as Harrods in London and Nike Town in Chicago are primary tourist attractions. Many destinations position themselves as 'shopping paradises' for tourists. London and Paris are known for their world-renowned department stores, while Hong Kong, Singapore and Thailand are recognized as major shopping centres in Asia. The development of the shopping sector is an important instrument in tourism promotion.

Shopping makes a significant contribution to the economy by generating income and employment in receiving regions (e.g. shopping in hotels, restaurants), generating regions (e.g. shopping at origin airports) and transitory regions (e.g. at airports, on-board shopping). Tourist spending represents a source of funding that can be used to develop retail areas, townscapes and streetscapes (Hall, 1994), and revitalize urban centres, deteriorating resorts and even rural areas (Jansen-Verbeke, 1991). In destinations known as 'shopping meccas', shopping represents a significant percentage of the visitors' expenditures.

Shopping will be a major activity in future leisure travel (Jansen-Verbeke, 1991). Many destinations will embark on it in search of success.

What is shopping?

Shopping is the act of purchasing goods. It can be an act of necessity or a utilitarian act, an act of pleasure, desire or even fun. According to etymologists, shopping is the process of going to shops to purchase goods and services. Others define shopping as a complex interaction of a shopper with (1) shops and the infrastructure of production and distribution; (2) social, cultural, economic and political life; and (3) commercial and cultural values. Shopping is an important element of commercial culture that influences the consumers' lives and stimulates sales. It is also an intertextual experience created by different cultural texts such as logos, brands, clothes, classes and genders. Shopping is about making choices and learning about desires and needs, human nature, the value of money, the purpose of life and work, and the influence of consumption on a society (Farrell, 2003).

Why do tourists shop?

Shopping is mostly about having fun, and is also about spending time rather than spending money (e.g. spending time in duty-free shops while in transit). It can bring relaxation, enjoyment, happiness and satisfaction into daily life. When on vacation, tourists are relaxed, have the time to browse and have money to spend, so they allow themselves the luxury of indulgence and escape into a fantasy that is often missing in their ordinary lives. They can immerse themselves in romance (a sunset cruise on the Caribbean), adventure and nature (fishing shops), culture (craft shops, book and music shops), fun and entertainment (rock cafés), seduction and desires (lingerie shops, sex shops), beauty (beauty shops, health spas), success (sports mart) and the chic casual mode (Gap, Banana Republic). Shopping is also about symbolic consumption. Purchased goods can symbolize and reinforce the sense of self. Tourists often shop to create self-identity and self-image, to express themselves and make sense of their lives. Although some tourists shop to get bargains (see Case study 15.1), many shop for pleasure. New clothes, books and perfumes make their lives more pleasurable and meaningful. In addition, tourists shop for social reasons – to see others and be seen, to bond with family and friends, to explore the relationships with others and engage in conversations with locals, and to find the sense of companionship. Many also feel they have to buy something for friends and relatives while on vacation.

From an economic perspective, several factors stimulate tourists' inclination to buy, including domestic taxes, import duties, the value of specific goods compared to that in the tourists' home countries, and the availability of duty-free stores. Duty-free or tax-free shopping in airports and on cruise ships offers an important incentive for tourists' propensity to buy goods, and contributes

Case study 15.1 The Amazing Thailand Grand Sale

The Amazing Thailand Grand Sale is Thailand's annual two-month shopping extravaganza which offers world-class shopping, a diverse selection of quality products and services, special discounts of up to 80 per cent off regular prices, and promotional offers extended by department stores and retail outlets in Bangkok and the popular tourist destinations of Chiang Mai, Pattaya, Phuket, Hat Yai and Songkhia. The event is one of the biggest in Southeast Asia. About 900 business operators participate, including retail shops, restaurants, tourist attractions, tour agencies, theme parks, golf clubs, sport clubs, spas, hotels and other forms of accommodation.

The event, organized by the Tourism Authority of Thailand (TAT), has been held every year since 1998. The objectives of the Grand Sale are to create an opportunity for people to visit Thailand and enjoy great discounts and deals, to stimulate domestic and international travel, to create revenue for the economic development of Thailand, and to enhance its image as a tourist destination.

(http://www.tatnews.org/tat_news/detail.asp?id=1931, and
http://www.tatnews.org/tourism_news/2166.asp)

to the popularity of shopping while travelling (Dimanche, 2003; Prosser and Leisen, 2003).

Changing shopping patterns

The last 20 years have created many more shopping opportunities. Today tourists not only shop in retail outlets such as small boutiques, large department stores and shopping malls, but also in train and bus stations, airports, on board big cruise ships, in hotels, restaurants, museums, theme parks and national parks, and even in banks, post offices and insurance companies.

The range of goods available has been broadened to go beyond typical mass-produced souvenirs such as postcards, stamps, maps, mugs, T-shirts, sweatshirts, local products (e.g. chocolate from Switzerland) and symbolic items (e.g. a minia-ture of the Eiffel Tower from Paris) to include such 'non-touristic' items as jewellery, leather goods, housewares, antiques, art, and duty-free and electronic goods. With the increased popularity of self-catering accommodation, tourists also buy a large number of grocery items (Timothy and Butler, 1995). Finally, tourists seek authentic craft souvenirs (Yu and Littrell, 2003) and cultural motifs in apparel (Asplet and Cooper, 2000).

The retail selection in airports has improved dramatically in recent years. Some airports offer otherwise hard-to-find regional goods. In Vancouver, British Columbia, for instance, travellers can buy plenty of high-quality Canadian goods, including salmon wrapped ready to travel, Canadian maple syrup, and Canadian-made clothing for cold weather. Houston's airports are the best spots to buy cowboy hats and boots, or other Western wear. International airports, most notably those in Europe, have become famous for their range of designer shops.

About 50 per cent of main airports' revenue is generated by retail rentals. Many international airports, such as London Heathrow, Singapore Changi and Dubai International Airport, have established themselves among the world's best for shopping.

Changing shopping needs and types of shoppers

While tourists constantly seek unique gifts and products, and are concerned about the price, brand names, product features and packaging, not all products are suitable for all travellers. Demographic, socio-economic and psychographic factors are important elements in understanding the needs of tourists-shoppers. The differences in shopping behaviour between the age, gender and socio-economic groups have been noted by some researchers (Jansen-Verbeke, 1987; Littrel *et al.*, 1994).

Similarly, cultural backgrounds influence tourists' shopping preferences and spending habits (Hobson and Christiansen, 2001). For example, Japanese shopping behaviour and patterns differ from those of Americans, Europeans or other Asians. The Japanese are very keen on detail, aesthetics, quality and service. They shop in groups, purchase more gifts for close friends and family members than the average tourist because of the cultural custom of *omiyage* or gift giving, and demand gifts that reflect the social position and age of the recipient. It is believed that significant profits exist in the sale of the right mix of products to culturally different tourist markets.

The shopper market itself is highly diversified. The major segments of shoppers and their purchasing motives are presented in Table 15.1. Increasingly a number of values are changing internationally, influencing the future of shopping and tourism as demonstrated in Table 15.2.

Table 15.1 Types of shoppers

Type	Characteristics and relevance to tourist behaviour
Bargain hunters	Seek clearance, seasonal, inventory reduction and factory sales; attend shopping events, travel to shopping destinations such as Hong Kong or Thailand
Browsers	Glance at random through merchandise
Compulsive shoppers	Addicted to shopping, highly oriented towards price, seek bargains
Convenience shoppers	Buy necessities and daily products such as groceries
Cool-hunters	Early adopters, seek new and trendy brands to impress friends
Depression shoppers	Make purchases to avoid depression or stress
E-shoppers	Shop for travel products online via the Internet
Impulse buyers	Make sudden purchases, swayed by emotions, easily influenced by the advantages of timeshare vacation units
Just looking window shoppers	Look for stuff to buy, gaze through windows; no commercial exchange occurs (one of the most popular tourist activities)
Tele-shoppers	Purchase via digital television

Source: Farrell (2003).

Table 15.2 Global values that influence the future of shopping in tourism

Values	General features	Tourist shopping purchases
Community	Public service	Products that create a sense of community and connect with the community (social events, social tourism)
Culture	Culture more important than money and material possessions	Cultural products (art, music, film, museums, galleries, concerts, cultural tourism, ethnic tourism)
Ecology	Importance of saving, conserving and protecting natural resources	Products that protect fragile environment and nature (eco-friendly products, ecotourism)
Education	Education is the best investment	Products that encourage learning experiences (books, guides, videos, educational tourism, interpretation services, special-interest tourism)
Family	Importance of family relations, support and love	Products that bond family together (games, sport and fishing products, family vacations, group activities)
Friendship	Importance of friendship – friends are forever	Products that allow people to spend time with friends and show appreciation (games, cards, gifts, wine, tea, jewellery, visiting friends and relatives)
Harmony	Social harmony	Products and services that create social harmony (social events, social tourism)
Humanitarianism	Caring for others, empathy, human rights	Products that compete with commercial market leaders (products for elders, disabled, unemployed, fund-raising events, donations, voluntary tourism, tourism for those with special needs, subsidized vacations, non-profit tourism)
Love	Importance of feelings, ethics and morality	Products that generate and teach feelings (poetry, music, art, romantic cruises, nostalgic tourism, nature-based tourism)
Safety and security	Importance of safety, security, social stability and order	Risk-free products and products that reduce risk (comfortable and safe clothing, transportation, sport and kitchen equipment, translating and guiding services, insurance)
Spirituality	Importance of inner values, inner peace, satisfaction	Spiritual and religious products that allow people to understand their inner self and the purpose of life (stones, crystals, tarot cards, bibles, religious books, spiritual retreats, wellness vacations, pilgrimages, trips to sacred sites)

Changing the way consumers shop

The Internet has transformed the way consumers shop. The development of sophisticated websites has offered the opportunity to see and experience products before purchase and also to obtain information about price, specific destination rates, seasonal discounts, hot hotel deals, car rentals and purchase conditions. Numerous websites, such as kelkoo.com, cheaptickets.com and discountflights.com, allow consumers to look for flights, a hotel or package holiday, and compare the prices of the product offered by a variety of suppliers. These websites not only enable buyers to find the best price from the convenience of their home, but also allow them to schedule own airline tickets, book accommodation, hire a car and purchase travel insurance. In the future, online sites will be able to access consumers with personalized messages and target special interests groups such as skiers, golfers or divers with customized offerings. Customers will be able to receive wireless messages and suggestions on products and activities related to their personal interests. Technology will allow suppliers to recognize a customer who visits their sites and tailor offers based on previous online behaviour or purchases. The use of wireless technology, including PDAs, cell phones and laptop computers with international reach, will provide new ways to shop for travel products and location-based services and products (Katz, 2004).

Shoppers are also encountering increasing automation in stores. Many stores now offer self-scanning and self-checkout, eliminating the need for a lengthy wait for cashiers. Customers in the United States have begun to use biometric identification to pay for their purchases. They place a finger in a scanner at checkout, eliminating the need for cash, cheques or credit cards. Soon, barcodes will be replaced by radio-frequency identification (RFID) technology.

Changing planning and geographic environments

Several major changes have taken place regarding shopping planning and environments in tourism. Shopping is a typical component of urban tourism, and inner cities and downtown areas have become major tourist attractions. The development of shopping districts has helped to rejuvenate some rundown inner city areas (e.g. The Rocks in Sydney). Hence shopping infrastructure and services in urban areas have been given more attention by urban planners and developers (Jansen-Verbeke, 1986). Factors that have been important in attracting visitors to retail stores include convenient location, wide variety of shops, good accessibility, pedestrian priority, attractive design, availability during leisure time, promotion, store image, hospitality (Jansen-Verbeke, 1991), display techniques, social interaction, and even friendly conversation with knowledgeable sales people (Littrell *et al.*, 1994).

Shopping mega-malls and large factory outlet malls selling higher-order goods like clothing or shoes have become tourist attractions and destinations for both locals and tourists. In addition to more traditional food courts, wide varieties of leisure attractions are being provided in large shopping areas and malls. Typical facilities include health clubs, play areas and water complexes.

Tourist Shopping Villages (Getz, 1993) as well as tourist-oriented centres (Wesley and LeHew, 2002) have become important planning concepts.

Case study 15.2 Cross-border shopping market assessment, UK

In 1999, 2.7 million UK residents went abroad for the purpose of shopping. This was equivalent to 5 per cent of all overseas travellers. The most important destination for cross-border shopping was France, visited by 92.8 per cent of cross-border shoppers. Almost all of the cross-border shopping market was channelled through the Eurotunnel Shuttle Services, while the short sea-crossing (Dover to Calais/Boulogne) ferry operators carried 1.1 million passengers. Eurotunnel Shuttle Services overtook the ferry operators as the most important route for cross-border shopping.

About 2.3 million of the UK's cross-border shoppers purchased tobacco or alcohol, or both. A further 11.2 million UK residents went overseas and purchased alcohol or tobacco for consumption in the UK. Wine was the most important product for cross-border shopping, followed by beer, spirits and tobacco. The value of cross-border purchases of wine and beer increased from £1.16 bn to £1.61 bn between 1999 and 2004. Total expenditure on alcohol and tobacco increased by 40.3 per cent, while the total number of visits involving purchases of alcohol or tobacco increased by 26.4 per cent. This rise was partly due to the abolition of duty-free taxes within the continent in 1999.

(http://www.researchandmarkets.com/reportinfo.asp?report id=3594)

Near-urban, resort and *en-route* communities have become viable shopping areas for attracting tourists (Getz *et al.*, 1994). Shopping arcades and entertainment complexes, themed spaces such as festival marketplaces, heritage sites, and cultural and waterfront attractions have been extended into popular shopping venues. Currently, rural shopping is emerging as an important tourism product. Many malls tend to be located in rural areas close to highways and major urban developments (Carmichael and Smith, 2004). In addition, big shopping malls and theme parks are increasingly merging together.

Regional differences and price fluctuations in neighbouring countries have increased an interest in cross-border shopping, particularly in North America (e.g. US–Canada) and Europe (Timothy and Butler, 1995). Cross-border shopping has brought numerous economic and social benefits to neighbouring countries (see Timothy, 1999; Case study 15.2).

New marketing strategies to attract shoppers to destinations

Shopping is a pull factor for destination attractiveness, and planners and marketers are increasingly developing and promoting shopping as a tourist product (Timothy and Butler, 1995). They consider a multitude of factors, including product design, features, value, reputation, retail outlets, service, methods of payment and price, outlet opening hours, attractive environmental surroundings, and distribution. They employ marketing strategies that enhance the appeal of shopping to tourists, such as promotional shopping tours for domestic and international tourists (e.g. Air France has marketed shopping trips from Europe to the US, and Asian travel agents have designed escorted shopping tours to Europe and Australia for their Japanese and Korean clients), development of unique shopping experiences, and aggressive marketing programmes adopted by shopping malls – including the introduction of mall entertainment.

Unique shopping experiences are created by making the store look like a market, streetscape or city square, or by enhancing the theme of the product by designing specific sights and sounds. For example, the Grand Canal Shoppes at the Venetian Shopping Mall in Las Vegas have been designed to resemble the city of Venice; complete with reproductions of the Grand Canal (with gondola rides and gondoliers) and St Mark's Square. More than 95 per cent of customers at the Grand Canal Shoppes are visitors enticed by the foreign ambience (Farrell, 2003).

Moreover, small events (such as local fashion shows, cooking classes and birthday parties) and big events (such as concerts featuring star performers live) have allowed tourists to combine shopping experiences with pleasure. For those who prefer more quiet and intimate moments, cafés, book and music shops provide havens in which they can relax, read literature, listen to music, and seek out new titles and CDs. Other special events that attract visitors are traditional or indigenous dancing, and arts and crafts festivals.

Shopper-tainment, the combination of retailing and entertainment, has been used by shopping venues to create a shopping experience. Active entertainment has become popular because it allows customers to participate in, as well as to watch, the event. Planners foresee shopping designed more for entertainment than for shopping. Retailing is becoming a real entertainment industry that attracts the local population and tourists. Further, shopping malls may be replaced by or blended with Disney-type venues and include amusement parks, golf courses, giant aquaria, waterfalls, trout ponds, rifle ranges, skating rinks, children's playgrounds, carousels, go-kart tracks, video golf, theme restaurants or health clubs, and many more. For example, since the Mall of America in Minneapolis-St Paul introduced an indoor amusement park, a Lego Imagination Centre, a wedding chapel, a radio station, a high school, a university and a medical clinic, it has attracted more visitors annually than all the national parks and national monuments combined (Farrell, 2003). The future will demand multigenerational shopper-tainment, serving the needs of different generations.

The hospitality industry has played an enormous role in providing entertainment and fun for shoppers. Restaurants and food courts have become an integral part of most shopping and entertainment venues. Themed restaurants offering Thai, Indian, Chinese or French foods have introduced diners to exotic meals that have become increasingly popular among locals and tourists alike. Also, dining experiences have been combined with live entertainment. For example, in San Francisco, Max's Opera Café has combined live performances and food with great success. Similarly, in Japan, indoor food theme parks have grown in popularity. The emphasis of 'eater-tainment' will be on enhancing the quality of the dining experience and enjoyment.

Fun has been introduced as a major element of shopper-tainment. For example, the Rainforest Café in Mall of America offers a virtual safari, exuding an atmosphere of adventure, featuring a 'native' cuisine of items like jungle safari soup and monkey business coconut bread pudding. The Café also sells safari clothing, toys and CDs. People return to the Rainforest Café for its ability to fulfil their needs for fun and a dream of a safari. Future shops will also likely showcase fun destinations to attract both locals and tourists.

Ethical concerns regarding shopping and future developments

Shopping malls promise to continue in popularity with the middle classes of North and South America and Central Europe, as well as among the emerging middle class in Asia – particularly women. However, shopping malls can create concern in societies with other than Western consumption ethics (e.g. in Asia). Western consumption culture threatens the Asian collective cultural values that bind people together, and causes the disappearance of old cultural traditions – especially among young people. The 'demonstration effect' that encourages spending rather than saving among poorer communities often causes serious material, social and human problems. Thus the development of big shopping malls may be discouraged in some countries in order to preserve cultural identity. Since the expansion of big shopping malls also threatens the survival of local small businesses, France has already imposed restrictions on the development of such malls.

As society becomes more environmentally conscious, it may also demand shopping venues that are ecologically friendly and designed in harmony with nature. The focus may be on ecological designs that fit with the design of nature (e.g. energy saving, free public transport for visitors), ecological buying practices (recycled packaging, paper conservation), humanistic designs (healthy products, organic production) and regenerative designs (improving nature by making human life beneficial to the biosphere). Shopping venues may become a centre for society and tourists, rather than centres for shopping. These venues may boast information centres, community and charity meetings, areas for speeches and voting, and include public theatres, health centres and childcare centres (Farrell, 2003). As the building of shopping centres also causes pressure on the urban infrastructure, environmental degradation, and traffic congestion on roads and within parking systems, the growth of mega-malls may have to be generally restricted in order to minimize the environmental problems. In order to attract tourists, the shopping villages that provide a variety of visitor services, facilities and tourist attractions may represent important tourist destinations.

Conclusions: new consumer values and ways of thinking about shopping

It is hoped that, as society becomes more globally oriented, it will re-evaluate its excessive consumption behaviour, develop new expectations, and demand new shopping experiences and benefits. The fear of the unexpected, such as wars, political conflicts, terrorism and incurable diseases, increases society's desire for safety, social stability and order. People will re-evaluate their use of time and choose a new balance between career and family, and work and leisure. It is hoped that such a shift in values will produce a new, less materialistic consumer, and a non-materialistic worldview that stresses the importance of ecology and living in harmony with nature and the community. In such a world, shopping will be about preserving natural resources and maximizing the quality of experience rather than the quantity of products purchased. Future traveller-shoppers will find self-expression in culture, ethics and morality, understand the importance of being healthy not only physically but also intellectually, emotionally and spiritually, and become more concerned about the planet, its resources, and its inhabitants all co-existing in peace.

The retail sector in the tourism industry has to respond to new trends in shopping. If retailers wish to attract tourists' attention and generate sales, they cannot be solely concerned with products, entertainment, special events, fancy meals and fun. Rather, they need to think about human values, the interplay between human activities and the planet, and try to respond to humanity's needs.

16

Gastronomy, food and wine tourism

C. Michael Hall and
Richard Mitchell

Introduction

Gastronomy, food and wine tourism has become
a rapidly growing area of tourism research and
tourism product development. From the perspective
of the consumer, food is an integral component of
daily life and therefore of travel. From a tourism production perspective, food offers potential for firm
and destination marketing opportunities, specialized
tourism products based on food experiences, and the
possibility of enhancing economic linkages between
tourism and agricultural production. However, there
is only a limited understanding of the market because
of the dearth of research into the demographic and
psychographic profiles of the consumer (Mitchell
and Hall, 2003), although greater attention has been
given to the development of food tourism.

Gastronomy, food and wine tourism defined

Gastronomy is the reflexive analysis of what we
eat. Food tourism can be defined as visitation to primary and secondary food producers, food festivals,

restaurants and specific locations for which food tasting and/or experiencing the attributes of specialist food production regions are the primary motivating factors for travel. Wine tourism is a subset of food tourism, as is gastronomic tourism, which implies visitation for specific high-quality tourism products. Such a definition does not mean that any trip to a restaurant is food tourism; rather, the desire to experience a particular type of food or the produce of a specific region or even to taste the dishes of a particular chef must be the major motivation for such travel. Indeed, such is the need for food to be a primary factor in influencing travel behaviour and decision-making that, as a form of special interest travel, food tourism includes what is described as 'culinary', 'gastronomic', 'gourmet' or 'cuisine' tourism, thereby reflecting consumer interest in food and wine as a form of 'serious leisure' (Hall and Mitchell, 2001). Figure 16.1 provides an illustration of the relationships between some of the various sub-categories of food tourism. The figure highlights the relationship between the level of interest in food and the size of the market. This is significant because the size of the market of tourists for whom food is a primary motivation for travel is actually quite small (Hall and Sharples, 2003).

The food tourism market

Strong evidence for a breakdown of the food tourism market along the lines of that illustrated in Figure 16.1 comes from research on visitors to four regions in the UK (the South West, Cumbria, Yorkshire and the Heart of England). According to research undertaken for the British Government (Enteleca Research and Consultancy, 2000), the UK holiday and visitor market can be broken into five groups:

1. *Food tourists* (6–8 per cent of domestic visitors (day visitors as high as 11 per cent) and 3 per cent of international visitors) – these people say that seeking local food and drink is a particular reason for choosing their holiday destination
2. *Interested purchasers* (30–33 per cent of domestic visitors) – members of this group believe that food in general can contribute to their enjoyment of their holiday and they purchase/eat local foods when the opportunity arises
3. *Un-reached* (15–17 per cent of domestic visitors) – members of this group believe that food and drink can contribute to their enjoyment of their holiday, are happy to try local food if they come across it, but at present are not purchasing local foods
4. *Un-engaged* (22–24 per cent of domestic visitors) – these people do not perceive food and drink as adding to the enjoyment of their holiday, but are not negative about trying local foods
5. *Laggards* (17–28 per cent of domestic visitors) – people in this group say they have no interest in local food and are unlikely to have purchased any on holiday.

Yet, given that regardless of what market segment visitors may fit into everyone has to eat, the role of food as part of the tourism experience and as a tourism product means that many firms and destinations are paying great attention to developing food-related tourism. Moreover, and just as importantly, changing

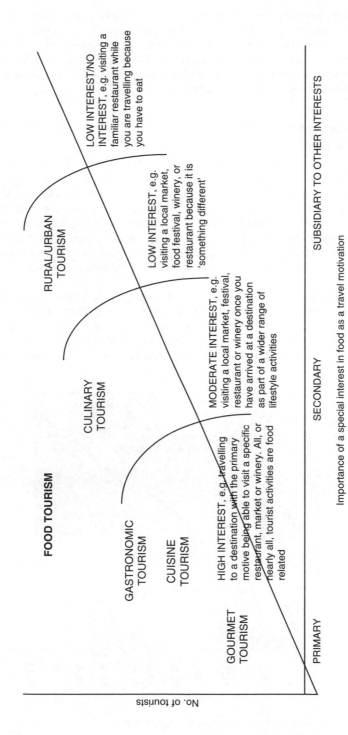

Figure 16.1 Food tourism as special interest tourism (Hall and Sharples, 2003)

patterns of food consumption, cuisine change and the awareness of food as a
component of contemporary lifestyle expressions also suggest that the number of
people overtly interested in food as a component of destination products is
increasing. The following chapter is divided into four main parts: the role of travel
in cuisine change; the influence of the media; changes in the role that tourism
plays in food production; and changes in consumption.

Cuisine change

Travel has long been an integral part of cuisine change. When people travel,
whether for migration, pilgrimage, trade or tourism, not only do they take their
food preferences with them but they may also take foodstuffs, plants and animals,
and knowledge regarding food preparation. This means that when people travel,
whether going to a destination or returning home, they influence both the food
environment they are travelling in as well as the foodways of those they interact
with. Foodways are therefore always changing, even though the proliferation of
'classic' cuisine styles as expressed in restaurants and cookbooks may sometimes
suggest otherwise.

Hall and Mitchell (1998, 2000) have argued that, since the medieval ages, three
major periods of cuisine change can be identified (Figure 16.2). The first wave was
the period of European mercantilism from the late 1400s to the 1800s, when sailing ships brought new foodstuffs back to Europe and provided ingredients for the
French, Italian and Spanish food traditions that we now think of as 'fundamental'.

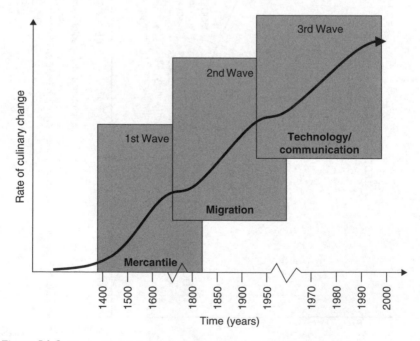

Figure 16.2 Waves of cuisine change (Hall and Mitchell, 1998)

For example, tomatoes, turkeys, corn, potatoes and peppers came to Europe and were later disseminated throughout the European empires. Peppers from the Americas became part of Chinese and other Asian cuisines through trading routes. Fruits, spices, vegetables and animals also became the stuff of trade, further leading to changes in foodways – for example, through the adoption of tea and coffee in Europe.

The second wave of food change was the influence of large-scale migrations from the seventeenth century through to the twentieth century. This occurred not only with the European settlement of the Americas, Southern Africa and Australasia, but also in more modern terms with the Irish and Scottish migrations as a result of the 'potato famine' and the 'clearances' respectively and, more recently, through the massive post-war migrations – particularly from Southern Europe to North America and Australia. Indeed, the migration of Italians and Greeks to Australia in the 1950s has been seen as critical for the development of a more cosmopolitan Australian attitude towards food and drinking, although this position has been challenged by Symons (1993: 12), who provocatively states: 'it is not even an exaggeration to say that multiculturalism also follows the new cuisine, and not the other way around'. More recent waves of migration from Asia to Australia and the United Kingdom have also created new waves of cuisine change, with Asian foods such as curry becoming accepted into the foodways of the host. For example, the Indian food business in Britain is worth over £3.3 billion a year. In 1987 there were some 4000 Indian restaurants; by 2002 there were more than 9000 (Palmer, 2002). Indeed, the arrival and growth of ethnic groups through transnational processes is a significant predictor of the development of restaurants that specialize in the cuisine of that group, albeit sometimes modified to meet the tastes of the wider market.

The third wave of the cuisine change is the present period of economic and cultural globalization, which will likely continue into the foreseeable future, in which advances in communication and transport technology have radically altered the rate at which food and information regarding food is relayed around the world (Figure 16.3) as well as influencing the potential development of fusion cuisine. Clearly, technology has always been a significant factor with respect to food production and consumption. The impacts that advances in transport (shipping, railways and automobiles), food production, preservation and retailing have had on what we eat have been described as leading to the 'homogenisation of the world diet' (Ripe, 1996: 4) or the 'McDonaldisation' of food (Ritzer, 1996). This means that, for those who can afford it, almost any foodstuff can be sent from one part of the world to another within 24 hours – and, arguably, that almost any restaurant can have 'local' food from almost anywhere. Perhaps just as significantly, it highlights the potential role of the media in influencing consumer purchasing and eating behaviour (Caraher et al., 2000). For example, in a survey of British consumers, almost six in ten respondents reported that their cooking habits had been influenced by celebrity chefs (Barkham and Gillan, 2004).

Media and food

The media has substantial influence in determining food product selection. The influence of celebrity chefs is often referred to as 'the Delia effect' after the

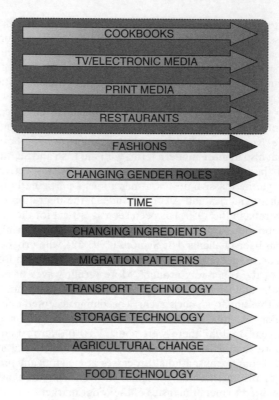

Figure 16.3 Factors additional to tourism that influence cuisine change
Source: Hall and Mitchell 1998

media chef Delia Smith, whose 1998 television programme *How to Cook* resulted in an extra 1.3 million eggs being sold in Britain each day of the series. More recently, in the first week that Sainsbury's supermarket sold Jamie Oliver-endorsed 21-day mature beef, 5000 packets left the shelves (Barkham and Gillan, 2004: 7). It is therefore perhaps no surprise that tourist agencies will often sponsor food programmes, while advertising is also used to connect travel with places. For example, many of the programmes on the Canadian and United States Food Network television channels are supported by regional and national tourism organizations. The promotion of food lifestyles via the media has arguably now become inseparable from travel for food as part of tourist experiences, or increased consumption of restaurant and takeaway food (Palmer, 2002). Such linkages between food and tourism are enhanced by the way that place is an important component in both food and tourism promotion, therefore creating opportunities for cross-promotion and awareness.

Moreover, travel itself is changing people's food tastes and contributing to new food products and patterns of consumption both at home and abroad. Holiday-making exposes tourists to new foodstuffs in many destination areas, while other forms of mobility, such as business and educational travel, have also led to increased interest in food as part of local cultures (Hall and Sharples, 2003). Indeed, food is now intimately related to lifestyle consumption, and is likely to remain so for the foreseeable future (Mitchell and Hall, 2003). Such a situation is somewhat ironic, given that fewer and fewer people in the developed world actually know how to cook – although it must also be acknowledged that for some people food is merely regarded as 'fuel', with no other associations of status or identity attached. Nevertheless, the new demands created for specific foods by tourist and leisure lifestyle consumption obviously have implications for food production.

Tourism and food production

Everyone has to eat. At the most basic level tourists therefore place demands on the food production chain. However, given the substantial restructuring of rural areas in much of the developed world, the food interests of visitors have become recognized as an opportunity to emphasize local foods and their production as an overt component of the tourist product, and to maximize the circulation of tourist spending in the local economy (see, for example, Canadian Tourism Commission, 2002). For example, the UK Countryside Agency (2001) developed an 'Eat the View' initiative to improve the market conditions for food products that contribute to the maintenance of the rural landscape. Under the initiative, the Countryside Agency aims to achieve a number of outcomes:

1. To inform consumers about the impact of their decisions on the rural environment and economy, and how they can take positive action to benefit the countryside
2. The development of systems for marketing/distributing/selling produce that will enable consumers to show support for local/sustainable production methods
3. The development of quality standards/accreditation systems to underpin markets for local/sustainable products
4. The development of local marketing/branding initiatives which will utilize unique features, such as rare animal breeds, local customs etc.
5. The development of new supply chain partnerships between retailers and producers which will increase the proportion of locally sourced/sustainable products
6. An increase in the proportion of produce sold through alternative markets to large retailers and bulk caterers (e.g. local collaborative arrangements)
7. An increase in the number of local/community-led food initiatives, creating stronger local markets for produce and strengthening links between producers and consumers (adapted from The Countryside Agency, 2001).

The potential for food tourism to stimulate local economies is substantial. For example, research on tourists in the UK suggests that between 32 per cent and 66 per cent of tourists either purchase or eat local foods during their visit, with the proportion being strongly linked to length of stay. Moreover, just as importantly, there is a widely held perception among respondents that the purchase of local foods helps the local economy (82 per cent) and that purchase of local produce helps the local environment (65 per cent). Importantly, 67 per cent of holidaymakers who took part in this research said that they were prepared to pay more for quality food and drink (Enteleca Research and Consultancy, 2000). Indeed, there is a number of significant advantages of food tourism for producers,

Table 16.1 Advantages and disadvantages of food tourism for producers (Hall *et al.*, 2003a)

Advantages

Increased consumer exposure	There is increased exposure to the product as well as increased opportunities to sample it
Increased brand awareness and loyalty	Brand awareness and loyalty is built through establishing links between the producer and consumer, and by the purchase of company-branded merchandize
Creation of customer relationships	The opportunity to meet staff and to see 'behind the scenes' can lead to positive relationships with consumers, which may lead to both direct sales and indirect sales through positive 'word of mouth' advertising
Increased margins	Margins are increased through direct sales to consumers, although the absence of distributor costs is not carried over entirely to the consumer
Additional sales outlet	Tourism provides another outlet for producers; for smaller producers who cannot guarantee volume or constancy of supply, this may be only feasible sales outlet
Product marketing intelligence	Producers can gain instant and valuable feedback on the consumer reaction to their existing products, and are able to trial new additions to their product range
Customer marketing intelligence	Visitors can be added to a mailing list, which can be developed as a customer database to both target and inform customers
Educational opportunities	Visits help to create awareness and appreciation of specific types of foods and food as a whole, and the knowledge and interest generated by this can be expected to result in increased consumption

Disadvantages

Increased costs and time	The operation of a tasting room or direct sales may be costly, particularly when it requires paid staff; while the profitability gap is higher on direct sales to the consumer, profit may be reduced if wineries do not charge for tastings
Capital required	Suitable facilities for hosting visitors may be prohibitively expensive for some small operators, especially as some types of added value production are capital-intensive
Inability to increase sales greatly	The number of visitors a business can attract is limited, and if a business cannot sell all of its stock then it will eventually need to use other distribution outlets
Opportunity costs	Investment in tasting rooms and tourist facilities means that capital is not available for other investments
Seasonality	Tourism, as with the production of food, is seasonal, and it is important to ensure that demand periods are complementary.

although some limitations can also be noted (Table 16.1). Tourism and hospitality operators and the wider region can also benefit from food tourism development (Hall *et al.*, 2003a) because:

- there is an association with quality products
- the non-standardized nature of food tourism reinforces 'authentic' tourist experiences, thereby allowing visitors to see beyond the shop front and establish strong relationships with a destination

- the existence of product (such as farmers' markets, direct sales opportunities, high profile restaurants and cooking schools and wineries) provides a motivation for visitors to come to an area, stay in accommodation and eat at restaurants
- the existence of product also helps to extend the length of visitors' stays because it gives them places to visit and activities to engage in.

Nevertheless, despite the potential of food tourism to stimulate production and maintain or even broaden rural diversification strategies, numerous barriers remain – with key issues being:

- measures to protect the intellectual property dimensions of food, wine and tourism
- difficulties in establishing networks between industries and sectors in which there has often not been much cooperation
- improving branding of destinations and food products from the same place
- ensuring that there is sufficient talent and knowledge in rural regions to provide the intellectual capital for development (Hall *et al.*, 2003b).

However, one final issue with respect to ensuring the positive development of food tourism is understanding the changing nature of consumption.

Food tourism and consumption

It is widely recognized that tourists provide a significant proportion of the market for restaurants and cafés around the world, with dining out often being cited as one of their main activities. One area in which some marketing research has been conducted is with respect to farmers, produce markets and farm outlets. Research by the UK National Association of Farmers' Markets suggests that the typical customer falls into the AB (upper/middle class) or C1 (lower middle class) socio-economic group – working people with high disposable incomes. Similarly, the US demographic surveys at farmers' markets have indicated that patrons are predominantly white females with above-average incomes, age and education. From a business perspective such a profile is significant, as this is the same profile as that of many food tourist target markets – such as those for cooking schools, and wine and food tours (Mitchell and Hall, 2003).

Research on 'wine and culinary' tourism conducted in North America (The Economic Planning Group of Canada (EPGC) 2002), similarly reported that the Lifespan Demographic Segments that rated highly on a Cuisine and Wine Interest Index were Affluent Mature and Senior Couples (Table 16.2). Interestingly, similar profiles have also been developed of wine tourists that also focus on the mature market, although in the case of wine tourism it is also often regarded as male-dominated. Nevertheless, research on wine tourism in New Zealand by Mitchell and Hall (2001a, 2001b) has substantially questioned the industry focus on the 'mature' male market by not only suggesting that there are substantial age and gender differences in wine interest, but also that the level of

Table 16.2 Demographics of high interest in cuisine and wine in Canada and the United States

Canada

- Young couples (married or living common law, 18–35 years, no children under 21 at home)
- Mature couples (married or living common law, 36–65 years, no children under 21 living at home)
- Advanced university degree (21 per cent high interest)
- Income levels of C$80 000 plus (24 per cent high interest)

United States
- Young couples
- Mature couples
- Mature singles (not married or living common law, 36–65 years, no children under 21 living at home)

Source: Derived from Lang Research (2001), and the Canadian Tourism Commission (2002), in Mitchell and Hall (2003).

knowledge is a significant factor in purchase and consumption that industry needs to respond to in order to ensure the development of new wine markets.

Developing the wine tourism market: Generation Y

Treloar et al. (2004) have suggested that substantial attention needs to be given to developing the Generation Y market in terms of future wine tourism consumption (an observation that applies equally as well to food tourism). Given Generation Y's presently relatively low income levels and interest in a wide variety of beverages and activities, it is readily apparent that cost and value for money are significant factors for this market. Cost impacts wine purchase decisions, and the decision to consume wine at all, as well as decisions to participate in wine tourism. Further, it was clear from this research that wine marketing efforts that are undertaken – including in-store promotions, wine reviews and awards, and bottle design alterations – have little impact on this segment, as previous experience and the influence of friends were found to be more important than those elements. The significance of the peer group suggests that marketing focusing on creating a personal or individual knowledge of the wine, one of the primary elements of the food and wine tourism product, could have an important affect on the purchase decision. Without such initiatives, wine consumption may further decline because of a perception that it is not relevant to contemporary lifestyles – with a consequent flow-on effect on wine and food tourism.

Conclusions

In order to maintain the development of food tourism products, it is essential to understand the changing consumption patterns of different cohorts as well as the role of food in contemporary lifestyles. We all have to eat, but the challenge for food tourism businesses is to ensure that they are producing something that visitors want to consume. Importantly, this means recognizing that there is only a small number of tourists who will travel just for reasons of food; however, there is a larger market of people interested in wine and food who could potentially become more committed to purchasing food and wine tourism products. In order to achieve this goal, a far better appreciation of food as part of lifestyle and consumer behaviour than at present will need to be a central focus, particularly given the increasingly competitive wine and food product offerings.

17

Travel/tourism: spiritual experiences

Yvette Reisinger

Introduction

The demand for spiritual and mental renewal, better health and identity has been increasing around the world. A growing number of people are turning towards spirituality, which is becoming an important motive for travel. Many destinations are promoting themselves in connection with spiritual motivations. Spiritual travel will change the nature of the tourism product on offer, and necessitate a new approach to tourism and tourism marketing.

Why do people turn to spirituality?

In the Western world, escalating civilization, technology, constant change, and being overworked, overfed and overstimulated by computerized automation have created some undesirable effects, such as anxiety among its citizens, identity crises, and feelings of isolation, depression and stress. Western societies are becoming more secular and distrustful of religion. People are getting tired of living a materialistic lifestyle. Some seek solace in activities that enhance their physical, mental and spiritual comfort (Smith, 2003a). Many decide to use travel as a form of escape from an ordinary, monotonous and often dangerous everyday life, to discover their own identity and their real sense of self. Tourists are increasingly drawn towards simpler, natural environments in which they can be more themselves, enhance personal growth, and experience enlightenment and spiritual healing.

In the future, travel and tourism may no longer be about sightseeing and material consumption but rather about getting in touch with oneself, with others and with the world at a deeper level. Tourists are demanding a new form of travel that fulfils a need for a temporary sanctuary for troubled minds and a way to balance mental well-being. The tourism industry can meet these needs by translating holiday experiences into spiritual experiences that enhance well-being and foster personal development. Spiritual tourism is becoming one of the most dynamically growing areas of the tourism sector.

Spirituality and spiritual experiences

The concept of spirituality is often mistakenly believed to be about church attendance or religious beliefs. As a result, spiritual tourism is sometimes referred to as religious tourism, which focuses on pilgrimages to religious places like the Vatican, Mecca or Jerusalem. However, there is a distinction between the concepts of spirituality and religiousness. Spirituality refers to the search for meaning, unity, connectedness and transcendence, the sacred and the highest level of human potential (see Table 17.1).

Central to spiritual experiences are concern and compassion for others, unconditional and altruistic love (Van Kamm, 1986), feelings of being grateful and blessed (Steindl-Rast, 1984), giving others the benefit of doubt and dealing with others'

Table 17.1 Definitions of spirituality

- Spirituality emphasizes the experience of relationship with the transcendent, a sense of unity with the transcendent, divine love experienced as affirmation that contributes to self-confidence and a sense of worth, divine intervention or inspiration, the perception that life consists of more than physical states, psychological feelings and social roles, the assumption that there is more to life than what one can see or fully understand, a sense of wholeness, inner harmony and peace. It addresses questions about life's meaning and allows looking beyond self (Van Kamm, 1986).
- Spirituality refers to looking for a sense of existence and its meaning, an ethical path to personal fulfilment, which includes experiencing oneness with nature and beauty and a sense of connectedness with self, others and a higher power or larger reality, concern for and commitment to something greater than self. Spirituality refers to a high level of faith, hope, and commitment to a well-defined worldview, strong belief system, principles, ethics and values; and love, joy, peace, hope and fulfilment (Hawks, 1994).
- Spirituality refers to transpersonal experiences such as intuition, psychic and mystical experiences, an expansion or extension of consciousness beyond the ego boundaries and beyond the limitations of time and /or space (Grof, 1976).
- Spiritual experience is 'any experience of transcendence of one's former frame of reference that results in greater knowledge and love, involves moving beyond one's own unhealthy egocentricity, duality and exclusivity towards more healthy egocentricity, inclusivity and unity' (Chandler et al., 1992).

faults in light of one's own, being generous of heart (Vacek, 1994), and accepting others as they are (Vanier, 1999).

Religiousness is concerned with systems of worship and doctrine shared within groups (Van Kaam, 1986), and with adherence to the beliefs and practices of an organized church or religious institution (Shafranske and Malony, 1990). While religion teaches people to search for an external God, spirituality internalizes this search and directs the mind to consciousness and one's own being (http://www. aznewage.com/spirituality.htm). Spiritual life can be fostered and nourished by religions (Van Kaam, 1986), so it may include various forms of religiousness; however, spirituality does not necessarily involve religiousness, and some people pursue and experience spirituality outside of religion. A central quality of spirituality is that it can affect people with no religious beliefs (Van Kaam, 1986). Likewise, it is possible to adopt various forms of religious worship and doctrine without being a spiritual person (Fetzer Institute, 1999). Many people identify themselves as being religious but not spiritual.

Meanings of spirituality

Spirituality has different meaning for each person (Hinterkopf, 1998), and it does not necessarily involve a higher power such as God, Christ, Allah, Mother Earth or universal energy. Some find spirituality in faith, unconditional love, living in the flow (the Tao), allowing (rather than controlling) and non-attachment (Lukens, 1992). Others experience spirituality in great joy, being supported by some greater power, or as a connectedness to the universe. Many experience spirituality by asking questions about the meaning and purpose of life, or intuitively understanding how to cope with life circumstances (Atchley, 2004). Some feel calm and spiritual when accepting another person's differences, and others, as they are. Spirituality may also be found in nature, art, ritual dance or choral music, and even in service to others or the environmental movement (Hinterkopf, 1998). The search for spirituality aims at reducing inner conflict and increasing a sense of peace with oneself, others and the world. It is always part of a quest for growth or change.

Spirituality also has different meanings in Western and Eastern societies. Western spirituality emphasizes a personal connection with God, higher power or the divine. Eastern and Native American spirituality refers to extraordinary events such as visions, near-death, past life and out-of-body experiences (Hinterkopf, 1998), and places more emphasis on a connection with all life and being part of a greater whole (Van Kaam, 1986). Also, in the West people often think of spirituality in terms of social unity, self-transcendence and love for others. However, for the Japanese, who are taught unity with other people and their environment and who do not use personal pronouns such as *I* and *you*, spiritual growth involves developing healthy egocentricity, a sense of individuality and separation from others (Hinterkopf, 1998).

Spirituality and tourism

Discussions of tourist roles often include the role of spiritual seekers who travel to learn more about themselves and the meanings of existence (Yiannakis and Gibson, 1992). Tourism 'provides people with the conditions for a constant search for ... spiritual enrichment' (Vukonic, 1996: 18). Tourism provides time and creates space, motivation, activity and a special environment (physical, social, cultural) that may translate holiday experiences into spiritual experiences. The characteristics of spirituality reflect important traits found in travel motivations, such as a quest for meaning, purpose, fulfilment, connectedness, nature, beauty or peace. Tourism offers events and activities that can fulfil these spiritual motivations. Visiting cathedrals or wilderness areas, for instance, enhances spiritual experiences and development.

However, some tourism motivations and activities are not necessarily spiritual, and some spiritual motivations or activities are not touristic. A key factor in determining spiritual motivation and activities is the attitude that individuals bring to their activities. An attitude of openness; the ability to be aware; a willingness to be more in touch with oneself, seeking balance in life between work and leisure; looking for physical settings that are natural, related to personal and human history or childhood; longing for solitude and silence; or pursuing activities that allow for being 'true to oneself' can enhance experiences of a sense of the universe, connectedness and one's presence, and contribute to spirituality. Peaceful natural settings (e.g. forests, gardens), remote wilderness areas, retreat camps or travelling with only the basics, as well as peaceful built settings (e.g. museums, libraries, monasteries) allow tourists to reflect, forget about daily commitments and facilitate their experiencing nature, being more sensitive to the things around them and more in touch with themselves. A wide variety of tourism activities, such as mountain hiking, canoeing or watching sunsets, allows tourists to experience quiet, appreciate the vast beauty of the natural environment and enhance spiritual experiences, as long as they help people to get in touch with themselves, be true to themselves and express their personalities (Heintzman, 2000, 2002).

Busy-ness, noisy settings and events, and urban environments detract from spirituality. Entertainment centres, live concerts, shopping malls, bars, video arcades and fitness classes keep a person busy in the material world and divert attention away from spirituality. Activities that have an element of tension (e.g. socializing with people one does not feel comfortable with) generate a negative state of mind. Similarly, spending time in artificial and plastic environments, such as theme parks (e.g. Disney World), is spiritually unhealthy (Heintzman, 2000).

However, some might argue that one may also experience spirituality at a rock concert or walking the happy streets of Disneyland. For some people, spirituality also comes from tragedy, death or danger. For example, a visit to the concentration camp of Auschwitz in Poland, and the atmosphere of horror when entering the 'shower rooms' and seeing the crematorium, may have a powerful influence on people's emotions and spiritual sensibilities. Similarly, a visit to the 'ground zero' area in New York and the recollection of the events of 11 September 2001, when thousands of people lost their loved ones to terrorist attacks, can generate a spiritual experience. Spiritual experiences can also be prompted by health problems, chronic illness, near-death experiences, suffering, stress, depression, tumult and chaos. Natural disasters, such as tornados or hurricanes, can offer spiritual experiences of the might of God or nature.

The age of change

Today, many long for a New World in which there is no disease, war, hunger, pollution, poverty and discrimination; in which the focus is on human rights, social justice, environmental preservation and conservation, ethical consumption, peace and universal religion; and in which people are concerned about the entire world rather than a single nation. Many believe in the importance of living in harmony with each other and the Earth, in sharing, non-violence and anti-militarism. They are convinced that in order to achieve this, humans may have to shift from consumerism and outside expression of themselves to inner change and a spiritual journey. Some believe in divine energy, transcendence of the entire universe, life after death, karma, invisible energy that surrounds objects and human body, the ability to heal ourselves and others, psychic powers and personal growth. They accept the existence of time travel (astral, spiritual, out of body; and physical travel back in time), outer space and non-human civilizations.

Those who seek such spiritual experiences often engage in astrology, channelling, aura and palm-reading, dowsing, numerology, psychometry, remote viewing, runes, tarot, listening to mystical music that transforms the consciousness into a state of meditation and trance, searching for past lives, out-of-body experiences (OOBE) and near-death experiences, searching for Earth mysteries (lights, leys, crop circles, energies), *feng shui* and geomancy, holistic health and medicine, and mental and physical techniques to advance personal potential and spirituality. Those who engage in the above practices are responsible for the growing interest in spiritual experiences, and constitute some of the market for spiritual tourism.

Spiritual travel products and experiences

In the future, an interest in spirituality may translate into high demand for spiritual travel products and experiences. Given all the different ways that people understand and experience spirituality, spiritual travel will take different forms, serve many purposes and have different meanings. Those who want to soak in cultural treasures or visit archaeological ruins or museums may include not only visiting heritage places or attending festivals in their travel itineraries but also participating in ceremonies and practising indigenous spiritual rituals, shamanism, and learning and understanding indigenous art, paintings or music. For example, Peruvian Amazon Jungle Journeys allows tourists to participate in healing rituals, purification diets and plant therapies.

Those who are interested in nature-based tourism products will extend their desire to see wilderness, flora and fauna to participation in nature-based activities such as bird watching and listening, swimming with dolphins, or even flower care to renew and rejuvenate their spirits. Others may seek spirituality in walking along beaches or snowy mountains, or sunset watching. There is an increasing demand for trips to experience Mother Nature. Tours in Alaska have surged in popularity in recent years; Alaska can offer a non-polluted environment, places off the beaten path, and guided and environmentally safe packages emphasizing social and environmental responsibility.

Those who are interested in rural products may seek trips to organic farms and regional producers to learn about the local produce and taste organic food. They may like to learn about growing fruits and vegetables, attend farm shows and harvest festivals, participate in food and wine tasting, take fishing and horse-riding trips, or go on bird and animal tours.

Since spirituality is an important component of overall health, the health/ wellness vacations and inner retreat centres (e.g. Hawaiian retreats) offering nature-based spiritualities, therapeutic activities, holistic healing, Eastern and alternative medicine, yoga and meditation are in high demand. Nutrition and workout programmes at retreat camps are sought. Trips to spa destinations to indulge in luxury pampering, beauty and body treatment, mud therapy, thermal water baths, massages, and cosmetic dermatology and wellness in general already experience high interest.

Vision quests are sought to learn more about the self, personal growth and life skills. Counselling, stress management, life and relationship strategies can be incorporated in tourism products as travellers ask for attitudinal healing and soul retrieval, exploration of their own energy centres, enlightening conversations with international healers and even card readings. Creative visualization, breath-work, imagery and awareness exercises can also be used to foster spiritual experiences and development (Chandler et al., 1992).

The expectations of religious tourists gradually change, and future activity will not be limited to pilgrimages and visitations of religious sites. New religious practices emphasize the importance of healing, optimism and psychic power. Tourists are expected to seek conversations with spiritual guides or chanting with monks when visiting temples. Monasteries can provide peaceful oases in which tourists will nurture body, mind and spirit, whilst churches can offer uplifting prayers to create the feeling of joy, the spirit of connection and the strength for personal re-creation.

A great deal of interest is already experienced in tours focusing on sacred and power sites and energy vortices. There is a very great variety of sacred places around the world (see Table 17.2). Many are cultural, but they also include natural sites as well as cultural landscapes. Some represent the delicate balance between

Table 17.2 Examples of selected types of sacred places

Type	Example
Ancient cities	Machu Picchu, Peru
Human-built places/monuments	Great Pyramids, Egypt; Taj Mahal, India
Labyrinth sites	Glastonbury, England
Oracle sites	Delphi, Greece
Places of apparition or visions	Fatima, Portugal; Garabandal, Spain; Guadaloupe, Mexico; Medjugorje, Croatia
Places of energy or mystical power of nature	Stonehenge, England; Sedona, Arizona
Places of remembrance	Auschwitz, Poland
Places sanctified by events in the life of a prophet or saint	Holy Land, Israel; Mecca, Saudi Arabia
Sacred bodies of water	Lake Titicaca, Peru/Bolivia
Sacred islands	Iona, Scotland; Easter Island, the Pacific
Sacred mountains	Mount Kailash, Himalayas
Sacred rocks	Ayers Rock (Uluru), Australia; Petra, Jordan
Shrines, altars, chapels, churches, temples	Temple of Artemis, Ephesus, Turkey
Sites of miracles and healing	Lourdes, France
Tombs of kings/saints/prophets/gods	Great Pyramids, Egypt

Source: Scheer, 1999; Shackley; 2001a.

Case study 17.1 A spiritual journey to Egypt

People who believe in the power of pyramids, crystals and meditation are travelling to Egypt in record numbers to visit the Great Pyramids, which are considered a source of great mysticism and energy. Unlike other tourists, they are not seeking a good time, but something more. Many believe in reincarnation, and that they lived in Egypt during ancient times. They want to visit the pyramids at night and during certain phases of the planets to chant and meditate. They pay a high fee for being able to participate in spiritually-oriented night visits to Egypt. Special tour groups are arranged to allow tourists to enter the pyramids before sunrise and meditate in the heart of the pyramids before dawn. There are 17 million people in the United States who believe in the power of the pyramids.

(http://www.cnn.com/World/9704/06/Egypt)

ancient traditions, modern society and nature – for example Ayer's Rock (or Uluru, as it's known to the Aborigines), which captures a sense of the sacred in the middle of Australia's outback. Many of the sacred sites, such as Machu Picchu in Peru, Stonehenge in England or the Egyptian Pyramids (see Case study 17.1), have become internationally renowned. Travellers like to visit sacred places to experience the hidden mysteries of the ancient metaphysical civilizations, their rituals and healing techniques; to gain inspiration, receive prophecies and other messages about what direction to take in their lives. Although the category of 'places of remembrance' includes sites that are not sacred in the conventional sense, these may also exert a powerful influence on spirituality as visitors respond emotionally to grief, pray, light candles and lay flowers (Shackley, 2001a).

Spiritual experts who understand the social, cultural and religious aspects of today's society and have knowledge of the sacred places and ancient civilizations will be needed to explain the purpose of spiritual places and activities. Spiritual visitors are expected to spend their time on meditation, sitting inside stone circles, meeting Sai Baba or exploring the Temple of the Dalai Lama, rather than just visiting the places.

Community engagement trips will be sought. Humanity trips will offer hands-on help to the poor and rural communities, to sick people, malnourished children, and all who are in need. More non-profit and fund-raising events of all kinds can be introduced to appeal to those seeking emotional and spiritual connection.

Spirituality-focused travellers will expect packages and services that encompass a whole range of spiritual activities and experiences. They will seek a wide variety of contemplative, enlightening, healing, therapeutic, interactive and personal development activities (Smith, 2003a). Creative cultural and educational activities, such as reading poetry, painting, writing, dancing and even singing, may also be used to create spiritual experiences and allow travellers to communicate with others and the outside world.

Leisure and recreation activities will increase in importance in creating spiritual experiences. Spiritual tourism products and services can be offered in combination with such activities as cross-country skiing, canoeing, camping, golf-ing, bicycling or hiking. For example, a combination of tennis and meditation, golf and yoga, swimming and hydrotherapy, sightseeing and colour and light therapy, or hiking and breathing therapy may become popular among particular market segments, leading to the widespread growth of all-inclusive holistic packages for special interest groups.

Spiritual products and services can be offered to tourists in many places – at ski centres, on international boat cruises, at conference centres, or in hotels. Tourists seeking spirituality may be attracted to one-day domestic experiences, or exotic travel to long-haul destinations that are almost impossible to reach (e.g. Maya sites).

Spiritual travel is gaining popularity among adults of all ages. Customized tours must be developed to meet every person's taste, age and activity level. Since women form the core clientele for spiritual travel (Attix, 2002), immediate atten-tion should be paid to women's tour groups and their spiritual needs.

Some spiritual products and activities can also be virtual. Prospective travellers can be provided with the chance to visit another planet or a sacred place, to climb Mt Everest or see the Mona Lisa or Picasso's paintings without leaving home. By using sensory stimuli and virtual reality, it is possible to create experiences close to the real feelings without travelling anywhere in the physical world. For exam-ple, computer technology already enables the State Hermitage Museum in St Petersburg, Russia, to provide people from all over the world with the virtual tour of the Hermitage, the magnificent buildings of the Winter Palace, the resi-dence of the Russian tsar, and its collections of works of arts.

In sum, it appears that the holistic approach to spiritual tourism will increas-ingly be adopted. Spiritual products and services can be offered by a variety of sectors of the tourism industry (e.g. hospitality, travel, visitor services), as well as by the recreation, leisure and sport industries.

Conclusion: the future of spiritual tourism

Outdated marketing strategies that focus on external attractions and activities such as luxury resorts, fun and entertainment no longer satisfy the growing hunger of those with unsettled minds. Even those who have finances to fulfil their needs will eventually find that something in their lives is missing and slipping through their fingers. Thus, tourism marketers may need to respond to the increasing human need for spirituality.

In the future, in societies where uncertainty has been brought into lives and ter-rorism is a sad reality, people will seek for answers to life problems in unusual ways. Spiritual tourism is one way to find these answers. A day at the spa or a trek in the Himalayas (see Case study 17.2) can take travellers out of their daily life and give them the chance to regenerate, connect and give back. It can also teach them how to be more fully aware, less task- and possession-oriented, and more being- or becoming-oriented. Spiritual tourism offers a break from the global problems of materialism, excessive consumption and environmental pollution; the disappear-ance of ethics and morality; and the declining value of social relations and friend-ships, philosophy and humanity. The concept of spiritual tourism contributes to a better understanding of the world and makes it a better and safer place.

Case study 17.2 The Kingdom of Bhutan

The Kingdom of Bhutan is a small country in the Himalayas – remote mountains that are referred as to the home of the gods and the immortals. The mountains offer a unique environment for communion with the divine through contemplation and meditation. Many ascetics, scholars, philosophers and pilgrims have travelled to the Himalayas in search of wisdom, inspiration, solitude and happiness.

The Kingdom of Bhutan offers rich spiritual, cultural and environmental experiences to its visitors. Its culture and traditional lifestyle are intact, and its environment is still pristine. The country is one of 10 biodiversity hot spots in the world, and one of the 221 global endemic bird areas. The Kingdom of Bhutan has been visited by saints, mystics, scholars and pilgrims for their personal enlightenment. In 2003, more than 6000 tourists visited the country. Tourists are allowed to travel on pre-planned, pre-paid guided package-tours only. The Bhutan has adopted a very cautious approach to tourism development to avoid its negative impacts on the culture and the environment.

(http://www.kingdomofbhutan.com)

18

Space tourism

Vaios Lappas

Introduction

Over the course of human history there has always been a strong drive to explore and travel to new and exciting places. Space exploration has captured the imagination of the general public for the last 30 years; it is only natural that people are now beginning to ask if and when they too might venture into space. Space and tourism have both developed at an equally rapid pace, and the potential of both together is definitely going to grow further.

Tourism has evolved significantly over the past few decades. Mass and specialised tourism have boomed, and new destinations, themes and adventures are being added continuously at a frantic pace. Similarly, space activities, and especially human spaceflight, have also developed dramatically over the past two decades. Although human spaceflight is currently the privilege of a few space-exploring nations, recent advances in space technology and entrepreneurship are about to change the *status quo*. China, with the assistance of Russian technology, was able to place an astronaut in space in 2003 in a fraction of the time that it took other space powers, such as the USA and USSR, to do this. The first credible private space-tourist venture is already a reality. The first space tourist, Denis Tito, flew in 2001 in a government vehicle, although his flight was privately funded, whilst in 2004 the first spaceship became a reality. However, there is a number of important questions which need answers in the near future – such as, can space tourism become a viable business? Can space tourism be easily accessible, affordable and a safe form of tourism?

The following sections present space tourism in its current form. A review of the technical, business and regulatory challenges is provided. The most realistic and practical form of space tourism is presented in the form of sub-orbital flights, along with the vision of a space community in the future of space tourism. Entrepreneurship is critical for both, and its effect on space tourism is just becoming evident: the first spaceship for space tourists is operational, and touching space with reasonable resources is no longer a distant dream.

The reason for space tourism

Humans have travelled and explored this planet ever since they first existed. People throughout the ages have enjoyed visiting or travelling, as time and funds have permitted. There have been various reasons for these constant movements. For some, there was the need or desire for new land and resources, or for new routes to known destinations. For others, there was religious, political, sports or social motivation. The need for adventure, travel and exploring is simply a fundamental part of being human. There are classic examples that associate certain entertainment, adventure and exploration locations with various social groups – for example, ancient Romans travelled to spas, many Russians enjoy vacationing at the Black Sea or in their country houses, many northern Europeans travel to the Mediterranean basin for a sunny break, and modern cruise ships tour most of the Earth's major waterways. Thus, over time a new leisure time pursuit and category of industry developed. The ideas of being a tourist and of tourism were born, leading to a large, profitable market with a healthy growth rate.

Why go to space?

Our society has progressed technologically and socially at an escalating pace. People have an increasing curiosity to visit, learn about and discover new places and challenges, and space is the ultimate frontier. Participating in adventure-related tourism activities such as climbing the tallest mountains of the world, taking wild nature safaris or flying around the world on different aircraft is very costly, but such adventures are increasing in popularity. Humanity is bound to reach its limits on Earth soon as the largest percentage of it has been explored and the remaining challenges and destinations are known. So, what is the next thing to discover? Is space the next most challenging, thrilling experience a human can have? Space seems to be the next natural step, at least physically, in our exploration, adventure and recreation activities.

The thrill of being selected to be strapped into a space vehicle and roar towards space, of freely floating in three-dimensional space and looking down at the Earth below, is at once sublime and euphoric. According to most astronauts and space travellers, it is hard to put their feelings into words; they are at once passionate and committed, perhaps beyond what surveys can capture. The dream of becoming a space explorer is a common one among young people all over the world (MSS, 2000). As they get older many go on to a variety of careers, yet the dream of travelling into space stays with them. For actor Tom Hanks, working on the film *Apollo 13* was fun because it let him live out his boyhood dream of being an astronaut (Myers, 2000).

Others go on to work on space projects but find their hopes of selection to fly fade as time goes by. Space tourism will offer these people the opportunity to realize their dream of space flight. The first tourists will not only be those who have always dreamed of being space explorers; adventure seekers and unconventional travellers will also want to be among the first to try such a grand undertaking, perhaps after having already travelled in Nepal and Antarctica. For them, travelling is about experiencing all the beauty life has to offer and seeking out that which is new, challenging and inspiring. The zero-G environment will offer them a new way to play, and being in orbit will provide a new view of their favourite playground, the Earth. While early space tourism may not be as physically rigorous as climbing Mt Everest, for example, it will appeal to the adventurous tourist because space is sexy – risky and unavailable to the mass market, only available to the dedicated, the unconventional and the daring (MSS, 2000).

The definition of space tourism

Space tourism is a new but rapidly developing concept. It is imperative that the term space tourism is defined. The first definition ever provided came from students of the International Space University, which studied Space tourism in detail in an interdisciplinary fashion as part of their summer project (MSS, 2000):

- Space: The empty area outside the earth's atmosphere, where the planets and the stars are (Cambridge Dictionaries, 2000). Although the frontier between the atmosphere and space is not officially defined, it is generally accepted that space begins 100 km from the surface of the earth.
- Tourism: (1) Provider-oriented definition: providing services such as transport, places to stay or entertainment for people (Cambridge, 2000). (2) Client-oriented definition: doing that which allows one to experience 'in reality' the pleasures imagined in one's dreams.

Thus,

- Space tourism: providing services for humans to access and experience space for adventure and recreation
- Space tourist: a person who travels to and experiences space for adventure and recreation (also space traveller, space client, space passenger).

The economics of space tourism

In addition to the motivation for space tourism owing to the basic human desire for adventure, travel and fun, there is also the possibility of economic motivation for the supply side. The economic rationale for space tourism is founded on two aspects: the first is the stimulation of the space industry and space exploration by opening a new market for reusable launch vehicles, and the second is the establishment of a new global industry. The only successful commercial space activities today are satellite communications and remote sensing. Although the emergence of mobile communications is leading to this industry's continued growth, satellite communications companies represent a small fraction of the market capitalization of the entire telecommunications industry, and satellite companies face competition from global optical fibre and local microwave systems. The satellite communications industry profits by using large (~2000–4000 kg) satellites with multiple transponders in geostationary/geosynchronous (GEO/GSO) orbits (~37 000–38 000 km) for a variety of applications – telephony, TV broadcasting, broadband Internet, storage and forwarding communications, to name just a few. The whole space industry is interrelated, in that the more satellites are built the more rockets and operations centres are required, increasing revenue and profits in the industry. The other successful space industry is the recently developed remote sensing industry. Although still in its infancy, multiple constellations of satellites placed in Low Earth Orbits (LEO) and equipped with multiple optical/radar sensors provide a high volume of information in varying resolutions (0.5 m–150 m) for customers such as farmers, the military, universities, urban planning organizations and government institutes/ministries. Space tourism has the potential to become a market itself, combining the size and specifics of the two industries it consists of – tourism and space. The development of a robust, safe and affordable spaceship that can carry space tourists can potentially capitalize on the great interest that exists in both industries. Tourism is one of the world's largest businesses, employing over 200 million people worldwide – or one in every nine workers. Tourism is the world's leading economic contributor, producing 10.2 per cent of the world's gross national product and generating the greatest amount of tax revenue at US$655 billion per year (MSS, 2000). Given the scale of the global tourism industry, there is huge economic potential for space tourism – but only if space transportation is safe and reliable, and the cost per passenger is substantially reduced. Based on the wide range of unique activities in space and the commercially vigorous nature of the tourism industry, the various aspects required to establish a robust space tourism industry would potentially initiate a whole new global paradigm, creating new business for companies in various industries such as entertainment, media, advertisement, insurance, investment, ground operations, and medical support. Technology and cost have been the largest obstacles to achieving a sustainable and affordable human presence in space. However, a number of existing activities that are related to the space experience are discussed in the following section (Collins and Ashford, 1986; O'Neil, 1997; Reichert, 1999; Crouch, 2001).

Space tourism as a business

The main 'space tourism' activities offered to tourists today are not truly space tourism, but rather space-related tourism. Space-related tourism in this context means adventurous and recreational opportunities that in one way or another are related to space (MSS, 2000). They may be physical (experiencing high/low/zero gravitation), visual (watching the stars, the sky or the northern lights, visiting museums or witnessing the launch of rockets/shuttles); or experimental (meteorite expeditions, rocket-/robot-building, running telescopes, virtual reality). These activities have the potential to raise significant funds for real space tourism developments, some currently planned by, for example, the X-Prize organization (Space Tourism Theme Park-X-Prize Cup) (X Prize, 2004).

Adventure-related space tourism

Some tourists demand more individual and extreme activities, and this has led to a large and diverse tourist market. Common to most adventurous tourists is the requirement for the impression of pioneering and potential risk. People are willing to pay a substantial amount of money for these activities, and it is expected that the first space tourists will emerge from this group of tourists.

Mountaineering expeditions and expeditions to the Himalayas, especially Mt Everest, are of growing interest to adventure tourists from all over the world. More than 600 climbers from 20 countries have climbed to the summit of Mt Everest (MSS, 2000). Permits cost thousands of US dollars (US$80 000 for a seven-member party in 2000), and are difficult to obtain (MSS, 2000). In some cases, waiting lists extend for years. The total price, including guides and porters, is close to US$1 million per person. Several companies offer trips to the Arctic and to Antarctica. The degree of extremity and prices vary a lot. Tourists can now fly from different cities in Australia to Antarctica on day trips in a B747-438 plane, crossing the South Pole, for prices ranging from US$1199 (tourist class) to US$3739 (first class) (Antarctica Flights Online, 2004). There are also ships that sail from South America (Argentina and Chile) to Antarctica, both cruising and on expeditions, and passenger prices range from US$4000 to US$10 000 (Quark Expeditions, 2000). Another indication of the growth in the number of adventure-seeking tourists is the large number of companies offering 'survival tours' in various deserts and jungles around the world. Rafting, scuba diving, parachuting and similar adventure activities are becoming more accessible today, and are big markets.

Some of the available activities can be classified as falling between 'regular' adventure tourism and space-related tourism. One example is meteorite expeditions to Antarctica. Meteorites have been falling to Earth for millions of years. In Antarctica they are well preserved, and it is considered to be one of the best places on Earth to find them. Some of these meteorites are from Mars and the Moon. On an Antarctica meteorite expedition tourists can search for and collect meteorites, called Stones from Space. The meteorites collected are used and studied by NASA or other research organizations, and cannot therefore be kept as souvenirs (Space Adventures, 2004).

Ground-based space tourism

One important and distinct feature of space travel is the experience of different gravity forces. During launch to and re-entry from space, a space tourist will experience a high gravitational force – several times higher than the gravity force on Earth. For the Space Shuttle, the maximum acceleration during launch is about 3 g (three times higher than on Earth), and for the Russian Soyuz it is slightly higher, about 5 g on re-entry. These conditions can be simulated on Earth in centrifuges. In the Yuri Gagarin Cosmonaut Training Centre in Star City, Russia, several companies offer rides in centrifuges for prices of around US$1150

(Space Adventures, 2004). In orbit around Earth (or other planets/celestial bodies), tourists within a spacecraft will have the feeling of zero gravitation or 'weightlessness'. In a Neutral Buoyancy Hydro Lab (essentially a huge, heated swimming pool) it is possible to experience something very similar to true weightlessness. The price for neutral buoyancy training is around US$7000 (Space Adventures, 2004).

Packages, such as cosmonaut training and space camps (Space Adventures, 2004), combine many activities related to space and space exploration. These give the tourist a broader picture of space exploration by providing a complete setting. At space camps tourists take part in all the different aspects of cosmonaut/astronaut life – eating freeze-dried space food, training in partial gravity simulators, learning mission control aspects and performing different jobs and tasks in the same way as real cosmonauts/astronauts would do. Cosmonaut training in Star City, Russia, gives the tourist access to different simulators, such as Mir, Soyuz-TM and navigation. It also includes rides in centrifuges and experience in a low-pressure chamber, as well as stellar navigation in a planetarium and walking tours and museum visits in Star City.

There is also a whole range of experimental and 'hands on' activities that are related to space. Just by looking towards the night sky, the stars, the planets, comets and meteorites, tourists get a feeling of space and the universe. Services provided for this kind of observation can also be considered as space-related tourism. In the Polar regions in the north and the south, companies offer Aurora (northern and southern light) watching (MSS, 2000).

Air-based space tourism

High and low gravitational acceleration can also be experienced in the air. Adventure tourism companies now offer flights in different jet fighters that are able to fly at very high altitudes and at high velocity. The MiG-25 and MiG-29 jet fighter planes can reach over 25 000 metres, and from this altitude it is possible to see the curvature of Earth. These jet fighter planes typically have a maximum velocity in the order of Mach 2.5, or 2.5 times the speed of sound. One of the most extraordinary aspects of space flight is the feeling of weightlessness. By flying a Russian Ilyushin-76 jet plane in a parabolic flight path, it is possible to create a zero-G environment for a short period of time. To do this, the parabolic manoeuvre starts from level flight at 8000 m. The plane is pitched up at approximately 45 degrees, and during this time the passengers feel an acceleration of up to 1.8 g. The engines are then throttled back, and the jet glides over the top of the path with just enough power to overcome air friction and drag. Everyone inside the jet experiences the sensation of free fall or zero gravity. Passengers have approximately 28–30 seconds of microgravity during the top of the parabolic path. During the parabolic flight, tourists get a chance to experience extended zero-G, and to play and to do experiments in this unusual environment (see Figure 18.1).

The challenges of space tourism

There are many legal, regulatory, economic and technical challenges that can prevent space tourism from being a viable business (Goodrich, 1987; Ashford, 1990;

Figure 18.1 Parabolic flights

Collins *et al.*, 1994; Smith, 2000). Binding international treaties and conventions can have a significant impact on space tourism activities. The liability treaty and the convention on registration are major issues concerning any private tourism activities in space, since they have the following implicit consequences:

- a state is entitled to prohibit any private space tourism pre-launch activity on its territory
- non-governmental activities in space tourism will require authorization and continuing supervision by the appropriate state party.

For example, any kind of private space vehicle will have to receive the full approval of the launching state. Thus the equivalent of an aircraft certification and licence will be required for space tourism purposes (MSS, 2000). The Liability Treaty dictates that any launching state is liable for any damage caused by its spacecraft, whether publicly or privately operated. This unlimited liability is due to the high risk of today's space activities, and has led governments to enforce very strict vehicle licensing procedures and safety regulations. Such liability philosophy is substantially different from the liability provisions applicable to the aviation sector, or to the established global passenger transportation industry. The hostile environment of space presents extremely varied human hazards, ranging from minor annoyances with non-operational or mission impacts, to severe and emergent life-threatening situations. These hazards span a wide range of events – some predictable, some less so. Examples range from expected physiological alterations to orbital debris impact during Extra Vehicular Activities (EVAs). However, the primary threats can be considered to fall into one of the following categories:

1. Cabin environment and altered atmosphere
2. Radiation
3. Microgravity (cardiovascular, neurovestibular, musculoskeletal).

The technical challenges of being able to have affordable, sustainable access to space are many and difficult to tackle. Current access to orbit is only possible via

Figure 18.2 Denis Tito (©Itar-Tass)

government means – using the Space Shuttle, which was grounded following the Columbia accident, the Soyuz spacecraft, or the Shanzou transfer vehicle designed by China and based on Soyuz technology. With a current cost of more than $20 000 per kilogram of payload, even assuming that governments will allow space tourists to travel, the cost is prohibitive. Denis Tito (Figure 18.2) and Mark Shuttleworth each paid $20 m to travel to the International Space Station via the Russian Soyuz vehicle – a cost that can be afforded by only a very few. Access to space for space tourists seems to need a combination of government incentives and private entrepreneurship in order for it to become reality. Without going into great technical detail, the current limited access to space and the technical complexity coupled with cost will not enable any sort of space tourism business today – at least not to the extent that space tourism can be considered a form of a mass product in the tourist industry. However, experience has shown that in situations where technical challenges and high costs prohibit us from achieving a goal, entrepreneurship can be a possible solution.

The future of space tourism

Space tourism is bound to expand in the near future. Although space hotels and mass access to space for tourists are still a dream, the first steps towards making space tourism a reality have already been taken.

The X-Prize and the SpaceShipOne

As with other aviation competitions of the past century, the X-Prize organization originated to promote spaceflight for regular people, in a frequent, affordable

Figure 18.3 (a) SpaceShipOne and its carrier, White Knight; (b) SpaceShipOne

and safe way, without government involvement. The $10 m (£5.7 m) Ansari
X-Prize was to reward the first team to send a non-government, three-person craft
over 100 km (62 miles) into space, and repeat the feat in the same carrier inside
two weeks (X-Prize, 2004). Although not in full orbit, this type of spacecraft will
be able to carry space tourists without having to go through time-consuming
preparations such as for Soyuz flights, will encounter weightlessness for minutes,
and will see the curvature of the Earth. Recently, and amongst 26 teams,
SpaceShipOne flew its two X-Prize flights on 29 September and 4 October 2004 –
the 47th anniversary of the launch of Sputnik, the world's first artificial satellite.
Carrying only its pilot and test equipment equal to the weight of two passengers,
SpaceShipOne claimed the X-Prize award (Figure 18.3).

SpaceShipOne was designed by aviation pioneer Burt Rutan, of Scaled
Composites, and financed by Microsoft's founder, Paul Allen. With only a cost of
approximately $20 million, both expect to recoup their investment through space
tourism ventures. Days after the first SpaceShipOne flight, Virgin's Richard
Branson announced his plans to launch a passenger service to space by 2007 on
his futuristic Virgin Galactic spaceline (Virgin, 2004). 'Two years ago people gig-
gled at the idea of space tourism in the foreseeable future, but we think it will be
happening by 2007', said Space Adventures' president, Eric Anderson (Space
Adventures, 2004). Space Adventures, the only firm in the world taking paid
reservations for sub-orbital passengers, says it is in talks with Branson and
several other companies regarding plans that would take their adventurous passengers into space. Rutan calls the project SpaceShipOne 'Tier One' – the sub-
orbital element of a multi-part programme to revolutionize off-planet travel.

SpaceShipTwo will be a five-person, sub-orbital vessel owned by a new venture
called Virgin Galactic, an offshoot of Virgin Atlantic Airways. The inaugural
flight is scheduled for 2007. Rutan and Richard Branson, Virgin's chairman, say
they will be aboard. The passenger list is also expected to include the winner of a
consumer promotion by soft-drink manufacturer 7 UP®, which plans to unveil
details of its competition in 2005. The company made the announcement following the completion of SpaceShipOne's landing. Ticket prices for the early flights
are expected to cost about $190 000, but Rutan and Branson said they expect
prices to fall rapidly as other companies stake claims in the space tourism
business. Branson has claimed that Rutan will build five vessels over the next
three years (Virgin, 2004). Tourists will fly even higher than SpaceShipOne's
record-breaking altitude of 69 miles, and will experience about seven minutes
of weightlessness. Every one of those passengers will have a much, much

Figure 18.4 (a&b) VSS Enterprise; (c) Expected view from VSS Enterprise

bigger window – a spectacular view. Branson emphasized the role of entrepreneurship: 'It'll be the most beautiful thing ever created by man. It's an adventure where we hope to make money because I don't think space has a future unless people make money' (Virgin, 2004). Branson added that profits from Virgin Galactic will be reinvested in space tourism development: 'We've done quite a lot of research; we think there are about 3000 people out there who would want to do this', he said (BBC, 2004). Designs for the Virgin Galactic craft are progressing on a weekly basis at Rutan's base in Mojave, California, and it is expected that by early 2005 the final design for the maiden Virgin Galactic ship, the VSS (Virgin SpaceShip) Enterprise (Figure 18.4), will have been signed-off.

Virgin's agreement with Rutan and Allen is not exclusive, however. Mojave Aerospace Ventures, the partnership created to develop SpaceShipOne and related projects, is considering offers from four or five other companies as well, Rutan said.

Orbital flights and space hotels

Besides the X-Prize there has been a flurry of space-related competitions, capitalizing on the success of the X-Prize. Although there have always been many plans to build space hotels, these futuristic concepts have never got further than the drawing board. There have been discussions between American firms and the Russian space manufacturer Energia regarding modifying and launching a dedicated habitable module for space tourism and other commercial work on the International Space Station; however, this has not materialized. However, is it possible that a form of a space hotel can be built in the near future using entrepreneurship?

A Las Vegas hotel magnate who is hoping to build the world's first commercial space stations launched a challenge in September 2004, offering $50 million to the creators of the first privately funded spaceship to reach orbit before 2010. Robert Bigelow, who owns Budget Suites of America, formally announced the long-rumoured prize just a day after the first privately funded spaceship rocketed out of the atmosphere and won the $10 million Ansari X-Prize, which was designed to spur commercial spaceflight. Bigelow acknowledged that reaching orbit would be much harder than briefly popping into space, as SpaceShipOne did. 'To be honest, I think it's a long shot', he said of any team's chances of winning the prize (CNN, 2004). In addition to the prize money, the winner of the America's Space Prize stands to gain contracts from Bigelow Aerospace to ferry passengers to and from its stations. Bigelow Aerospace plans to launch its first space modules on commercial rockets in late 2008 or early 2009, and to send up the first crews by 2010. The company plans to make a profit by selling standardized space-station modules, complete with life-support systems and living quarters, for $100 million each. Bigelow sees industrial and medical research as the most important uses for the modules, but says they could also serve as space hotels. Bigelow will front half of the $50 million America's Space Prize, and is seeking sponsorship for the other half. To win the contest, which is limited to US-based ventures, a team must build a five-seat spacecraft without government money and send five astronauts into orbit above the Earth twice within 60 days.

Conclusion

> Benz created the car but it was Henry Ford who is remembered for making it available to the masses; Charles Lindbergh's flight across the Atlantic was marvellous but the enduring legacy is the airline industry he inspired.
>
> (Virgin, 2004)

We are at the frontier of engineering and rocket building and, despite our restricted, although highly successful technological advancements, there are today many limitations that prevent us from having more regular and cheaper flights to space. Owing to the limitations of rocket and structural materials technology available today, it is not possible to construct a single-stage rocket that can effectively deliver itself or a spacecraft into orbit in the same way as an aeroplane carries passengers.

Unfortunately space transportation is still very expensive, and only the USA Space Shuttle and the Russian Soyuz capsule can carry humans into space today – at a high cost of about US$20 000 per kilogram. A few people have already done it as paying passengers on the Russian spacecraft Soyuz. The fare was as steep as the ascent – $20 million for the first man who did it. Nonetheless, Futron, a management consultancy in the US, has estimated that the business could generate annual revenues of more than $1 billion by the year 2021. The largest area of demand, it says, is likely to be for cheaper 'sub-orbital' flights – short trips into space and back. Sales for that type of trip could be as high as 15 000 passengers a year by 2021. These forecasts were based on a survey of what the company called 'affluent' Americans. With even a short trip likely to cost anything up to $100 000, they will need to be affluent (Futron, 2004)!

The recent massive success of the X-Prize can hopefully be used as a springboard to more affordable and frequent access to space, even if orbit insertion is not achieved. It seems that entrepreneurship is needed in order to take a novel, innovative and interdisciplinary approach towards making space tourism a reality. We are at the very frontier of space tourism. We have sent humans into orbit, and with the incredible pace of technological advancements the time to address the issue of safe, affordable and frequent access to space is getting closer than ever.

Part Three: New Industry

19

Intermediaries: travel agencies and tour operators

Dimitrios Buhalis and
Dorota Ujma

Introduction

Technological turbulence re-engineers the distribution and intermediation of tourism products and services. Will tourism intermediaries exist in the future, or will they disappear? Is it likely that travel agencies will stay in the market, taking over the responsibilities of tour operators – or the other way round? These questions are not new, yet the answer is even more unclear. Boundaries are becoming blurred, and whoever is going to survive the changes needs to deliver the value customers are looking for.

The linkages between tourism suppliers and their potential customers are imperfect. Therefore, intermediaries exist to improve distribution by bringing buyers and sellers together. Tourism intermediaries have been discussed in textbooks as well as specific texts and articles (see, for example, Buhalis and Laws, 2001; Buhalis, 2003; Cooper *et al.*, 2005). Traditionally, tourism intermediaries are classified in three broad categories that reflect their functions: Outbound Travel Agencies (OTAs), which

Table 19.1 Roles undertaken by different intermediaries

	Outbound travel agents	*Tour operators*	*Incoming travel agents*
Before trip	■ Dispense advice on destinations ■ Identify consumer needs ■ Present available offers to consumers ■ Sell the product and provide documents	■ Contact suppliers and travel agents ■ Organize charter flights and pre-book accommodation ■ Put packages together ■ Market products	■ Provide links between destination suppliers with tour operators ■ Package together and distribute
During trip	■ Cooperate with TOs and incoming travel agents on smooth running of holidays ■ Look after customers by providing secure point of contact ■ Provide information and directions ■ Sell value-added services, such as excursions	■ Deliver transportation and supervise delivery by principals such as hotels and attractions ■ Responsible for local handling ■ Deal with local authorities ■ Handle special requests	■ Provide transport and local excursions
After trip	■ Review the travel experience and receive feedback ■ Monitor satisfaction levels ■ Handle complaints ■ Keep customer profile for future trips	■ Review the quality of products and services ■ Review the travel experience and receive feedback ■ Monitor satisfaction levels ■ Handle complaints	■ Improve/change products on offer

are retailers; Tour Operators (TOs), which are aggregators, package creators and wholesalers; and Incoming Travel Agencies (ITAs), which are handling agencies or destination management companies (in charge of fulfilment at the destination as well as providers of transfers and excursions). Tourism intermediaries undertake a number of key functions; they:

■ increase the efficiency of the process of exchange globally
■ adjust the quantity and type of products with consumer demand
■ undertake routine transactions and establish a payment mechanism
■ facilitate the searching process and identify the best product
■ reduce transactional links between suppliers and potential clients.

Table 19.2 Distribution costs and benefits for principals

Benefits	Costs
■ Wider coverage of markets	■ Loss of margin (paid to TA//TO)
■ Convenient points of sale for customers	■ Loss of marketing control/power over the process
■ Lower marketing/operating costs	■ Risks ownership
■ Wider product range	■ Intermediaries' economic motivations
■ Knowledge of markets	■ Ultimate customer service is beyond the supplier's control
■ Consideration of customer finance	■ High priority given to intermediaries rather than customers
■ Handling of customer needs, communication and complaints	

Source: based on Christopher (1992).

The competitiveness and prosperity of the three groups of intermediaries are largely dependent upon their ability to add value that customers would be willing to pay for. Therefore, value creation is the linking element in the distribution chain for channel members. Table 19.1 demonstrates the key roles of each intermediary before, during and after travelling.

Bastakis *et al.* (2004) note the contribution/value creation generated by TOs for a variety of players in the channel. Consumers mainly gain because of the reduced price of travel, a common culture and language shared with a TO. This provides the feeling of security and better understanding of their needs, guidance and assistance at the destination and quality control. Destinations and principals gain increased accessibility and international visibility, marketing, an extended season and sometimes support for sustainability. Although all types of suppliers are represented by travel intermediaries, small and medium-sized tourism enterprises (SMTEs) are particularly dependent on intermediaries for distributing their products. Distribution generates a number of costs and benefits for principals (Table 19.2).

Poon (2001) states that new trends emerging in tourism and technology change the process of value creation by influencing the relative position of players. Tourism is an ideal candidate for the application and diffusion of information communications technologies (ICTs) (Bennett and Buhalis, 2003). The industry is highly dependent on technological change and global concentration. Multimedia, audiovisual and computerized marketing tools are increasingly presenting more accurate and timely information on which consumers build expectations of enjoyment, and which enhance their motivation to travel. The future of tourism intermediaries is closely related to these developments, and there is dynamic change.

The future of tourism channel intermediaries

The Internet has revolutionized information provision and purchasing patterns globally. Rosenbloom (1999: 451) refers to electronic marketing channels as 'a whole new paradigm for distribution channels, a very different kind of "animal" that will profoundly reshape marketing channel structure'. This enables both principals and intermediaries to develop eCommerce strategies and to adopt a variety of electronic distribution channels. In response to the competition from online agents, leading travel suppliers developed their eCommerce strategy to attract direct sales. In September 2004, 53 per cent of British Airways' short-haul leisure flights were booked online on ba.com, with 38 per cent via the travel trade. These data are in contrast to April 2002, when the trade share was 54 per cent, with 20 per cent booked via the web. Direct contact is easy through the Internet, and additional requirements can be discussed via e-mail or on the telephone. Wide use of credit cards simplifies the transaction, and language and cultural barriers are being addressed through globalization. The travel suppliers also formed industry alliances to strengthen their own position, and the companies created also offer the broad range of products demanded by customers. The best known are as follows (Buhalis and Licata, 2002; O'Connor, 2003):

- Orbitz – created by five American airlines, this is airline focused, but also offers hotel and car hire
- Opodo – formed by nine European airlines, this offers a variety of travel products with the main emphasis placed on airlines
- Hotwire – this follows the Priceline technique, and offers products from the same segments as Orbitz
- TravelWeb – developed by five major hotel chains and a reservations technology provider, this focuses on hospitality products, offered mainly by hotel chains.

Therefore, the future of distribution channels needs to be discussed alongside the application of ICT to evaluate how electronic channels will affect the future of tourism intermediaries and what the strategies for survival should be.

Travel agencies

The role of travel agents, first in domestic and then in international markets, is predicted to decline. It has become relatively easy to find information about destinations and suppliers globally. Customers may see the agent as somebody who comes between them and their host, adding little value and interrupting rather then helping. Internet adoption, globalization and international integration of travel companies have accelerated this trend (Buhalis, 1998).

Observing the historical development of travel agents, it can be seen that they have demonstrated a flexible approach to changes. Since the 1930s, travel agents have been successfully adjusting to accommodate a number of threats. Bitner and Booms (1982) saw many years ago that travel agents were endangered. They predicted that travel agents' roles would change because there would be more competition in the industry. New competition from technology, new systems and banking companies emerges and strong consolidation occurs in the tourist market. They therefore suggested that travel agents must develop their use of marketing techniques (especially knowing their clients), product line analysis and information

Case study 19.1 'Travel Agents Fighting Back', UK

The Travel Technology Initiative's 2004 Spring Conference, 'Travel Agents Fighting Back', demonstrated that travel agents need to adapt their business models and harness technology to guarantee their long-term survival. Truly empowered travel professionals understand that their experience, coupled with one-to-one relationships with their customers, is their greatest asset. By developing these benefits to a travel counsellor role, they can improve service and profitability. They also benefit from the use of ICT tools to support sales and monitor performance. Agents can beat tour operators at their own game by contracting, packaging and selling their own products. Smaller agents should take advantage of their collective buying power, and build consortia to pool resources and negotiate better rates with suppliers. Improving service should transform the agent into a customer-focused 'independent travel expert' who adds value to the process and may charge fees for consultations and transactions. Agents should focus on improving their productivity through automation, whilst gaining more control over the content offered to consumers and adding value by choosing the right partners. Improved communications and effective customer care are key to future survival and prosperity.

(Source: Richer, 2004.)

systems, knowledge of travel destination and suppliers, and how to interact and negotiate successfully with them.

Travel agencies are fighting back by demonstrating expertise and by adding value to the process (see Case study 19.1). The key information-exchange role of the retailer has been a primary factor in shifting the balance of power in the chain of distribution away from the manufacturer to the retailer (Richards, 1995). The role of experiential information, provided in 'educationals' for agency staff, is important in making product choices and for adding value. Experienced travel agents are often the best option for complex itineraries or inexperienced travellers. The personal approach, 'hand-holding', call-back and calling centres, providing quality of service, and adding value to the channel alongside multi-channel strategies can save the intermediaries from extinction. However, unless agents demonstrate expertise and experiential information in relation to their clients' needs, they risk the situation where their customers become more knowledgeable than themselves. Nevertheless, changes in OTAs (Table 19.3) are inevitable.

Agents should move with the times and ensure they are using the Internet to their advantage by:

- dynamically packaging customized tourism products for their clientele
- developing websites and indexing them with search engines
- embracing change by knowing the tools available and using them efficiently
- choosing partners carefully to maximize value added
- developing linking relationships with other channel players
- creating special sets of fees for services on offer.

Table 19.3 Changes in travel agents' business

- High concentration of travel agents through mergers and acquisitions or alliances/ consortia of small, independent agencies
- New technology-based entrants (Expedia.com or Lastminute.com)
- Greater reliance on technology than on the travel agents' services by the public
- Commission capping and service fees
- Bypassing of the agent by the customer because of service fees
- Flexibility of e-commerce allows travel agencies to package tourism products dynamically
- Internet-based reduction of intangibility, reducing reliance on agents for information
- Suppliers' websites allow direct access for consumers

Source: based on Poon (2001).

Many online travel agencies have emerged using ICT developments. Online agencies have become successful by utilizing two strategies: the merchant model, similar to strategies used by tour operators (bulk purchase at discount prices and sales with an added margin); and dynamic packaging (O'Connor, 2003). Travel has become one of the most popular and most expensive products sold online. The larger online travel sites offer multiple products from a variety of principals. Mergers, once observed in the high street bricks-and-mortar travel agencies, have dominated the online environment, and the bulk of online travel sales are concentrated on a few companies. In 2004 in particular a number of mergers and acquisitions took place, bringing consolidation to the online players. The biggest online travel groups emerging are:

- InterActive Corp (including Expedia, Hotels.com), which is linked with a global distribution system (GDS) WorldSpan
- Travelocity, owned by Sabre
- Priceline, the originator of the 'name-your-own-price' business model; which bought Active Hotels
- Lastminute.com, which acquired HolidaysAutos, MedHotels, Lastminute.de and several other players
- Cendant, including Orbitz, ebookers and OctapusTravel.com
- Opodo, owned by Amadeus.

In challenging times, agents should not lose hope regarding the viability of their businesses but adapt to the environment in which they have to compete. They need to negotiate the best deals with travel suppliers, and to harness ever more sophisticated technology in order to specialize and survive.

Tour operators

Tour operators make a significant contribution to the tourism value chain. Their position between the supply side, represented by principals, and the demand side, represented by travel retailers and consumers, gives them the advantage over these two groups. TOs can support other members as well as cause conflicts, owing to a variety of factors (Table 19.4).

Table 19.4 Channel members' requirements and conflict resolution techniques

Tour operators: support	Tour operators: conflict
■ Large TOs offer a sense of security and financial consistency by sharing their expert knowledge of the market	■ Low level of TOs' commitment to destination areas and the lack of loyalty
■ Direct SMTEs to productive investments and create mutually beneficial synergies	■ Pressure by TOs for lower prices
	■ 'Coerciveness' of negotiations
	■ Lack of human contact and 'high touch' involvement
■ Smaller TOs offer better relationships through personal contact and communication, and mutual appreciation and respect	■ The absence of a local incoming agent as the result of the introduction of vertically integrated with TOs incoming agencies that operate in accordance with their parent companies' strategies and tactics

Source: Bastakis *et al.*, 2004.

Chandler (2000) analyses the consolidation in the UK tour operating business, where the dominance is clearly marked by the big four operators – which control more than 60 per cent of the market and are totally vertically integrated. Four out of 1444 fully-bonded British TOs control 53 per cent of the licensed charter flight capacity and 40 per cent of the high street retail outlets, and influence over 70 per cent of them (Bastakis *et al.*, 2004). The four major players (Thomson (TUI), Airtours (My Travel), Thomas Cook (JMC) and First Choice) have entered the 'acquisition trail' and are now responsible for sales of 80 per cent of package holidays, 66 per cent of flights and over 50 per cent of retail distribution (Reynolds 1999: 7). TUI and Thomas Cook, the two German tour operators, and the British MyTravel now dominate the European leisure market (Buhalis, 2000). Vertical integration is increasingly common, with the same companies controlling tour operators, retail agencies, airlines and hotels – both inventory and securing the distribution system. Naturally, they sell their own 'in-house' packages through directional or 'switch selling' practices (O'Brien, 1998; Hudson *et al.*, 2001).

Tour operators, particularly the large ones, are increasingly seen as 'inflexible monsters' that have outlived their sell-by date. MyTravel announced a deficit of £800m in 2004, and most other integrated operators had financial difficulties. The full vertical integration they were once so proud of has become a heavy burden with considerable overheads and risks attached. The development of the Internet and the availability of both information and special deals on each component challenge their hitherto unique position regarding packaged tourism products. Although consumers do not benefit from the discounts achieved through the bulk purchasing of tour operators, they can benefit from special offers and discounts offered by suppliers as well as by not paying for administrative costs, brochures and commissions. Tour operators should work hard to demonstrate the value-added services that justify their profit margins. They have started de-packaging their products and distributing individual components through the Internet. They are attempting to reinforce their own role by using user-friendly computer systems, de-packaging and repackaging tourism products, and linking together principals and retailers. In contrast, small players are strengthening their position by

Case study 19.2 TUI UK shake-up

TUI UK has consolidated its holiday group, airlines and tour operations, dropping its Britannia and Lunn Poly brands. It has also reduced its London office base and fired 800 people. The key points of the shake-up are as follows:

- All planes will be rebranded Thomsonfly, with the fleet expanded and refurbished
- Internet distribution will encourage the seat-only market
- There will be a shift in emphasis towards selling through 'dynamic packaging' and through direct channels
- The Lunn Poly travel agency network will be renamed Thomson Holiday Shops and continue to be reduced, with shops reviewed as leases expire rather than a mass closure programme
- A review of summer holiday brands and overseas services will take place.

(Source: www.tui.com, and http://www.e-tid.com/pm.aspx?article_id=22409&show Live=1&useCache=1, 29 Sep 2004.)

not only being able to develop their product range to match the needs of an increasingly specialized market but also using the Internet to promote and distribute their products widely in the marketplace.

Case study 19.2 describes TUI's efforts to strengthen its role.

Intermediation, disintermediation, reintermediation and dynamic packaging

Technology creates both opportunities and threats to tourism intermediaries, as it changes the manner in which information is communicated and purchases are made throughout the channel. Intermediation is emerging as one of the most dynamic arenas of travel and tourism. Standard packages are still popular, although agents are increasingly adopting dynamic creation of holidays. However, as a result of speed and connectivity, the boundaries between various channel players are getting blurred. Companies are refocusing and taking on a variety of responsibilities that earlier belonged to interdependent channel players. Intermediation will become more challenging in the future, and only players that can add value will be able to survive in the long run.

There are two conflicting trends in distribution, namely disintermediation and reintermediation. Buhalis (2003) defined disintermediation as the elimination of intermediaries within the distribution channel, propelled by electronic means that enable consumers to access and transact directly with suppliers and destinations. The Internet enables consumers to 'package' their own trips by collecting inventory from individual suppliers and supporting B2C (Business to Consumer) eCommerce.

However, the reality has not conformed to the theory of disintermediation; quite the opposite (Rosenbloom, 1999: 452). As electronic channels provide opportunities for further expansion, both horizontally and vertically, new intermediaries emerge in the channel structure. Reintermediation refers to the development of the electronic means of existing players to communicate and transact, and also to the emergence of new players that use electronic means to add value and distribute tourism products (Buhalis, 2003). This involves either a new electronic intermediary, or new methods for existing channel members that use technology for eCommerce. Most traditional intermediaries have developed their Internet presence to support B2B and B2C transactions.

New entrants into the industry, such as Expedia.com or Lastminute.com, have taken roles of both tour operators and travel agencies and have both captured a significant proportion of the market, as well as expanding it. It has become almost second nature for travellers, especially in the USA, to turn to websites such as Expedia.com, Orbitz.com and Travelocity.com in planning a trip. New search engines have also been created to scan the travel agents' sites, the airlines, and car rental agencies to find the best prices. Cheapflights.com, Kelkoo.com, Mobissimo.com, Kayak.com and FareChase.com search about 150 travel sites, including those of low-cost airlines, which rarely show up on GDSs and travel portals.

Eager to earn commission from hotels and car rental companies, in order to compensate for the limited commission or fees from airlines, eMediaries launched dynamic packaging, enabling consumers to amalgamate tourism products and to save money by giving up some of their margin on individual products (Buhalis and Licata, 2002). Dynamic packaging also empowers channel members to interconnect and transact in a B2B (business to business) or B2B2C (business to business to consumer) environment using tools to support the exchange of information involved in creating an itinerary from multiple components. Several standards are emerging to simplify interconnectivity and interoperability between selling and buying partners. Lastminute.com has launched a website for agents to package its products dynamically, which is making both a generator of revenue and a competitor out of the travel agent. In reality, therefore, both disintermediation and reintermediation occur in the market, with online expansion fuelled by both an expansion of the market and a migration from offline intermediaries to online trade.

Power and conflict resolution in tourism distribution

Understanding channel management is important in predicting the future of tourism players. Relationships in distribution channels reflect all the interactions, processes and flows taking place between those companies involved in exchange of products and services (Ujma, 2002).

Channel relationships include elements of both cooperation and conflict (Stern *et al.*, 1996). Principals, travel retailers and tour operators often share information, ordering systems and promotional budgets. Each channel partner should offer services that are desired by the other partner, to enhance cooperation. Each organization is interrelated in the value chain, but remains independent, often leading to conflicting objectives and requirements (Christopher, 1992: 129). There are several causes of conflict. Obviously, the accrual of profit by one channel partner pre-empts the allocation of the profit to other partners.

The availability of alternative partners, performance incentives and contractual terms may also result in conflicts and often determines who is the channel leader (Laws, 1997; Buhalis and Laws, 2001).

The better the relationships between channel members, the more benefits are usually achieved. Anderson and Weitz (1989) argue that balanced power relationships imply greater stability, and to avoid destructive conflicts the channel members should regularly monitor the performance and satisfaction levels of all channel members. For example, a successful evolution of inter-organizational relationships between travel agents and hotels is dependent upon the level of business done with a certain partner (Medina-Muñoz *et al.*, 2002; Bastakis *et al.*, 2004). The development of stable and harmonious relationships between players in the channel determines mutual benefits.

Conclusions: the future of intermediation

Due to the complex nature of tourism products, the Internet revolution and the high reliance on a service component, the significance of the usual eight flows (Stern *et al.*, 1996) available in any other distribution channel changes. These flows include information, negotiations, financing, ordering, payment, physical ownership or possession, promotion and risk-taking. Information becomes one of the most important flows, as it represents the product and therefore helps customers to make the decision about the purchase. Information will therefore lead competitiveness in the future.

To be successful in the future, tour operators should be flexible and innovative in predicting and delivering products required by customers. ICT can help to distribute products to both sides of the channel – travel agencies and consumers, as well as suppliers. Therefore, tour operators can use de-packaging and repackaging techniques to respond to changes in demand patterns and to add value to the customers' experience.

Travel agents need to ensure that they are providing a professional advisory service. Customers are becoming more knowledgeable, and need to be convinced that travel agents add value to their experience. Travel agents can use multi-channel strategies as well as expertise to address specific requirements expressed by customers. ICT offers an effective tool to package specialized products dynamically. Incoming agents can also develop specialized services at their destination and sell them globally through the Internet.

The key factors for success in the future for intermediaries will be flexibility and innovation in providing added value to tourism products and services. ICT should be used to develop and distribute these offerings globally, through user-friendly interfaces and interoperable systems. Successful intermediaries will emerge as customer-centric value creators.

20

Transport and transit: air, land and sea

Anne Graham

Introduction

Transport is an essential element of tourism, and provides the vital link between the tourist generating areas and destinations. Moreover, transport provides the means of travelling around the destination. Transport itself can also be the main reason for travel – for example with canal trips or steam rail travel. Some transport services are provided exclusively for tourists, such as cruises, whereas others, like rail and air, are offered to different passenger and freight markets.

Reference is often made to the 'Travel and Tourism Industry', which acknowledges the close link between tourism and transport. Good accessibility, which is determined by the transport services provided, is a fundamental condition for the development of any tourist destination (Prideaux, 2000). Conversely, the transport industry can be a major beneficiary of tourism because of the additional passengers that may be generated. In order to benefit from such two-way relationships, these linkages must be fully recognized. For example, the economic benefits that can occur as the result of increased tourism need to be considered when air transport policies or airport expansion are being evaluated

(Papatheodorou, 2002; Forsyth, 2003). Moreover, conflicts can arise if different goals and objectives are set. Particularly in some less developed countries, there may be aviation policies designed to protect the commercial and financial interests of national airlines. These may hinder the growth of tourism.

The role of the different modes

Historically transport has played a vital role in the development of tourism. Domestic tourism in Europe was revolutionized by the development of the railway in the nineteenth century, and by the private car in the second half of the twentieth century. Similarly, the introduction of aircraft jet technology after the Second World War directly led to the emergence of the charter and tour operating industries, and consequently in a dramatic growth in foreign holiday-taking.

For some journeys the transport modes compete for tourist traffic. At other times the transport operations may be complementary, such as rail links to airports, and fly-drive or fly-cruise holidays. The car is the most popular means of transport for domestic and short-distance international tourism to neighbouring countries, as it offers convenience, flexibility and accessibility that public transport cannot match. The use of other surface transport modes, such as rail, bus and coach travel, has generally declined at the expense of car travel.

Aviation has virtually replaced the need for the use of sea transport for long-distance leisure travel. However, there are two types of sea travel, namely short sea ferries and cruise shipping, which remain popular. The highest concentration of international ferry routes is in Northern Europe and between North Africa and Southern Europe. The cruise industry has changed significantly since the

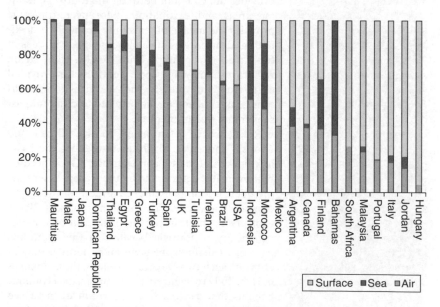

Figure 20.1 Destination arrivals by mode of transport, 2001
Source: WTO

1960s, when most of the liners were positioned in the Caribbean and appealed to wealthy and elderly tourists. Sophisticated purpose-built vessels are now used, and mass-market tour operators have developed cruise products. This means that the industry is much more diverse in terms of the destinations served and the spread of ages, incomes and interests of the passengers.

Air travel tends to be the dominant mode of transport for international and long-distance travel. It is particularly important in South America and Asia, where there tend to be large distances between tourist origins and destinations. Figure 20.1 shows the share of arrivals by mode of transport, with most variation being largely explained by the geographical characteristics of each country.

Changing industry structures and competitive environments

Privatization and competition

In recent years the links between the transport industry and the public sector have been loosened because of trends towards privatization and liberalization. This means that, in some areas of the world, competition between and within different forms of tourist transport has increased and a more customer-focused approach has been adopted.

For an increasing number of governments the privatization route has been followed primarily to reduce the burden on public sector expenditure and to encourage greater operating efficiency. In the airline industry a number of national 'flag' carriers (such as Air Canada, Qantas, LanChile and Lufthansa) are now totally privatised, whilst others (such as SAS, Malaysia Airlines and LOT) are partially privatized with the state retaining an interest. However, many airlines from less developed countries still remain under total government control (Doganis, 2001). Similarly, a number of full or partial privatizations have occurred at airports, including the London airports, Rome, Frankfurt, Vienna, Copenhagen, Zurich, Sydney, Melbourne and Johannesburg, although again many still remain in public hands (Graham, 2003).

The trend towards air transport deregulation began in 1978 with the US domestic market. Many more markets have been subsequently liberalized or deregulated. In some cases this has been as the result of the adoption of more liberal bilateral air services agreements between governments – as has occurred on a number of the North Atlantic and Pacific routes. In the European Union (EU), deregulation has been achieved with a multilateral policy that evolved over a number of years with the introduction of three deregulation packages. Since 1997 any carrier based in the EU can fly any route between two countries with virtually no controls on pricing or capacity.

The nationality rules contained within the bilateral air services agreements, which exist almost everywhere except within the EU, mean that traffic rights are lost if two international airlines merge. It is primarily for this reason that airlines have stopped short of total cross-border mergers and takeovers and have formed alliances instead. Even when Air France took an 80 per cent share of KLM in 2004, the two airlines kept their own identities to enable them to maintain their traffic rights. However, a significant development here is the possible establishment of a Trans-Atlantic Common Aviation Area (TACA). Discussions between the European Commission and the US Government were at very early stages in 2004, but any eventual agreement could have wide-reaching implications for the structure of international aviation operations. Ultimately this could lead to the relaxing of the nationality rules, which would then allow the airline industry to operate more like any other global industry (Doganis, 2001).

A major consequence of the more liberal air transport regulatory environment has been the development of the no frills, low-cost carrier (LCC) industry. Such airlines offer a basic product with high seating density and minimal in-flight service, and tend to use cheaper airports. They achieve high utilization, and mostly sell direct (primarily through the Internet) with no paper tickets, which further reduces their costs (Lumsdon and Page, 2004). The origins of the sector lie within the US with the airline Southwest, and there are now many other LCCs operating in the North American continent, such as Air Tran, Frontier, Spirit and jetBlue and Westjet. In Europe, Ryanair and easyJet were the first LCCs to become established in the late 1990s, primarily operating routes out of the UK and Ireland. The sector is still dominated by UK and Irish services, but mainland European services are growing rapidly. According to AEA, they accounted for 14 per cent of all scheduled seats in 2002 but this rose to 29 per cent in 2003. Overall within Europe in 2003, 16 per cent of all seats were on LCCs compared to just 4 per cent in 2000. There are many new start-ups in Europe, with competition being particularly strong in Germany with new airlines such as Germanwings, Hapag-Lloyd Express, Air Berlin and Germania Express. European Union enlargement in 2004 has encouraged a number of new Eastern European start-ups, such as Wizz and SkyEurope. The low-cost movement has also begun to spread rapidly from North America and Europe to other parts of the world. This is particularly the case in Asia-Pacific, where the LCC sector includes AirAsia, Virgin Blue, Freedom Air, Jetstar and Tiger Airways. Other examples are Air Deccan in India and Gol in Brazil.

Whilst the traditional airlines have faced their worst economic crisis since 2001, by contrast the established low-cost airlines such as Southwest, easyJet and Ryanair have managed to maintain high levels of profitability. However, there have also been many failures, and it is very unlikely that many of the start-up carriers will survive because of the increasingly competitive climate both amongst the LCCs and with the more traditional sector, where an increasing number of airlines such as Aer Lingus and BA have changed their short-haul strategy in order to compete more effectively. Others have set-up their own low-cost subsidiaries such as Ted (United), snowflake (SAS) and Qantas (JetStar). The European charter airlines have also felt threatened and some have moved into this business with LCCs such as myTravelLite or Hapag-Lloyd Express (Dennis, 2004). The net result of these developments is that the distinction between traditional 'flag carriers', LCCs and charter airlines is becoming increasingly blurred.

Surface modes

With surface modes there have also been attempts at increasing competition. A key issue for railways has been whether to maintain common management of services and infrastructure or whether to separate these. In countries such as the USA, Japan, Brazil and Mexico, common management has remained, whereas the European Union favours separation. As a result of this, a number of European countries such as France, Germany and the UK now have this separation. In some countries, for example Scandinavia and the UK, there has also been rail privatisation, but not with the success that was envisaged. More competition between coach operators has also been permitted in some areas, again for example in Scandinavia, and in the UK where there has been total deregulation and privatization of the state-owned operators (Page, 2003a, 2003b).

Horizontal and vertical integration

Within many of the transport sectors there has been a trend towards increased concentration, with a relatively small number of operators providing most of the capacity. The key perceived advantages of such concentration or horizontal integration are cost savings through economies of scale; marketing advantages through brand awareness and widespread coverage; and technological development opportunities that would not be available to smaller operators. In many cases this expansion has occurred across national borders, and so a much more international or global transport industry is emerging.

One of the most important developments in the global arena is the emergence of the international airline alliances. The major alliances are the Star Alliance, SkyTeam and oneworld (Figure 20.2). Alliances enable airlines to undertake joint scheduling, marketing and code-sharing, to offer combined frequent flyer programmes, and to share facilities such as check-in, airport lounges and reservation services. Costs may also be reduced through combined purchasing, operational synergies and the rationalization of services.

The cruise industry is now also highly concentrated. The top three parent companies are Carnival (see Case study 20.1), Royal Caribbean and Star, who dominate the cruise industry and account for 80 per cent of the worldwide cruise market (*Cruise Industry News*, 2004). Consolidation has also occurred within the car-hire sector. Likewise, airports have been expanding beyond national boundaries and buying or operating other airports. For example, the UK-based company BAA is involved in the operation of airports in Australia, Italy, the United States,

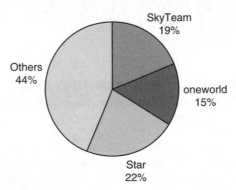

Based on 2003 revenue passenger kms (RPKs)

Figure 20.2 Global airline alliances market shares
Source: Airline Business

Case study 20.1 Carnival Cruises, USA

The trend toward consolidation within the cruise industry is well illustrated by Carnival Corporation plc, which is now the largest cruise company in the world. It was formed in 1972, and since the late 1980s has followed a strategy of expansion through acquisition. For example, it acquired the Holland America line in 1989, the Seabourn cruise line in 1992, Costa Cruises in 1997 and the Cunard Line in 1998. In 2003 it merged with P&O Princess Cruises, which at that time had the third largest global share. This expansion policy has meant that Carnival now controls twelve different key brands, which enables it to appeal to a diverse range of market segments and to achieve a very wide geographical coverage. Passenger numbers rose from 2.4 million in 1999 to 5.0 million in 2003. The next largest cruise company, Royal Caribbean Cruises, carried 2.9 million passengers in 2003. Of a world cruise fleet of around 250 ships, Carnival owns around 75.

(carnivalcorp.com)

whilst Copenhagen airport has interests in Mexico and Britain, and Amsterdam airport in Australia and the US (Graham, 2003). Some coach operators have recognized the need to coordinate services internationally, such as with the Eurolines brand, which offers coordinated long-distance services of 35 European coach companies (Page, 2003b).

One of the results of a more liberal surface transport economic environment has been the integration of different modes of travel and the development of multi-modal transport operators who provide bus, coach, and rail services. In Europe these include UK companies such as Arriva, Stagecoach and Firstgroup, and Transdev in France (White, 2002). The links between transport and other parts of the tourism industry through vertically integrated companies have also been strengthened with, for example, tour operators owning cruise ships. There are even airport examples such as in the UK, where Norwich airport owns a network of travel agencies and charters aircraft; Coventry airport (the base of Thomsonfly) is run by TUI; and the owners of London Manston have bought a share of Eujet, start-up LCC.

Emerging operational and technological trends

Operational developments

One of the ongoing major operational advances in transport has been the development of high-speed trains for long-distance travel. These began in 1964 with the Japanese 'Shinkansen' network, which continues to expand. This was followed in Europe in 1983 by the introduction of the TGV service between Paris and Lyon, and subsequently to many other French destinations. There are high-speed operations in other European countries, and it has been a European Union priority to assist in the development of a pan-European high-speed rail network, known as the Trans European Network System (TENS). An example of this is the THALYS service that operates between Paris, Brussels, Cologne and Amsterdam (Page, 2003a). In the more distant future it may be that magnetic levitation or 'maglev' technology will be used to provide very rapid rail services.

Within the shipping sector increasingly larger vessels, both for cruising and short sea ferries, have been introduced which have reduced unit costs and brought service quality benefits and lower prices to the tourist. Some of the latest ships, often known as 'floating resorts' because of the wide range of facilities offered, have a capacity of five or six times the original purpose-built vessels of the 1970s. Cunard's *Queen Mary 2*, the world's largest cruise liner at 151 000 tonnes and with a capacity of 2600 passengers, came into service in 2004, as did Princess's three new sister ships, each with a capacity of 2500–3500 passengers.

The airline industry, unlike the cruise industry, has not experienced any major changes in passenger capacity since the 1970s, when the Boeing 747 appeared. The other key development around this time was the arrival of supersonic Concorde aircraft. This did not have the dramatic impact that was originally envisaged, and in 2003 the last remaining operational aircraft were withdrawn from service. As regards a successor, Boeing was considering the development of a high-speed, long-range aircraft called the Sonic Cruiser, but it eventually abandoned this idea primarily due to lack of interest from the airlines. The two major aircraft manufacturers, Airbus and Boeing, have rather different views of the types of aircraft that will be needed in the future. Airbus believes that the growth in passenger numbers on dense routes will be accommodated by providing large aircraft at major airports, being operated on a hub and spoke basis; thus it is building the double-deck 550 passenger A380 aircraft. By contrast, Boeing considers that there will be a greater passenger demand for smaller aircraft, on a point-to-point basis, from more local or regional airports, and is consequently developing the 200–300 passenger 787 Dreamliner. Looking further ahead, space tourism is a concept that has attracted much interest (Crouch, 2001). It appears to have become closer to reality recently – in October 2004 Richard Branson of Virgin announced plans to build five 'Virgin Galatic SpaceShips', and the rocket plane SpaceShipOne shot to an altitude of more than 100 km for the second time inside a week to claim the $10m Ansari X-Prize.

Security

Since the events of 11 September 2001 and other terrorist attacks such as the Madrid train bombings, the provision of safe and secure transport services has been an issue of high priority. Within the air transport industry some of the most sweeping changes have occurred in the United States, where security services were previously relatively lax. However, these have resulted in a 'hassle' factor at airports which is thought to have put some passengers off flying or to have encouraged them to travel by different modes. Elsewhere in the world security has also been tightened, with a major issue, particularly in Europe, being whether the state or industry should provide the funding (ACI Europe, 2002).

Various airports have begun to use biometric identification. This uses unique physical characteristics to ensure that a passenger or member of staff is known.

Such techniques can be as simple as a specialized identity card, or as sophisticated as the recognition of retina patterns, fingerprints or speech. Then there is the provision of security measures on board the aircraft, which is a very controversial area. Strong views have been voiced both for and against certain procedures, such as the positioning of armed sky marshals, the arming of flight crew and the locking of cabin doors.

Information technology

It is not just regarding transport operations and security, but also in the area of sales, distribution and reservations, where technological changes have had a major impact. Traditionally the majority of air and cruise travel tickets have been bought through travel agents, whereas for other modes many tickets have been bought directly from the transport operator – particularly with surface transport, where many passengers just 'turn-up and go'. However, since the late 1990s there has been strong pressure for airlines to reduce their commission costs and this, coupled with the development of the Internet as a viable alternative means of distribution, has meant that more and more airline tickets are being sold direct. In the USA now many airlines pay no commission at all, and in Europe a number of airlines are doing the same. The airlines have also managed to reduce their costs by moving towards ticketless travel or e-ticketing.

There has been a huge growth in indirect Internet sites, such as online travel agent, consolidator or consumer bid pricing sites, which are used by the transport sector. The airlines have also set up airline portals, such as Orbitz in the US and Opodo in Europe. It is now possible in a growing number of countries to get real-time information by mobile telephones or online services regarding transport schedules. Also, in order to encourage transport integration between the modes and to make the public transport option more attractive, various joint information systems have been developed. An example of this is Traveline, a partnership of local and national government and transport operators that provides passenger information about all British public transport services. Information technology has also impacted on the product on offer, with an increasing number of airlines and other operators such as railways providing WiFi links for laptops and access to online services.

The net result of these developments is that information technology now plays a key role in the provision of customer service for transport operations, before the trip (through Internet sales), during the trip (through product enhancement) and after the trip (through allowing benefits such as frequent flyer points or other loyalty schemes).

Coping with growth and pressures on the environment

Congestion on the roads or in the skies can be a major problem for tourists, as can overcrowding within passenger terminals or stations. If new infrastructure is to be provided, funding is often an issue. Traditionally, much of the finance has come from public money; however, this option is becoming progressively more difficult with growing pressures on public sector expenditure. Hence there is the need to turn to the private sector, either through the privatization process or through some type of public/private funding partnership. Examples of such partnerships include the new airport in Athens, which was opened in 2001 and built by a company owned 55 per cent by the Greek Government and 45 per cent by a private sector international consortium. When expansion is not possible or not considered desirable for environmental reasons, market-based measures to ration demand, such as the pricing mechanism, may be possible. This is the reasoning behind the vehicle congestion charges that have been introduced in a number of cities including London, Singapore, Melbourne, Oslo and Toronto.

Many of the environmental problems facing tourist destinations such as historic cities are often due to the huge proportion of visitors that come by car. Various destinations, such as Canterbury in the UK, have responded by introducing traffic management schemes as part of a broader visitor management process (Laws and le Pelley, 2000). These may involve the provision of park-and-ride facilities, enhanced public transport provision, pedestrian priority and traffic calming. Coach operations may also have to be considered, with possible solutions being special coach drop-off/pick-up points or designated coach parks. Traffic management schemes have also been introduced in National Parks and other popular countryside areas (Graham, 2000).

Transport operators of all modes are under mounting pressure to introduce policies aimed at reducing noise, fuel consumption and emissions. With growing concern about global warming and greenhouse gases, more and more attention is being directed at the emissions impacts – particularly of air transport. It is estimated that the global warming effect of aviation, which currently represents around 3.5 per cent of all emissions, could rise to 4–15 per cent by 2050 (IPCC, 1999). There are increasing demands for aviation to pay for the full cost of the damage that it causes. This is a difficult issue, since international regulations prohibit the taxing of aviation fuel, but other possible alternatives include emissions charging or trading (CE Delft, 2002). Encouraging switching from air to rail transport for short sectors could also be an option.

Conclusions

The predominantly state-controlled transport industry of the past is very gradually being replaced by a more competitive and consumer-focused industry. However, with the overall trend towards greater concentration and globalization, it is debatable whether greater competition will actually be maintained in some sectors. There is also a growing number of tourists who are looking for a different or personalized experience and are shying away from these mass-market products. Hence there will always be the need for niche services such as yacht cruising or long-distance luxury rail travel.

Choosing between different modes of transport will become increasingly more complex in the future owing to a number of new developments. These include the speed and time required to complete the door-to-door trip, the changing channels of distribution, the emergence of low-cost products (see Case study 20.2). The increased sophistication of on-board services and after-sales loyalty schemes, more stringent security measures and their associated costs, and health concerns, for example, act as a threat for airlines because of DVT or as an opportunity for

Case study 20.2 EasyGroup, UK

EasyGroup, a private holding company for a number of 'easy' products, has developed the concept of low cost travel further than any travel company. The first and largest 'easy' company, easyJet, had its inaugural flights in 1995 from London Luton to Glasgow and Edinburgh in Scotland. By April 2004, it was offering 151 routes from 44 European airports. Passenger numbers have grown from 30 000 in 1995 to 20.3 million in 2003. More than 95 per cent of these were direct bookings on the Internet. Since 1995, a number of other low-cost transport services have been offered. The car-hire company, easyCar, began operations in 2000, and this has lower costs by offering only direct booking (again with more than 95 per cent online in 2003), no refuelling services, a standardized fleet and high utilization. Customers pay extra for car cleaning. In 2005 easyCruise is due to be launched, and the traditional cruise product will be simplified by providing more basic cabins and charging for food, drink and additional cleaning. Another new transport company, easyBus, was established in 2004.

(easyGroup.com)

cycling holidays. Undoubtedly a key factor will be environmental impacts, which could result in increases in the cost of air travel or force changes in modal split as more destinations introduce measures to manage car use. Overall changes in transport have always had a fundamental impact on tourism development, and there seems no reason to believe that the situation will be any different in the future.

21

Hospitality megatrends

Peter Jones

Introduction

At the heart of the industry lies a simple idea – the provision of hospitality. This act of hospitality – providing people with food, drink and somewhere to sleep – is almost certainly thousands of years old. Even today the tribes who live as hunter-gatherer societies habitually offer hospitality to travellers and strangers whom they encounter. However, the nature of modern hospitality is now of a much larger scale than ever before and it is conducted in richly diverse ways and in many different settings.

Based on an analysis of the major forces that have shaped the industry in the past, the hospitality industry of the future will have the following features:

1. Hospitality operations will continue to be located close to transportation nexuses
2. Asia will be the major growth area
3. New and innovative concepts and products will be designed to appeal to emerging lifestyle groups
4. There will be strong branding across all sectors of the industry
5. Hotel and restaurant chains will continue to be significant in the industry, but so will small and medium-sized enterprises
6. Process design will continue to evolve
7. Environmental responsibility and sustainability will be features of the industry

8. Crisis management and asset security will have a higher priority
9. The Internet will play a greater role in hospitality operations management.

The development of the industry: forces driving change

The single most important influence on the provision of hospitality is travel. The moment that people leave their own homes, they need other people to provide them with food and drink to sustain them and somewhere to sleep. Thus inns, and eventually hotels and restaurants, developed. Such places were then frequented by local people in order to hear about what was happening in the world, as travellers were the sole source of news up to the 1800s. Hence, understanding the reasons for travel and the means of transportation are key to understanding hospitality.

Reasons for travelling

In medieval Europe, travelling was confined to the very rich or the religious. However, from the 1300s onwards travel was increasingly undertaken for commercial reasons – to buy or sell products or services. This led to the development of the roadside inn. Travelling for pleasure was confined only to the wealthy up to around 1850, but the working man and his family began to travel for a holiday as a result of the industrial revolution, urbanization, and the development of the railway. During the summer, British trains were packed with families travelling from cities to seaside resorts such as Blackpool, Skegness, Brighton and Torquay, whilst in the winter the Alpine regions attracted skiers. Today people travel for a variety of motivations, including business and meetings, leisure, religion, culture, visiting friends and relatives, education and health.

Transportation

The influence of transportation on hospitality is one of size and speed. Put simply, over time the means of transportation have increasingly grown larger and faster. By transport becoming larger, more people than ever before can travel and, moreover, new types of traveller emerge. As transport becomes faster, people can travel much greater distances.

In 1754, the road journey by coach between London and Edinburgh took ten days in the summer and twelve in winter (Jackman, 1962). Over time road travel got faster, but people did not travel straight through and continued to stop off overnight. In the 1700s and 1800s small towns like Grantham had more than ten inns, which could accommodate as many as 300 people and as many horses. A very similar pattern is evident in Europe and the United States today, with clusters of hotels, motels and inns located at major points along major highways, with the same importance to the local economy as in the 1700s.

In the mid-1800s, rail travel began. It was faster, cleaner and more reliable than coaches, especially over long distances. A new feature introduced on rail transport was the notion of dining whilst travelling. Pullman developed the first restaurant

---

Case study 21.1 The British fish and chip shop

Walton (1994) explains that 'the arrival of steam {power} for the {fishing} fleets and the development of icing equipment produced a massive expansion in supplies of cheaper forms of sea fish'. At the same time, the working classes had a general rise in their incomes. This left disposable income for luxuries like the fish supper. By 1910 there were around 25 000 fish and chip shops in Britain, and by 1927 that number had risen to a peak of 35 000. Up to two-thirds of all the white fish being landed was sold though these outlets. Even today there are still 8600 fish and chip shops in the UK, despite concerns about the healthiness of deep-fried foods.

---

cars, but they quickly became a feature of all long-distance train journeys. This period also saw the growth of large hotels at all major rail stations, often adjoining the concourse itself, as at St Pancras with the Midland Grand Hotel.

Meals were also served on the very earliest form of air transport – airships and aeroplanes (Jones, 2004). In the 1920s, Imperial Airways (one of the forerunners of British Airways) was the first to introduce what might be recognized today as in-flight services. Just as with road and rail transportation, hotels have been built at airports. Major airport hubs will have a considerable lodging infrastructure – for instance, at London's Heathrow airport there are now 16 hotels providing over 3000 bedrooms.

Disposable income

Although travel and transportation have been important, the growth of the middle class and an increase in wealth has also been a major driver of growth within the industry. The key influence that this has had is on the growth of hospitality establishments aimed not at the traveller but at local people. People started going out for drinks and meals. The story of fish and chip shops in the UK (see Case study 21.1) illustrates this.

The hospitality industry in context: contemporary issues

Scale of the industry

The sheer scale of the hospitality industry is breathtaking. On any given day around the world, 500 million people will buy a restaurant meal and 300 million will sleep away from home. A single restaurant chain, McDonalds, now has over 25 000 restaurants worldwide. In a single year, 1 billion passengers are fed on aeroplanes. More people are fed in hospitals each day than make up the entire population of France. Food and drink is provided to people in every imaginable setting outside the home – at work and at leisure, in schools and hospitals, on trains, ships and planes, and whilst sitting, standing or walking. People who wish or need to sleep away from home also have a wide range of different places in which to spend the night – hotels, hostels, hospitals and halls of residence, to name but a few. In the USA more than 50 per cent of meal occasions involve the consumption of food and drink prepared outside the home, and this will also be the case in the UK before the year 2020.

Complexity of the industry

Whilst the concept of hospitality is quite simple, hospitality operations are challenging to manage. This is for three main reasons – their process type, cost structure, and market features. In terms of process, most hospitality operations are a combination of customer processing operations (CPO), materials processing operations (MPO) and information processing operations (IPO). Allied to the notion of process type is the fact that from a financial perspective, hotels have a mix of cost structures based around the provision of service (rooms division), 'manufacturing' (foodservice) and retail (bars). The implication of this is that some management skills apply in one context but not another – for instance, production planning is important in manufacturing, inventory management is essential in retail, and forecasting is a key element of service operations.

Segmentation

In the early stages of the hospitality industry, one establishment – the roadside inn – provided all three elements of the hospitality experience: lodging, food and drink. The same establishment also served all market segments, albeit that the wealthy stayed in rooms with four-poster beds whilst their servants were put up in attic rooms, and their grooms slept with the horses in the stable. Over time two things happened. First, the provision of food and drink was separated from lodging, and thus restaurants and public houses (bars) were created. Second, each of these types of hospitality business began to be designed for specific groups of people, or market segments. Originally segmentation was based on social class, expressed largely through how much someone could afford to pay. Five-star hotels were for the upper class, whilst guesthouses and boarding houses were for the working class. Over time, other factors influenced segmentation. For instance, when Marriott decided to develop a budget concept, Fairfield Inns, they deliberately designed it to meet the needs of the so-called 'road warrior'. This is the commercial traveller who spends more than 200 days staying away from home.

Not-for-profit hospitality

It should also not be forgotten that there are significant sectors of the industry where both accommodation and foodservice are provided for people who have little or no choice but to stay or eat away from home – in hospitals, schools and universities, workplaces, prisons and so on. Today these places have facilities, décor and service styles very similar to those found in the commercial sector.

The major trends: the hospitality industry of the future

Location, location, location

Hotels will continue to be built in the major types of locations – urban centres (mainly for business travellers), resorts (mainly for leisure travellers) and along-side major transportation networks or hubs such as airports. Restaurants and bars will be more ubiquitous, with most being located very close to their market and a few exceptional places being 'destination' restaurants owing to the reputation of their cuisine or some other factor. Some destination-based concepts use location as their unique selling proposition. Jules Underseas Lodge in Florida is reputedly the world's first underwater hotel, although it can accommodate only a maximum of six guests (www.jul.com). Other unusual concepts include 'ice hotels, which are literally carved out of ice; haunted hotels and guesthouses; and hotels built in trees (treehouses).

New and emerging markets: Asia leads the way

Much of the growth in the industry will take place in Asia. This is because the economic and social forces that drive change are very great in this region. For instance, by 2010 it is forecast that one-half of all the world's airline travel will be in this region. Many of the major American and European chains are investing heavily in India and China, but there is also strong growth in hotel chains based in the region, such as Taj and Oberoi, Shangri-La and Mandarin Oriental.

Lifestyle segmentation

Today and in the future it is more likely for a hospitality product to be designed for market segments based on lifestyle. Thus there are family restaurants, sports bars, and boutique hotels (aimed at the fashion conscious). For instance, the boutique Hi Hotel in Nice, France, has:

> Uberhip style with individually designed rooms interpreting themes like
> 'white & white', 'monospace' (think bright primary colors and cubes), and
> 'outdoor terasse' (smooth wood floors, white sheets and sky-blue walls).
> The restaurant features organic, raw and vegetarian options; all food is
> self-serve, in mason jars for guests to mix and match.
>
> (www.hotels.about.com)

This trend will continue in the future. As new lifestyle groups emerge, hospitality products – lodging, foodservice and bars – will be developed to reflect this

Case study 21.2 Hooters restaurants, USA

One excellent, sometimes controversial, example of a lifestyle-driven restaurant brand is Hooters. As their website explains:

> Hooters is the Atlanta-based operator and franchiser of over 375 Hooters locations …. The casual beach-theme establishments feature '50s & '60s jukebox music, sports on television, and a menu that includes seafood, sandwiches, salads and spicy chicken wings. Hooters, system-wide, generates and averages 72% of its sales from food, 5% from merchandise, and 23% from beer and wine. Notably, Hooters does not serve liquor. The element of female sex appeal is prevalent in the restaurants, and the company believes the Hooters Girl is as socially acceptable as a Dallas Cowboy cheerleader, *Sports Illustrated* swimsuit model, or Radio City Rockette. The Hooters system employs over 25 000 people – over 15 000 of which are Hooters Girls. Hooters characterizes itself as a neighbourhood place, not a typical family restaurant. Sixty-eight per cent of customers are male, most between the ages of 25–54. Hooters does not market itself to families, but they do patronize the restaurants.

(www.hooters.com)

(see Case study 21.2). For instance, a hotel has recently been opened in London that is exclusively for children.

Branding

As markets become more and more segmented, more and more choice is created for consumers. In order to stand out from the crowd, major companies develop brands that are easily recognizable (see Case study 21.3). Branding has been a key to the success of the large chains such as Hilton and McDonalds, and will continue to be important into the future – especially so that lifestyle groups can identify the hospitality businesses that have been designed for them.

Chains and small businesses

One of the reasons for the growth in brands is a parallel growth in large hospitality firms. The two have gone hand-in-hand, and will continue to do so. The brand reassures consumers that the standards and the system will be the same wherever they may find the operation – so whether you are in Bangor, Wales or Bangor, Maine or Bangkok, the hotel or restaurant will be identical.

Except … there are subtle differences between lodgings and foodservice. Most hotel chains, especially at the top end of the market, are aimed at the international traveller. Hence international hotel chains do have properties and services that are very similar wherever you might stay. However, foodservice chains are

Case study 21.3 Sodexho brands, UK

Our brand portfolio brings a new excitement to catering, helping you to reduce or even eliminate your subsidy by increasing sales and creating strong customer loyalty. Foodservice brands have become one of the strongest influences on the High Street in recent years. In shopping centres, airports and motorway service areas, they have proved irresistible. Now brands are opening up new opportunities for our clients and customers throughout the business and industry, healthcare, leisure and education sectors. The attraction of brands is simple – they deliver consistent food quality, a high standard of customer service and outstanding value for money in an attractive environment. Customers know exactly what to expect and they get it every time. The financial case is proven. Brands strengthen the loyalty of regular customers. They attract, and keep, new customers. They bring excitement and provide the food and service style that customers want, increasing spend per head. In the UK, we have these brands in more than 1000 locations. Each brand has increased customer patronage, increased sales volume and customer satisfaction and reduced clients' catering subsidies.

(www.sodexho-uk.com/segments/brands)

less reliant on tourists than on the local population, and hence they adapt their operation – especially the menu – to reflect local tastes. For instance, beef is not eaten in India, which is a challenge for McDonalds, so their menu has Chicken Maharaja instead of the Big Mac, and a range of vegetarian options not found in other countries.

Despite the growth in international chains, the industry continues also to have a very large number of small businesses. Indeed, the growth of the Internet has enabled small hotels and restaurants to promote themselves highly effectively in competition with the big brands. The relative ease of entry into the industry means that SMEs will continue to play a significant role in hospitality. Many entrepreneurs in tourism and hospitality are lifestylers, rather than rational business people, providing a number of challenges.

Trends in hospitality process design

In hospitality operations process design, Jones (1988) first identified three key trends: production lining, decoupling, and customer participation.

Production lining refers to the concept of breaking down production activities into simple tasks so that they may be organized on a production-line basis. It has long been argued that services in general are moving towards more industrialized processes. Indeed, this has actually been termed the McDonaldization of society (Ritzer, 1996).

Decoupling refers to the idea of separating, both in place and time, back-of-house from front-of-house activity. Often the rationale for doing so is that one or the other (usually back-of-house) can be production-lined. For instance, a number of health authorities in the UK have created one large central production kitchen for a number of hospitals and introduced cook-chill, so that the kitchen may produce 5000–6000 meals for transportation the following day to five or more different hospitals.

Customer participation is otherwise known as self-service. Many hospitality operations now enable their customers to do things for themselves that were previously done for them. It is possible to check into a hotel by using a swipe card system, to select salad items from a self-help salad bar, and to check out of a hotel using the in-room television set.

Jones (1996) has subsequently identified two further process trends in the industry – the development of so-called micro-units, and the dual or multi-use of physical infrastructure. Micro-units are foodservice outlets of a very small size, aimed at serving often limited and/or captive markets. They include outlets in petrol filling stations, cinemas, sports stadia, the workplace and so on. Their growth derives from the fact that more traditional sites are now unavailable and demand for eating out continues to grow.

The final trend of dual or multi-use of infrastructure is sometimes a consequence of devising micro-units. By enabling a brand to be delivered inside a small 'footprint', it can then be incorporated into an existing outlet. For instance, the table service restaurant chain Little Chef has incorporated micro-Burger King units alongside the main restaurant.

All of these will continue into the future. The concept of production lining is likely to be extended by the use of the Internet to enable customers to order online so that their meal is ready for them when they arrive at the restaurant or on board the train or plane. Decoupling has now been extended into outsourcing so that more than one firm is involved in the operation's processes. High-profile restaurateurs operate hotel restaurants, and cleaning companies clean hotel bedrooms.

Sustainability

Many existing hospitality businesses are concerned about the environment, and this is likely to become more significant in the future (see Case study 21.4). Hotels are being built from environmentally-friendly materials, and policies are in place to 'reduce, recycle and reuse' as per the International Environmental Hospitality Initiative.

Security and assets

Security and assets have been recognized as two of the five major challenges to the industry in this new millennium by the International Hotel & Restaurant Association (IH&RA 1996). Events since the start of the new millennium have underlined this – 11 September 2001 in New York, SARS in Asia, foot and mouth in Britain, hurricanes in the Caribbean, and the 2004 tsunami disaster in the Indian Ocean have all greatly impacted on the industry.

Clearly, there is little the industry can do about such external occurrences except to ensure they have crisis plans and contingency marketing plans for responding to a decline in demand. However, customers do expect that hotels are

Case study 21.4 The environmental pod hotel

According to Thomson Holidays, who hosted a 'Future Forum':

> The hotel of the future will be a fully transportable super pod containing rooms of varying sizes that can be dismantled and which will have a disposable waste unit. The holiday pod can be packed up easily and moved to any location in the world, be it the South Pacific, the Arctic or the desert. The pod's construction materials will allow it to be developed away from the area, before being transported to its final location. Each pod will be pre-fabricated and self-sustaining. The pod will contain different sized rooms that can be upgraded or downgraded according to travel budgets. Inside the rooms, 'active' walls and floors will show changeable images, enabling guests to set whatever mood they wish, be it an ocean view or a jungle look out. All waste produced by the hotel will go into a unit at the base of the structure, so no blemish will be left on the environment after it has moved on.

(www.tui-uk.co.uk/press/news_releases)

safe places to stay, and hotel companies need to ensure that they have appropriate security measures – not only to safeguard their guests but also their employees and the property.

Integrating technologies

The development of integrated systems based on the Internet will increase 'virtual management' (O'Connor, 2000, 2001; Buhalis, 2003). This is the case in the airline industry, where the two global catering companies have both developed Internet-based systems to manage the supply chain – eGatematrix and eLSGSkychef (Buhalis, 2004). Likewise, specialist application service providers are providing new services for hospitality chains. For instance, eProductive enables hotels to manage their labour scheduling process online, with considerable gains in productivity and efficiency.

Conclusion

In this chapter, nine major trends have been identified. It is argued that the forces that shaped the industry today will be the same forces that shape it tomorrow. However, the world is turbulent, politically, socially and environmentally, so it is unwise to predict the future without some form of caveat.

22

Attractions megatrends

Pierre Benckendorff

Introduction

Tourist attractions are frequently described as the key components of a destination's tourism industry. While they have received increasing attention from researchers, attractions continue to be poorly understood, with research lacking conceptual sophistication and depth (Richards, 2002). Tourist attractions serve two key functions in the tourism system: they stimulate interest in travel to a destination, and they provide visitor satisfaction (Gunn, 1994). Yet the role of tourist attractions in the post-modern world is changing. Consumer demands and competitive innovations are driving this change, which is resulting in a more multifaceted, fragmented attraction sector. Tourist attractions are proliferating in terms of form, location, scale and style. The following discussion explores our current understanding of tourist attractions and also a series of trends that will influence attractions over the next twenty years.

Understanding tourist attractions

Before proceeding with a detailed discussion about the future of attractions, it is useful to pause for a moment to consider exactly what we mean by the term 'tourist attraction'. The term is difficult to define for two reasons. First, it is difficult to determine the number of visitors that have to travel to a site before it can be classed as an attraction. Secondly, the purpose for visiting a site may determine whether it should be classed as an attraction (Swarbrooke, 2002). These technicalities are further complicated by the diverse and disparate nature of the attractions sector. While various definitions have been suggested, they vary in terms of their purpose, disciplinary approach, applicability and simplicity. Walsh-Heron and Stevens (1990) provide one of the most comprehensive and widely cited definitions of a tourist attraction. They suggest that an attraction is a feature in an area that is a place, venue or focus of activity that:

1. Sets out to attract visitors and is managed accordingly
2. Provides a fun and pleasurable experience and an enjoyable way for customers to spend their leisure time
3. Is developed to realize this potential
4. Is managed as an attraction, providing satisfaction to its customers
5. Provides an appropriate level of facilities and services to meet and cater to the demands, needs, and interest of its visitors
6. May or may not charge admission for entry.

Leiper's (1990a) definition of an attraction, adapted from MacCannell (1976) and Gunn (1988a), stands apart from those of other authors by implicitly identifying an attraction as a system consisting of three elements: a tourist or human element; a nucleus or central element; and a marker or informative element. A tourist attraction system comes into existence when the three elements are connected. Richards (2002) provides empirical support for this view of tourist attractions, and observes that Leiper's system does not adhere to the conventional view that tourists are 'pulled' towards attractions; rather they are 'pushed' by their own motives.

Figure 22.1 presents a framework of a tourist attraction. The framework incorporates the three key components of an attraction (MacCannell, 1976; Leiper, 1990a). An attraction cannot exist without a tourist with a motive to travel. Tourists gather information about an attraction using series of markers. There are three types of markers that may compel a tourist to visit an attraction in search of a satisfying experience. The first is an awareness marker that brings the attraction to the attention of the tourist – Leiper (1990a) calls this the generating marker. An example of an awareness marker may be a website or brochure about the attraction. A second type of marker is a transit marker or, more simply, a piece of information that the tourist encounters while *en route* to the destination – an example may be a roadside billboard. The final type of marker is located at the core resource, and is ambiguously referred to as a 'contiguous marker' by Leiper (1990a); however the concept can be broadened to describe markers that provide a context for understanding the attraction. They create a sense of place and help visitors to understand the attraction through interpretation. It is through the use of context markers, such as signage, brochures and interpretation, that visitors can conceptualize or derive meaning from the attraction.

The attraction itself is made up of a core resource, variously described as the sight (MacCannell, 1976), nucleus (Gunn, 1988a; Leiper, 1990a) or imagescape (Wanhill, 2003). The core resource is frequently conceptualized using a two-dimensional construct consisting of a natural–manmade dimension and a site–event dimension. The framework presented in this chapter adopts a slightly different approach, and uses a 'natural–cultural' dimension and a 'temporary–permanent'

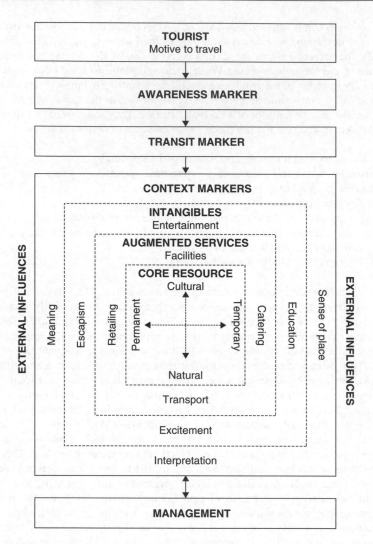

Figure 22.1 A framework for understanding tourist attractions

dimension. The natural–cultural dimension recognizes that attractions are not only based on tangible natural or manufactured attributes, but that cultural elements such as individuals (past and present) and customs can also be attractions. The temporary–permanent dimension implies that while some attractions are permanent, the core resource may change. Furthermore, this dimension recognizes the temporary nature of events as attractions. Figure 22.2 provides examples of core attraction resources that can be conceptualized using this construct.

In many attractions, the core resource does not exist without a range of augmented services that support visitor activities (Swarbrooke, 2002; Wanhill, 2003).

Cultural

Archaeological site	Festival
Historic/museum site	Museum/art exhibit
Art gallery	Theatre performance
Theme park	Musical recital
Garden	Religious event
Shopping centre	Sports event
City centre	

Permanent ←————————————→ **Temporary**

National Park	Volcanic eruption
Landscape	Coral spawning
Fauna	Wildlife migration
Flora	Astronomical event
	Meteorological event

Natural

Figure 22.2 Conceptualizing the core resource of tourist attractions

Gunn (1988a) referred to this aspect as the 'zone of closure'. Augmented services may include basic visitor facilities such as restrooms, retail outlets, food and beverage facilities and transport infrastructure. The importance of intangible elements such as education, entertainment and excitement, and escapism has also been recognized by several authors (Wanhill, 2003). It is the desire to seek out these intangible experiences that initially motivates tourists to travel. The core resource provides a setting for activities that result in the creation of visitor experiences.

While other models of attractions imply that they need to be managed, this component is explicit in the framework presented. While it is certainly true that some natural attractions are not managed, a vast majority of attractions is maintained either directly or indirectly by managers or regulatory frameworks. Even the most pristine natural attractions (temporary or permanent) are subject to management regimes imposed by conservation or government agencies, albeit with varying levels of success. Attraction management, therefore, is aimed at ensuring that the needs of current visitors are met and that the resource core is preserved for future visitors.

The final aspect of the framework presented in this chapter is the recognition that tourists, managers and the core attraction resource are subject to external influences. It is these external influences that are ultimately responsible for the emergence of new trends in attractions.

Major trends in tourist attractions

Attractions change over time owing to physical deterioration and as a result of changing consumer needs (Gunn, 1988a). The following section attempts to identify and synthesize some of the key developments that have the potential to impact on tourist attractions. The discussion focuses first on the broad 'external' influences that are generally beyond an organization's influence. These trends are presented using the STEEP framework (Socio-cultural trends, Technological trends, Economic trends, Environmental trends and Political trends). Following this, the discussion turns to a consideration of trends that are 'internal' to the attractions sector.

Socio-cultural trends

Of all the forces that will change the world over the next generation, demography is arguably the most important. Some of the most pervasive socio-cultural trends influencing tourist attractions include:

- the decline of traditional families and the increasing influence of females and children in making leisure decisions
- the ageing of populations in key generating markets
- increasing cultural diversity
- multiculturalism emerging from globalization
- continued growth in more frequent, shorter trips
- the increasing sophistication of visitors seeking quality experiences in education, entertainment, excitement and escape
- disenchantment with lifestyles that focus on work and material possessions, and growing demand for experiences that incorporate spiritual elements, personal fulfilment and time to appreciate family.

These trends are caused by the complex interaction of a number of social factors, and will result in a number of challenges for tourist attraction operators. Lack of children, or an increase in the average age of women at childbirth, means that young couples have more discretionary time and income. Singles and couples may view travel as an opportunity to meet and interact with people. Smaller family size means that the family unit has greater flexibility in their activities, and more money to spend on recreation and entertainment. Tourist attractions may need to re-evaluate the types of services and packages that are offered. For example, the standard two adult-two children 'family' ticket may no longer be attractive to the market place. Furthermore, these trends may create a demand for activities that are less family oriented, or leisure products that provide child-minding services.

The effects of an ageing population on tourism have been extensively studied, and some commentators have suggested, rather naively, that with above average wealth and relatively few demands on their time, the elderly will make up an ever-larger part of the tourist market. These views, however, seem to ignore the reality that retired travellers will need to survive in a world of inflation, increased living costs, diminished government support and increased life expectancy. In other words, older travellers will get less for their money and will need to spread their savings over a much longer twilight period than past generations. Furthermore, some governments are contemplating an increase in the official retirement age, somewhat diluting the view that the retired market will have a great deal of disposable time. Chapter 4 in this volume explores this social development more fully.

A well-established tradition of accepting immigrants and assimilating them into a broader mainstream culture in English-speaking nations such as the

United States, Canada and Australia has caused populations in these countries to become more culturally diverse. Increased cultural diversity creates several challenges for attraction operators. First, the influx of new cultures may gradually change domestic visitor markets, in terms of both visitor preferences and expectations. Secondly, a multicultural society encourages international visiting friends and relatives (VFR) travel, and it would be reasonable to suggest that the mix of VFR travellers to a particular destination may change. A third challenge for tourist attractions is the need to be sensitive to cultural differences. For example, should tourist attractions remove pork from food menus, or should prayer rooms be provided in theme parks to meet the needs of Muslim travellers?

Technological trends

The pervasive nature of technology impacts on the business environment of tourist attractions both directly and indirectly. The direct applications of technological advances benefit the attraction sector in terms of business efficiency, product development and marketing. Technological innovations and directions of research over the next twenty years can be envisaged with reasonable accuracy because many prototypes and technologies already exist in the laboratory. Some of the technological developments that may impact on tourist attractions include:

- the use of computerized booking systems, smart cards, and electronic security to control visitor flows and to free up staff to interact with visitors
- the creation of interactive multimedia experiences using technologies such as audio, lighting, animatronics, simulations and virtual reality
- advances in online technologies such as real-time video, virtual tours and web-based interpretation to encourage visitation and remote visitor interaction
- the use of online technologies that support spontaneous travel decisions by allowing visitors to book at the last minute, perhaps at a discounted price
- the use of virtual reality and technology to enable reconstructions of cultural heritage attractions
- advances in genetics that raise the possibility of enhancing tourist attractions by ensuring that plant and animal species are more resilient, or by 'resurrecting' recently extinct species to create new attractions.

The way in which tourist attraction visitors will respond to the use of technology is a serious challenge for attraction operators. Sheldon (1997) suggested two polar responses to technology, using a high-tech/high-touch paradigm. She proposed that some travellers, grouped under high-tech, would have an expectation of higher levels of automation. Conversely, high-touch travellers would view technology as being destructive to the tourism experience. In reality, anecdotal evidence suggests that most travellers fall somewhere between these extremes.

Economic trends

There are perhaps as many opinions about the future of the world economy as there are commentators; however, a few consistent viewpoints are worth exploring here. Economic trends that may create new challenges and opportunities for attractions include:

- the continued spread of globalization, creating a need for attractions to be globally competitive while maintaining a local flavour
- changes in the spending of discretionary income on various leisure products, including in-home entertainment (e.g. increased spending on home theatre systems, game consoles, computers), shopping and broader leisure opportunities (e.g. cinema attendance)
- an increased tendency for tourism businesses to focus on yield, rather than visitor numbers
- the emergence of an increasingly wealthy middle class, with the means to travel, in countries such as China and India.

While tourist 'production' is linked to local conditions, tourist attractions cannot avoid being influenced by globalization. Some tourist attraction operators will need to confront the issue of globalization, as they struggle to remain competitive in the global environment while delivering authentic, personal visitor experiences.

From a micro-economic perspective, there is an increasing recognition that growth in visitor numbers is an inadequate measure of tourism performance. In Australia, some attraction operators have shifted their focus towards promoting business strategies that optimize the yield potential of different market segments. For the attraction sector, this would suggest a focus on increasing the profit earned from each visitor. This could be accomplished in a number of ways, as follows:

1. Increasing entry prices – a decision that may result in decreased visitor numbers. Decreased visitor numbers in some attractions may lead to lower operating costs, thus increasing the yield per visitor.
2. Creating a number of complementary sources of income from visitors. Examples include admissions, refreshments, souvenirs and merchandise, photos/videos of visitor experiences, and so forth.
3. Implementing marketing strategies to target wealthier clientele.
4. Using technologies to reduce operating costs – examples include the use of energy and waste minimization technologies in attractions.

Environmental trends

The combined growth of the human population and increased energy consumption has created pressures on remaining natural environments. While this has triggered a number of responses from groups with varied interests and goals, most commentators agree that the awareness of environmental impacts has increased over the last 20–30 years. This has resulted in two related trends of relevance to tourist attractions:

1. Greater pressure on attractions to deliver products and services in an environmentally responsible and culturally sensitive manner
2. An increased desire to visit attractions that conduct their business in an environmentally-friendly manner, or attractions that have a strong environmental theme.

The shift toward sustainable experiences has created a positive outcome for nature-based attractions. However, as concern for environmental issues continues to grow, demands for even greater environmental controls are inevitable – especially in relatively pristine regions or at sensitive cultural sites. This creates a challenge for tourist attraction operators, who will need to manage the constraints imposed on businesses due to environmental concerns. Some attractions have developed strategies to minimize water and energy consumption; others have responded by offering activities that alleviate environmental impacts by serving as a substitute for actual visits to sensitive sites.

Political trends

Perhaps the most challenging issue confronting attractions in the present political climate is the need to offer visitors a safe and predictable environment. The threat of terrorism is particularly acute for attractions such as national monuments or those that offer a setting where large numbers of people gather. Furthermore, attractions such as theme parks, which flaunt Western values and excesses, may also be terrorist targets. In the broader context, some tourist attractions are highly sensitive to the international movement of visitors and are therefore vulnerable to developments in international politics.

Internal attraction sector trends

An important attraction trend in both the United Kingdom and the United States is the emergence of integrated leisure complexes. These centres combine retail, leisure, entertainment, catering and accommodation into integrated complexes designed to have broad market appeal (Middleton, 2001). Global examples include Bluewater Park and Trafford Park in the United Kingdom, and West Edmonton Mall in Canada (Case study 22.1). Allied with this concept, albeit on a larger scale, is the emergence of 'Fantasy Cities', or Urban Entertainment Destinations (UEDs). Faced with the decline of urban centres, a number of cities have transformed central business precincts into settings that offer shopping, dining, entertainment, education and culture in a predictable and secure environment (Hannigan, 1999). Examples include Las Vegas and Times Square in the USA, and Darling Harbour in Sydney. UEDs have six common features (Hannigan, 1999):

1. They are developed around themes, usually drawn from sport, history, or popular entertainment
2. They are usually aggressively marketed, often with the help of large corporate sponsors (e.g. Nike and Coca-Cola)
3. They operate day and night
4. They offer an array of standard entertainment 'modules', such as themed restaurants, multiplex cinemas, high tech amusements and megastores
5. They are physically, socially and economically isolated from the local urban environment
6. They offer a postmodern environment constructed around technologies of simulation, virtual reality and the thrill of the spectacle.

Case study 22.1 West Edmonton Mall, Canada

West Edmonton Mall exemplifies the integrated leisure complexes described in this chapter. The facility is a 49-hectare (121 acres) super mall that includes 800 stores, 110 restaurants, an ice arena, a water and amusement park, an aviary and aquarium, a dolphin lagoon and a hotel with 354 rooms. The centre is the only place in the world where visitors can experience indoor bungee jumping. West Edmonton Mall also boasts the world's largest car park (holding over 20 000 cars), indoor lake, indoor wave pool (2 hectares) and indoor amusement park (37 000 square metres). In addition to providing a secure environment for visitors to engage in a wide variety of activities, the organization has shown a strong commitment to the environment by utilizing technologies which reduce energy and water wastage. The success of the mall is based around the concept of providing an environment that offers a compelling mix of retail, leisure, entertainment, catering and accommodation.

(http://www.westedmall.com/)

Such trends place traditional tourist attractions in competition with specialist leisure and entertainment destinations. Both Middleton (2001) and Stevens (2003) have commented on the decline in visitors to traditional attractions. This decline has been attributed to intense competition from a wide range of rapidly emerging, innovative leisure products. The decline in visitor numbers, combined with decreasing public capital and revenue funding, has encouraged some tourist attractions to expand their revenue streams into areas such as conference venues, events and off-site activities.

Innovative attraction strategies

In order to compete, operators in North America, Europe, Japan and Australia have developed increasingly innovative attraction strategies. These attractions have moved away from the traditional stand-alone attractions toward multifaceted facilities offering a dense spectrum of recreational opportunities. Specific trends that can be identified from these attractions include:

1. Use of theming. Built attractions are making use of extensive theming and technology to enliven visitor experiences. Disney has long been a leader in this field, but other attractions are successfully developing themes based around nature, culture, history, fantasy, industry, agriculture and sport. These themes are often supported by high-tech rides, interactive displays and a diverse mix of recreational opportunities. Table 22.1 indicates the long-term growth of this style of attraction in the United States.
2. Managing visitor satisfaction and entertainment. There is increasing emphasis on visitor satisfaction and entertainment in heritage attractions. This trend is driven by live theatre, living history and frequently changing programmes and exhibits. Historic theme parks, such as Sovereign Hill in Australia (see Case study 22.2), exemplify this trend.

Table 22.1 Yearly attendance and revenue estimates for the US amusement/theme park industry

Year	Attendance (millions)	Revenue (US$billions)
2003	322	10.3
2002	324	9.9
2001	319	9.6
2000	317	9.6
1999	309	9.1
1998	300	8.7
1997	300	8.4
1996	290	7.9
1995	280	7.4
1994	267	7.0
1993	275	6.8

Source: International Association of Amusement Parks and Attractions, 2003

Case study 22.2 Sovereign Hill, Australia

Sovereign Hill is a multi-faceted visitor attraction that depicts the Australian town of Ballarat ten years after the discovery of gold in 1851. The attraction offers an excellent example of a 'living' museum presenting the mining and social history of Australia's gold-rush era. Visitors are presented with a living gold-rush town spread over 25 hectares (60 acres) of land. The township consists of over 60 buildings that are brought to life by more than 300 costumed staff, 200 costumed volunteers and around 40 horses. The museum enhances visitor experiences through role-playing and personal interaction with characters, buildings and artefacts. This is supplemented by a modern orientation centre that utilizes audio and video to acquaint visitors with a background of the 1850s gold rushes.

After-hours use of the site is enhanced by a 90-minute 'Blood on the Southern Cross' sound-and-light show, which features state-of-the-art lighting and dazzling special effects. Furthermore, the museum has extended its core product by hosting small to medium conferences and meetings, as well as large group functions and special occasions such as weddings. The facility also offers on-site accommodation through the Sovereign Hill Lodge.

(http://www.sovereignhill.com.au/)

3. Providing interpretation and education. A proliferation of interpretive signage, guided tours and interpretive centres is increasingly common, particularly at natural attractions. The use of roving staff to provide explanations of exhibits or settings is an innovative illustration of this trend (Pearce, 1998).
4. Managing people and capacity. Technology is being used in high-density visitor attractions to facilitate visitor flows, to enhance visitor comfort and to reduce resource stress (Pearce, 1998). Disney's FastPass system is an example of this trend.

5. Enhancing professionalism. Leading tourist attractions are becoming increasingly sophisticated in their management of visitors, markets, service and presentation (Swarbrooke, 2002). One clear indication of this trend is the increasing sophistication of attraction marketing campaigns and concerted efforts to encourage repeat visitation through membership programmes and discounts for local residents. The market-niche orientation of some attractions also exemplifies an increasingly professional approach to the marketplace (Pearce, 1998).

6. Creating multiple use facilities. There is increasing recognition by attraction managers that the core resource can be exploited or further developed for multiple uses. Attractions are increasingly being used for film sets, weddings, festivals and other special events (Pearce, 1998). Some attractions have added accommodation and conference facilities to increase the utility of the resource. In addition, attractions are extending their opening hours, or have developed all-weather facilities that expand the use of the resource. Some attractions are open 24 hours a day. Singapore Zoo has been particularly successful with the development of night-time safaris.

7. Cooperative alliances. A broader economic trend stemming from globalization has been the merging and blending of companies with similar markets, goals or philosophies. When compared with the hospitality and transport sectors, tourist attractions have undergone very little corporatization. In the short to medium term, alliances and cooperative arrangements between attractions and other players in the tourism industry may be a more common form of collaboration. The concentration of attractions into corporate holdings or alliances would suggest a rapidly changing environment in which attractions will need to pool resources to counter their competitors. This trend may manifest itself in the clustering of attractions, or the sharing of market intelligence and marketing initiatives (Pearce, 1998). An extension of this trend is the emergence of single-entry tickets for clusters of attractions.

Conclusion

The next twenty years will see remarkable changes in the nature of the tourist attraction sector. The term 'attractions' will encompass a much wider array of facilities offering multifaceted leisure and entertainment opportunities. Successful attractions will require new forms of management and organizational configurations to deal with an increasingly sophisticated marketplace.

23

Culture, heritage and visiting attractions

Bob McKercher and Hilary du Cros

Introduction

While people have always travelled to learn about different cultures, cultural tourism has been recognized as a distinct product category only since the mid-1980s. Today it is arguably the most popular form of special interest tourism, yet at the same time it finds itself at a crossroads. Cultural tourism remains a little understood phenomenon, driven by hyperbole and hope. Moreover, a number of tourism and other economic development pressures pose real threats to its asset base. This chapter reviews the current state of cultural tourism and identifies emerging issues that will affect its future development.

A definition of cultural tourism

A working definition of cultural tourism is:

A form of tourism that relies on a destination's cultural heritage assets and transforms them into products that can be consumed by tourists.

That cultural tourism is a form of tourism should be self-evident, for the adjective 'cultural' qualifies the noun 'tourism'. Yet some stakeholders see it as a form of cultural heritage management that can be used to achieve different objectives. Such confusion leads to misunderstandings, poor decisions to pursue tourism and a heightened risk of failed products. A community's, region's or nation's cultural heritage assets form its foundation, setting it apart from other forms of tourism. Heritage includes both tangible and intangible assets. Existing structures, modified facilities and purpose-built attractions are examples of tangible assets. Their scale can range from a single building to entire cities and, arguably, countries. Intangible assets include traditions, customs, stories and manifestations of past and continuing cultural practices and collective knowledge.

Tourist consumption occurs as a result of the transformation of these assets into products, either through their physical modification to cater to visitors or their promotion by the tourism industry (with or without modifications). Most tourists are usually short-term visitors, travelling mostly for recreation, whose knowledge of the destination is often limited. Consequently, they seek products that are easy and non-threatening to consume, even though the underlying experience may be challenging.

There are three types of consumption. Passive consumption occurs when tourists visit and observe, but do not interact – as in the case of photographing historic streetscapes. Active consumption of activities or experiences strongly associated with the intangible values of the asset occurs when they visit museums, art galleries and theme parks, or when they see live performances. Active consumption of experiences, not normally associated with the intangible cultural values of the asset, can occur through, for example, dining in restaurants and nightclubs located in renovated historic buildings.

Cultural tourism today

Many parallels exist between the growth of cultural tourism in the 1990s and that of ecotourism some ten to fifteen years earlier. Many lessons can therefore be learned from the ecotourism experience about managing assets, phantom demand, and myths about 'new' types of tourists seeking 'new' types of meaningful experiences.

Integrating cultural heritage management and tourism

Tourism and cultural heritage management (CHM) represent discrete sets of stakeholders with specific roles to play in the sustainable development of this sector, as summarized in Table 23.1. Tourism has assumed the role of product transformer and developer, marketer and guide. The CHM sector, on the other hand, owns and manages the assets and must deal with the impacts of visitation. Each has traditionally performed its job in isolation from the other, with little overlap or interaction, often resulting in conflict.

Most people in tourism understand little about cultural heritage management. This sector includes tradition bearers, custodians, the local community, heritage

212

Table 23.1 Comparing cultural heritage management and tourism

	Cultural heritage management	Tourism
Structure	■ Public sector oriented ■ Not for profit	■ Private sector oriented ■ Profit making
Goals	■ Broader social goal	■ Commercial goals
Key stakeholders	■ Community groups ■ Heritage groups ■ Minority/ethnic/indigenous groups ■ Local residents	■ Business groups ■ Non-local residents
Economic Attitude to assets	■ Existence value ■ Conserve for their intrinsic values	■ Use value ■ Consume for their extrinsic appeal
Key user groups	■ Local residents ■ Often school children	■ Non-local residents
Background of professionals working in the sector	■ Social science ■ Arts degrees	■ Business/marketing degrees
Use of asset	■ Value to community as a representation of tangible and intangible heritage	■ Value to tourist as product or activity that can help brand a destination
International political bodies/ NGOs	■ ICOMOS/ICOM/ UNESCO – promote conservation of culture	■ WTO/WTTC – promote development of tourism
National NGOs	■ National Trusts/Heritage Trusts/indigenous and ethnic organizations	■ Tourism trade associations/ tourism industry bodies
National/regional political/ bureaucratic bodies	■ National, state and local agencies and some museums concerned with heritage management, archives	■ National, state and regional tourism bodies tasked with product development, promotion and maximizing returns from tourism
Stakeholders	■ National organizations for heritage professionals/ local historical groups/ religious leaders	■ National tourism trade associations, other industry bodies

Source: McKercher and du Cros, 2002

professionals, cultural heritage managers and public sector heritage agencies. It traces its roots to the early 1800s' heritage preservationist movements, triggered by a (re)discovery of the value of culture and an ensuing growing political interest. Today, its main goal is conserving a representative sample of our diverse tangible and intangible heritage for future generations, in recognition of the speed at which the world is changing.

Cultural heritage management is a structured process guided by a series of international charters, declarations and conventions created by the following organizations:

1. ICOMOS – International Council on Monuments and Sites
2. UNESCO – United Nations Educational, Scientific and Cultural Organization
3. ICCROM – International Centre for the Study of the Preservation and Restoration of Cultural Property
4. ICOM – International Council of Museums.

These instruments focus on issues pertaining to the limits of permissible change to fabric and settings, and their relationship and meanings to local communities. Tourism use is emerging as a key issue, for it can overwhelm assets or place pressure on owners/managers to modify them in such a way that their cultural context is damaged. Moreover, excessive tourism use can stress assets beyond their abilities to absorb change. The WTO *Global Code of Ethics for Tourism, 1997* and the ICOMOS *Cultural Tourism Charter, 1999* call for tourism to work closely with others in the community to protect and preserve natural and cultural heritage assets to ensure a sustainable future for both (see Case study 23.1). Both organizations are currently working together on a manual to mitigate the impacts of congestion at heritage assets.

Better understanding of the market

Much of the early work on the cultural tourism market focused on quantifying participation rates without any acknowledgement that differences existed between cultural tourists. As a result, some fantastic figures were promulgated about the size

Case study 23.1 Partnerships: Rivers of Steel, NHA, Pennsylvania, USA

Through the efforts of local communities, the United States Congress and National Parks Service, 23 National Heritage Areas (NHAs) have been established. This designation requires collaborative partnerships for development, tourism marketing and heritage conservation. The Rivers of Steel National Heritage Area (ROSHA) in Pennsylvania focuses on heritage assets connected to steel manufacturing and related industries. It aims to revive the region's post-industrial economy by promoting tourism and economic development based on its historic industrial heritage. The development of the new Homestead Works National Park, comprising the Carrie Furnaces (the last of the giant blast furnaces from the Homestead Works) and the Pump House (site of the violent 1892 Homestead Steel Strike), is one of its initiatives.

Since 1996, ROSHA has received over $3.9 million in National Heritage Area funds and leveraged more than $23.5 million in other public or private funding. With the creation of the new Park, the Heritage Area is expected to attract 840 000 visitors annually and to generate revenue of nearly $60 million per year.

(For more information see: http://www.riversofsteel.com/default.aspx – Rivers of Steel Heritage Area (ROSHA), (2004) National Heritage Area, Pennsylvania, USA)

of the market and the importance of culture in the overall travel decision-making process (McKercher and du Cros, 2002).

A more realistic understanding is now emerging. Richards (1996a) cautions that not all tourists visiting cultural attractions can automatically be classified as cultural tourists, while he (1996b), Silberberg (1995) and a study in Pennsylvania (DKS, 1999) showed differences based on the importance of cultural heritage as a trip motivator. Others also began to recognize that tourists visiting the same attraction could have quite different experiences (Timothy, 1997; Kerstetter *et al.*, 1998; McIntosh and Prentice, 1999).

McKercher and du Cros (2002) combined the two dimensions of importance of cultural heritage as a trip purpose (centrality) and depth of experience, to categorize cultural tourists into five groups:

1. Purposeful cultural tourists (high motivation/deep experience)
2. Sightseeing cultural tourists (high motivation/shallow experience)
3. Casual cultural tourists (modest motivation/shallow experience)
4. Incidental cultural tourists (low motivation/shallow experience)
5. Serendipitous cultural tourists (low motivation/deep experience).

Purposeful cultural tourists represent only a small portion of the total cultural tourism market (about 10 per cent of cultural tourists), and they seek quite different experiences to other cultural tourists. They travel to learn about cultural heritage, and seek out museums, art galleries and out-of-the-way attractions. The majority, on the other hand, fall into the casual and incidental cultural tourist segments. They travel for fun and recreation, and visit cultural attractions for their recreational values as one of the many activities they pursue.

Pressures and impacts

Likewise, the understanding of impacts is also becoming more sophisticated. While overuse remains an issue, under-use and inappropriate use are also recognized as threats. Under-use occurs when significant investment has been made to develop attractions, but few people visit (see Case study 23.2). Low visitation results in low revenue for ongoing conservation and interpretation work and, more importantly, may produce diminished local support for maintaining attractions if ongoing public sector funding is required to keep them operational. Adverse impacts can also be noted when visitors engage in inappropriate activities. These activities range from littering or taking photographs when asked not to do so, to more significant impacts such as scratching or souveniring artefacts from ancient sites or showing little respect for local cultures and traditions.

Product assessment and commodification

Overuse, under-use and misuse are symptomatic of deeper planning and management issues that can be traced back to a poor decision to pursue tourism. There is a naïve belief that any locally significant historical or cultural asset can be a tourist attraction, when in fact only a few possess the necessary attributes. Consequently, a framework for assessing tourism potential needs to be applied more stringently.

Case study 23.2 A failed cultural tourism attraction – the Murray River paddle steamer, Australia

Community support for heritage was especially strong leading up to the Australian bicentennial in 1988. Residents of the regional centre of Albury, Australia, caught the spirit and built a replica of a Murray River paddle steamer as a community-based project, in the hope that it would become a major tourist attraction afterwards. The boat is authentic in nearly every detail. However, it has failed as a tourist attraction. Ultimately the local city council assumed ownership, and since then has had to provide an ongoing subsidy to keep it operational.

Why did it fail? There are many reasons. First, it appears that neither a business plan nor a marketing strategy was undertaken to see if such a project was viable. Second, the ship is too authentic, necessitating high maintenance and running costs. Third, seasonality was not considered – instead of operating year-round, the effective operating season is less than six months. All in all, the paddle steamer is a fine heritage asset but does not work well as a tourism product.

(For more details, see McKercher, 2001.)

One approach is to consider market appeal and robusticity. Market appeal examines how much interest tourists have in visiting, by considering such features as uniqueness, accessibility, and the ability to retain tourists for extended periods. Robusticity examines the asset's ability to cope with increased visitation by examining the physical state of repair, the potential to harden the site and, importantly, whether traditional users and the local community want to and will be affected by increased visitation. Four outcomes, with different management options, emerge from this framework:

1. High market appeal/high robusticity
2. High market appeal/low robusticity
3. Moderate market appeal/moderate robusticity
4. Low market appeal.

Where the tourism potential is high and the asset is robust, tourism can take a leading role in management. Cultural heritage management considerations must dominate fragile assets, regardless of their tourism potential. Likewise, tourism should not be pursued if market appeal is low. Where some market appeal exists and the asset is moderately to highly robust, opportunities exist for a more equal relationship between tourism and cultural heritage management objectives.

Future trends for cultural heritage and attractions

A number of issues will affect the development of cultural attractions in the next decade, including:

- broadening of the market
- greater breadth of products

- interpretation
- congestion.

Broadening of the market

The market will continue to grow, with growth occurring mostly in the casual and incidental segments. Jones and Robinett (1998) caution their theme park clients not to become too serious about the cultural message, or the parks can cease to be fun. Managers and asset owners of museums, art galleries and historic sites will also need to shape their experiences around the needs of pleasure visitors, but must always be mindful of their strong moral imperative to ensure that presentation is accurate and culturally sympathetic.

Asia in general, and China in particular, will emerge as the single greatest source of international tourists within the next ten years. As a result, the traditional Eurocentric approach to cultural tourism will need to change. Additionally, these tourists will have different needs, as, aside from language, many will have limited international travel experience. Existing products will have to be modified and new products developed specifically for these consumers. In addition, different signage and more culturally sensitive food and beverage outlets will also be required.

Greater breadth of products

The range of products will continue to expand, with demand for intangible heritage seeing particular growth (see Case study 23.3). Intangible heritage is typically presented through festivals and events, or by joining specialty tours that provide some form of controlled interaction with local residents. However, as the desire to have new and more authentic experiences increases, minority cultures, especially in developing destinations, may find they have become tourism commodities, often without the consent or full participation of the affected community. One solution is to remove the intangible asset from its context to showcase it in cultural theme parks and performances. However, doing so can alter its cultural values for the producer/custodians by turning heritage into performance, and at the same time reducing the sense of authenticity for the tourist.

A series of new niche products will also emerge, especially among the purposeful segment. Thanatourism (penal colonies, massacre and war sites etc.) and dark tourism (slavery sites) are now emerging, with much heavier themes at their base. While numbers remain small, few problems will arise. However, as their popularity increases, the risk to capitalize on market opportunities may result in their message being compromised for the sake of ease of consumption. The message cannot be compromised for the less involved casual and incidental segments; instead, they must be made aware at some point in their decision-making process that the visit will challenge their preconceptions about human nature and history. Sacred sites also need special care with marketing and interpretation (Shackley, 2001b). Attractions that do not do this well show little respect for the cultural value of the asset, and miss an opportunity to raise the awareness of tourists without alienating other visitors.

Case study 23.3 Intangible heritage – Arita/Imari potteries, Japan

Intangible heritage is often difficult to commodify and conserve. One excellent example is that of the potters who produce Arita/Imari porcelain in Japan. The communities of Arita and Imari on Kyushu Island are listed as nationally significant, and several of the Arita potters are rated as National Treasures under Japan's intangible heritage legislation. Although legislation does not necessarily bring greater protection or invigoration of intangible heritage, it does provide a basis for more general recognition of the role of special individuals as 'transmitters of traditions'. The areas' surrounding natural landscape of forested hills and quiet ambience is reflected in the artistic style of Arita/Imari porcelain.

At peak times the Arita and Imari townships attract around 700 000 tourists, mostly from Japan. Facilities and infrastructure are unobtrusive. Parking is limited to residents only, and accommodation is provided outside the townships. The townships' artistic heritage is reflected even in small things, such as site plans that are made of locally manufactured tiles. The heritage asset has retained its place in Japan's art history, and is dynamic enough to train and provide work for potters and other community members while satisfying the needs of the tourism sector.

(For more information, see *UNESCO managing living human treasures*, available at www.unesco.org/culture/heritage/intangible/treasures/html_eng/method.htm.)

Interpretation

The presentation of culture for tourist consumption will also face additional challenges. Technology developments provide new and exciting opportunities for presenting materials. Already, some commercial firms have begun to offer guided tours using Bluetooth technology. Visitors turn on their mobile phones, and as soon as they walk past a concealed transponder (inside or outside structures) their number is dialled automatically and a message about the site feature is sent. This technology is still in its infancy, but it heralds an emerging trend of on-demand information. Reconstructions and virtual reality technology also present new ways of presenting aspects of heritage assets.

Technology heightens the role of information gatekeepers in providing the link between the tourist and the experience. The gatekeeper role usually falls to the tour guide, whose main criterion for employment is a valid bus driver's licence. Most are self-taught, and often have limited knowledge about the cultural significance and values of the attraction being visited. Attraction managers and the cultural heritage community must take a more dominant role in information provision before, during and after visits.

Congestion

Congestion and uneven demand pressures will continue to affect this sector. Peak periods strain resources, while troughs can limit income and employment opportunities. Some attractions will need to engage in de-marketing to transfer demand to shoulder seasons. Destinations as a whole will also need to adopt strategies to shift demand from over-utilized to under-utilized attractions through the creation of heritage trails, bundling, and the promotion of a wider variety of attractions.

Conclusions: the future of cultural heritage attractions

What does the future hold for cultural heritage attractions? Decisions made in the next few years will determine whether cultural and heritage tourism will achieve its potential to be economically, culturally and socially sustainable, or if it will go down an unsustainable path providing benefits for some, at great costs to others. The following issues will determine which path it follows:

- resolving difficulties between tourism and cultural heritage stakeholders
- developing workable intangible heritage protocols and policies, and implementing them
- creating new and innovative strategies to manage tangible heritage
- recognizing and catering to the needs of emerging markets, including China
- undertaking realistic assessments of the potential of attractions, especially in rural and remote communities that have little else to offer
- adopting holistic destination management policies to shift demand from over-used to under-used attractions.

The resolution of these issues is the responsibility of all stakeholders involved in cultural tourism, including asset managers, the tourism industry and the tourists themselves. Each of these has a strong social and moral contribution to make to ensure that our valuable cultural heritage assets are conserved for future generations.

24

Entertainment and new leisure tourism

Melanie Smith

Introduction

People are increasingly living in 'money rich, time poor' societies in many Western developed countries; therefore their leisure time is becoming more and more precious. The need for escapism from a long-hours working culture has stimulated the demand for new forms of entertainment and recreation. People are apparently undertaking more leisure activities than ever, but they tend to be of a shorter duration. A lifestyle of leisure has been created, where time is sacrosanct but affluence is growing. Contrary to predictions that leisure time would increasingly take place within the home, it seems that new leisure consumers are more interested in going out than staying in. It also appears that there has been a noticeable rise in the number of holidays being taken within contemporary leisure time. According to a report by Tyrell and Mai (2001), experiences and memories now mean more to contemporary consumers than products.

This chapter will focus on a growing sector of new leisure tourists. This is a relatively young breed of tourist, who is seeking escapism, entertainment and fun. Time may be limited, but disposable income levels are high. Relative levels of comfort and security are sought, but a thrill-seeking disposition may motivate the tourist to look for diverse, often fantastical experiences. This may include visiting themed attractions, adventure lands, cyberworlds or simulated destinations.

What is new leisure tourism?

The breakdown of tourism, leisure and everyday life

Many people, especially in Western societies, are now living in the era of what post-modernists have called 'de-differentiation', or the breaking down of boundaries between previously distinct activities. As stated by McCabe (2002), the boundaries between tourism, leisure and recreation are becoming more difficult to define; thus tourism increasingly represents a microcosm of everyday life. Many tourists are actively engaging in the kinds of activity that they could quite feasibly do at home (e.g. shopping for global brands, eating international fast food, watching sport on satellite TV). Media pervade some people's lives to the point that they watch their favourite soap opera or football team play while they are in beach bars abroad. Work and leisure are scarcely differentiated as tourists increasingly check e-mails, carry around laptops, and are glued to the ubiquitous mobile phone whilst on holiday!

A recent debate in Britain run by the *Guardian* newspaper questioned whatever happened to the dream of the leisure age. Many people have become complicit in a 'willing slave' culture of overwork and they are burning out. Tyrell and Mai (2001) similarly note that the concept of a 'leisure society' is something of a misnomer at a time when leisure time is more limited than ever before! However, people seem to be taking more and more holidays to compensate, averaging two breaks per year, with over a million Britons taking at least five holidays in 2004 (*Guardian*, 2004). It seems that escapism through tourism is big business.

New leisure and tourism experiences

Several authors have suggested that post-tourists or new leisure tourists want to engage in more fantastical experiences that surpass anything they could find at home. They are seeking the 'hyper-real' (Eco, 1986), 'extra-authenticity' (Boniface and Fowler, 1993) or sites of 'fake authenticity' (AlSayyad, 2001). These might include theme parks, adventurelands, simulated destinations, themed attractions, and giant leisure and retail complexes.

In many ways, such attractions can be viewed as more sophisticated variations on the leisure activities popular with the typical mass seaside tourist (e.g. pleasure beaches, amusement arcades, end of the pier shows, illuminations). In most cases consumers have become more discerning in their tastes, expectations are higher and the provision of good quality entertainment venues has surpassed anything a struggling seaside resort could provide.

New leisure tourists are often seeking to visit landscapes that correspond to Barber's (1995) concept of 'McWorld', where a number of familiar global brands are clustered under one roof. These could be viewed negatively for being standardized and placeless (i.e. they could be anywhere in the world and are not specific or unique to one place). After all, if everywhere starts to look the same, then the question might quite reasonably be asked, 'why travel?' However, many destinations offer themed attractions which combine global brands with unique features, such as special rides, simulated environments, and micro-destinations. They are all very different from one another, and are branded accordingly. Nevertheless, the fact remains that they could often be placed anywhere, regardless of geographical and cultural context. However, visitors will go there because they are 'one of a kind' in the world, or they are the biggest and best of their kind.

New leisure and tourism attractions

Rojek (1993) identifies four kinds of tourism and leisure attractions that feature in the landscape of postmodernism. These are:

1. Theme parks
2. Literary landscapes
3. Blackspots
4. Heritage sites.

Such attractions would be of interest to the new leisure tourist – especially theme parks, with their increasing technological sophistication and diversity. Theme parks, particularly Disney parks, are viewed as safe, secure and dependable. New leisure tourists are arguably not particularly adventurous, and expect certain levels of comfort and security when they travel. However, within this framework they are then apt to thrill-seek. Rojek (1993) refers to the 'thrill factor' provided by fast rides, and the way in which time and space are dissolved in a diversity of spectacles and experiences.

Literary, film and television landscapes offer a unique blend of reality and fiction. Many tourists are keen to follow in the footsteps of their favourite soap stars, actors or literary characters. The media-driven obsession with the cult of the celebrity has also fuelled a desire to emulate famous people and to simulate their glamorous lifestyles (e.g. the television series *Footballers' Wives* and *Sex and the City*). This is coupled with a growing interest in 'real life' issues. For example, visits to recent 'blackspots' or sites of atrocity (e.g. Ground Zero in New York) afford tourists an experience which allows them to watch history in the making, like an extension of 24-hour news.

Many heritage sites offer a somewhat sanitized or glamourized version of history, which focuses on entertainment rather than education. This may include 'living history' – for example, where actors dress up and act as key figures from the past. Such developments can (and have) been heavily criticized. However, these are the kinds of attractions increasingly favoured by the new leisure tourist, who is not seeking genuine cultural interaction or authenticity but merely wants to be diverted and entertained. Museums have also been criticized for becoming more and more like theme parks, as they have often been forced by economic imperatives to offer consumers a more entertaining experience that competes with other leisure attractions.

Who are the new leisure tourists?

Urry (2002) suggests that people seek to experience in reality the pleasurable dramas they have already experienced in their imagination. He goes on to argue that reality rarely lives up to expectations, and that consumers therefore become insatiable in their quest for novelty. Similarly, Sarup (1996: 128) states that 'under postmodern conditions, there is the exhilarating experience of ever new needs rather than the satisfaction of the still-existing ones'. The new leisure tourist consequently seems to have a rather short attention span. Tyrell and Mai (2001) note that consumers are actually engaging in more leisure activities than ever before, despite a time deficit, but these activities are inevitably of a shorter duration. Urry (2002: 83) refers to the concept of a 'three minute culture', which is characteristic of the media and its televisual influence, and Bayles (1999) describes life as 'channel zapping'. New leisure tourists arguably need constant, changing stimulation in order to hold their attention. This might include bigger and faster theme park rides or more realistic simulations in cyberspace, virtual reality and technological interaction. It might involve a more diverse choice of retail outlets or activities within shopping and leisure complexes. In short, the new leisure tourist is a restless thrill-seeker who is constantly hankering after the next sugar rush, be it a new ride, a new purchase, a casino flutter, or an extra large Coca-cola!

Tyrell and Mai (2001) describe the new leisure age as one in which the individual is king and independence is valued highly. Therefore, even family holidays are taken in an environment where the family can arrive together but individuals can do their own thing on arrival. They cite the Center Parcs concept as an example of this phenomenon.

Table 24.1 sets out and compares some of the characteristics of the new leisure tourist. Whereas cultural tourists tend to be well-educated, earnest seekers of 'authentic' culture and communities, post-tourists tend to enjoy more playful tourism and leisure experiences (Smith, 2003b). New leisure tourists take this a stage further, often engaging in fantastical experiences that are far removed from reality.

It can be seen from Table 24.1 that the new leisure tourist differs significantly from the cultural tourist. There is no pretension to being interested in local societies and cultures – in fact, many of the environments visited are simulated (i.e. they are representations of real or imagined places and contain no local people). New leisure tourists are escapist, and will generally try to leave work behind whilst on holiday (although they may not be able to resist checking e-mails and answering the mobile phone). However, the pursuits engaged in may well be little more than an extension of the technology- and media-fuelled activities of home. As mentioned previously, the new leisure tourist is easily bored and needs constant stimulation, fun and entertainment. Some activities may be sociable and involve friends or families (e.g. shopping, sport, theme parks), but in many cases the new leisure tourist is keener to interact with simulated worlds and experiences than with real people. Representations are preferred to reality. Therefore, the new leisure tourist may enjoy visiting a model village or destination to a real one. Not only does it save time, but it also affords a more sanitized, comfortable or glamourized experience than any real place. For example, many theme parks seem to simulate environments like Egypt's Valley of the Kings, an Arabic souk or the jungles of Africa, and offer 'safe' interactive experiences there.

Table 24.1 Characteristics of the new leisure tourist

Cultural tourist	Post-tourist	New leisure tourist
Keen on notion of travel and personal displacement	Enjoys simulated experiences, often in the home	Keen to escape from home and overwork culture
Actively seeking difference	Little differentiation between tourism, leisure and lifestyle	Seeking experiences more 'fantastical' than at home
Seeking objective authenticity in cultural experiences	Acceptance that there is no true authentic experience	Looking for 'extra' or 'fake' authenticity
Concerned with existential authenticity and enhancement of self	Treats the commodification of the tourist experience playfully	Wants to forget about self and be entertained and have fun
Earnest interaction with destinations and inhabitants	Ironic detachment from experiences and situations	Likes interactive experiences, but of a technological nature
May have idealized expectations of places and people	Little interest in differentiating between reality and fantasy	Aware that what they experience is not 'real', and little interest in local people
Interested in 'real' experiences	Interested in 'hyper-real' experiences	Actively travelling in 'hyper-reality'
Disdain for representations and simulations	Acceptance of representations and simulations	Loves representations and simulations

Table 24.2 Typical profile of a new leisure tourist

- Relatively young (15–45 years, but the influence of children is also significant)
- High disposable income
- Individualistic/independent
- Escapist on holiday but work-obsessed at home
- Enjoys luxury, comfort, security
- A thrill-seeker but in a controlled environment
- Compulsive consumer
- Short attention span
- Interested in new technology and media
- Fascinated by cult of celebrity

Of course, tourist profiles are never fixed or static, and people may choose to be a cultural tourist at one time and a new leisure tourist at another. For example, single people and childless couples may be more likely to pursue cultural activities than families with young children or teenagers, who often seek out new leisure attractions. At certain points in time, people might prefer to seek escapism, entertainment and fun than education (e.g. when life and work have become particularly stressful). Thus new leisure tourism is life-stage and mood driven, and typologies can only indicate collective trends rather than individual preferences and proclivities. However, as a generalization, the profile of a new leisure tourist often has the characteristics described in Table 24.2.

Tyrell and Mai (2001) suggest that there is a current expansion of the leisure market away from the typical consumer age range of 15–44 towards an older age group of 45–64. This group is increasingly affluent with fewer time constraints. Whereas the last 40 years appear to have been dominated by the influence of youth culture, the future looks set to change. However, it could still be argued that the new leisure tourist market as described in this chapter tends to be dominated by younger consumers. The influence of children on their parents' choice of tourism and leisure activities is also very significant.

Where do new leisure tourists go?

Soja (1989) describes postmodern cities like Los Angeles as being a place where all places are (i.e. they contain many of the world's major cultures and communities). It is therefore not surprising that many new leisure tourists head for cities to enjoy the diversity on offer. In a cosmopolitan environment they can take the best of international cuisine, fashion and shopping opportunities, often in so-called 'mega-locations'. They may visit themed spaces, which conveniently cluster leisure attractions together. For example, Edensor (2001) describes the way in which tourist space has become increasingly themed, especially in areas like Leicester Square/Piccadilly Circus in London, where the everyday and the extraordinary are mixed in attractions like Rock Circus, Sega World, Planet Hollywood and the Fashion Café.

Howard Schultz, the founder of Starbucks, popularized the concept of the 'Third Place'. Home is seen as the 'First Place' and work as the 'Second Place'. The Third Place becomes a location for interaction, blending commerce, community, relaxation, ethics and hedonism (Tyrell and Mai, 2001). Starbucks coffee shops were designed with this principle in mind, and it is not difficult to see how this has been extended to shopping malls, leisure centres and theme parks. The Third Place is comfortable, convenient and safe, but it also offers the excitement of consumption, entertainment and interaction, and can be a place of fantasy and self-discovery. For example, Sarup (1996) refers to the shopping mall as an alternative life-world in which people can create different selves or identities.

There are, of course, whole new leisure destinations in the form of theme parks or themed attractions (e.g. Las Vegas or Santa Claus Land – see Case study 24.1). The majority of theme parks seem to combine a number of fast rides with simulated, interactive environments, as well as multicultural shows. Examples include the well-known Disney theme parks in the USA and France, Port Aventura and Terra Mitica in Spain, and Gardaland in Italy. Some theme parks are based on fairy tales (e.g. Efteling in the Netherlands), on specific fictional characters (e.g. Parc Asterix in France), or on well-known celebrities (e.g. Dolly Parton's 'Dollywood' theme park in the USA). Water parks such as the 'Wet n' Wild' chain in the USA, Brazil and Mexico are becoming more popular. Some parks are based on media and film, such as Universal Studios in Florida and Japan, and Movie World in Spain, or include simulations of space visits – for example, the Kennedy Space Center in Florida, and Futuroscope in France.

It is also interesting to consider other new leisure destinations, currently emerging, which would not be categorized as either theme parks or themed attractions. Case study 24.2 gives an example of one of the newest and most fascinating new leisure destinations in the world.

Case study 24.1 Santa Claus Land, Finland

The figure of Santa Claus is one that attracts numerous international tourists, and
not only at Christmas. Rovaniemi in Finland is perhaps the most famous destination for Santa Claus fans, as it is home to Santa's Workshop, Santa's Village
and Santa Park, where children can attend Elf School and go on sleigh rides, as
well as meeting Santa Claus himself. In 2001, the Chinese developed a second
Santa Claus Theme Park in Jilin province during China's International Snow and
Ice Festival, claiming it was 'the second hometown of Santa Claus after Finland'.
Better known still, perhaps, is the Santa Claus Land Theme Park in Indiana,
USA, where Christmas is celebrated all year round. Santa Claus attractions are
typical of new leisure tourism as they focus on a fictional character, but one who
seems real enough in the minds of visitors to warrant an 'authentic' context in
which to live and be visited!

(http://www.santaslandnc.com/
http://www.santapark.com/)

Case study 24.2 Dubai: a fantastical new leisure destination

Mitropolitski (2004) states that 'It's no exaggeration when Dubai is often compared to Disney World or Las Vegas'. The architecture of Dubai could be described
as fantastical and unique. The famous Burj Al Arab 'seven star' hotel is shaped
like a sailing boat, for example. The hotels are some of the most luxurious in the
world, appealing to the new leisure tourists' desire for comfort and quality service. Restaurants offer the best of international cuisine, the most famous of
which seems to be the underwater fish restaurant in the Burj hotel. Most of
Dubai's leisure consumption takes place within sumptuous shopping malls.
Theme parks such as the Wild Wadi Water Park have been developed within hotel
complexes. However, the future projects planned for Dubai are even more spectacular. These include:

- Dubailand – incorporating Adventure World, Aqua World, Snow World, Space
  and Science World, Vacation World, Shopping World, Family City World, Mid-
  Ages World, and a space hotel.
- Palm Island – a man-made island complex currently under construction near
  Dubai's coast. It is envisaged that a second development called World will
  aim to create a map of the world out of 223 man-made islands. Both devel-
  opments will be visible from space.
- The Hydropolis Hotel – an undersea hotel.
- The world's largest indoor ski slope – to be built in the desert!

(http://www.uae-pages.com/tourism/why-dubai.html
http://www.dubaicityguide.com/tourism/attractions.asp)

New leisure tourism: future perspectives

It is clear that new leisure tourism is dominated by consumers who are short of time but keen to engage in as many activities as possible in order to maximize their precious leisure experiences. Their high disposable incomes allow them to take more and more holidays, and to be more discerning and demanding in their tastes. Consequently, the desire for comfort, luxury and quality of service is paramount, but so too is the need for escapism, entertainment and fun. New leisure consumers are clearly keen to leave home and the demands of work behind, but destinations are required to become more and more sophisticated and exciting in order to attract them. Therefore fantastical tourism projects are being developed as a means of differentiating and branding destinations in a competitive marketplace. Future new leisure tourists are likely to be older, with even more time and money on their hands. As everyone becomes more technologically literate and media-orientated, it will be interesting to see how the attractions sector responds. Given that many natural and cultural destinations are being destroyed by the impacts of tourism, new leisure destinations in the form of simulated environments may also offer the most sustainable form of tourism development in the future!

25

Destination management organizations and actors

Mara Manente and
Valeria Minghetti

Introduction

In the last two decades, the steady development of tourism from both the demand and the supply sides has brought to light the issue of destination management. As stated by Gunn (1988b: 11):

> tourism distributes markets to products (travel destinations) rather than the opposite ... This difference means that the product areas, the places to which we travel, are more difficult to plan, design and manage.

The growth of tourist flows and the differentiation of tourists' motivations and requirements on the one hand, and the creation and organization of supply to meet customers' expectations and specific market segments on the other, have a heavy impact on the evolution of the destination and then on the local environment as a whole. The main problems here are first, matching the preservation of natural and cultural resources (and the community identity) with their tourist use; and secondly, building a consensus among different stakeholders, who usually have diverging interests and goals, in order to coordinate their actions.

Given these elements, destination marketing and management represent key strategies for both mature and emerging destinations, in order to satisfy an ever-demanding consumer, ensure sustainable development and positive impacts, and then gain, hold or win back a strong position on the global tourism market.

Understanding this approach and the opportunities it offers becomes a priority for public/private organizations and tourism suppliers at national, regional and community levels. However, in spite of the popularity that these concepts and tools are currently enjoying in academic circles, their diffusion, understanding and use among tourism operators is still low, if compared to the benefits they can bring to each business and to the destination as a whole.

Tourism organizations and, above all, SMEs are not completely aware of their role in the creation and management of local supply, of their influence on the destination image and then on the customer's experience. In addition, they are not conscious of being a system or of the importance their interactions have in organizing the product and then determining the destination competitiveness on the market (Manente and Cerato, 2000). This chapter provides a contribution to this field, discussing the main issues emerging from defining the destination as a system.

Defining destination, destination management and destination marketing

Approaching the topic of destination management and marketing requires, first of all, a definition of the concept of destination. According to *Webster's Dictionary*, the term 'destination' is used to denote 'the place set for the end of a journey' – i.e. a geographical area (a location, a resort, a region, a country, etc.) where the traveller intends to spend time away from home.

For economic and marketing sciences, a tourist destination is more than a mere geographical place. It is an amalgamation of products, services, natural resources, artificial elements and information that is able to attract a number of visitors into a place (Leiper, 1995; Bieger, 1998). As stated by Keller (2000):

> tourists perceive a destination or the service offered in the context of a destination, as a whole. The package of services is often impossible to separate from the geographical place. Destination and product are thus identical.

The shift of focus from the destination as a 'tourist place' to the destination as a 'tourism product' or, better, as a system of products, depends on the perceptions of the stakeholders directly and indirectly involved. Actual and potential tourists, public administration, local private tourism activities, non-local tourism activities and the host community usually have diverging objectives and needs.

From the point of view of tourism demand, tourists can have different ideas of the destination and of the benefits they can receive, according to their culture, system of values and socio-economic status. The assembling of different tourism components is made according to tourists' preferences, motivations and expectations (Gunn, 1988b; Hu and Ritchie, 1993). Consequently, a tourist destination can be defined as a collection of experiences gained by the traveller' (Gunn, 1972: 11). It can be seen as a packaging of products and services partly created by public and private operators. The core is not the single attraction in itself, but a combination of factors made through the tourist's consumption experience (Leiper, 1990b). The overall travel experience to a destination also involves the activity of many tourism businesses, public organizations, intermediaries etc., and the development of actions and programmes directed toward specific functions.

From the supply side, the destination can be defined according to two different perspectives:

1. As a tourist place, i.e. a place where tourist activities have been developed and then tourist products are produced and consumed
2. As a tourist product and then as a specific supply involving a set of resources, activities and actors of a territory as well as the local community.

All these issues lead to the conclusion that the 'destination' is a fuzzy concept that cannot be defined *a priori* once and for all. This is why the understanding of a tourist destination and then the analysis, planning, management and control of the destination development do require a systematic and interdisciplinary approach.

In this context, destination management and destination marketing are two distinct but interrelated concepts. Destination management implies both governmental/decisional and functional competences (planning, organization and control of business activities), which should be generally performed by the public sector. The main objective is to manage and support the integration of different resources, activities and stakeholders through suitable policies and actions. This can create a unique system of tourism products that meets the needs of different categories of clients and ensures sustainable growth, combining private profit and general economic development with the preservation of the host community's identity and quality of life (Manente and Cerato, 2000). This concept is broader than that of destination marketing, which is concerned with the overall promotion of destination image and the distribution of local tourism products (Dolnicar and Mazanec, 1998; Keller, 2000).

Understanding the destination as a system

The presence of a wide range of stakeholders who interact with and within the resort, each one with diverging interests and different perceptions of the destination, make it very hard to plan coherent development of the destination.

The key issue is to harmonize the variety of interests/perceptions on the one hand and of tourism products on the other with the identity of the destination, in order to create an integrated system of tourism supply.

As mentioned by Laws (1995), system models, useful for understanding the destinations through a multidisciplinary approach, have been developed by Mill and Morrison (1985) and Leiper (1990b). All these contributions can be synthesized into a simpler definition of a destination system as 'a group of actors linked by mutual relationships with specific rules, where the action of each actor influences those of the others so that common objectives must be defined and attained in a co-ordinated way'.

Such a systematic approach first implies that it is important to be aware of the interactions among the destination stakeholders and of the effects that the competitive environment has on the destination system. This means analysing the positioning of destination products, the characteristics of destination resources and the destination's potential, and how these resources are developed, planned, organized and managed. The main objective is to fulfil market segments' expectations by providing specific products and experiences. Secondly, this approach requires understanding of what different stakeholders expect from the destination system outputs (Figure 25.1).

As outlined in Figure 25.1, the consumer's perception of the destination is influenced by the destination image, which derives from both the destination's identity and the local actors' marketing strategies (Gartner, 1989). In addition, the positioning of the destination in the tourist's evoked set is affected by exogenous stimuli (media, opinion leaders, word of mouth, etc.) (Um and Crompton, 1990). Tourism operators can try to drive the consumers towards a unique image, acting on their motivations, involvement, learning and attitudes. This image should be coherent with the destination's product mix, so as to appeal to different market segments. In turn, actual and potential tourists may influence the product development by searching for information, assessing different product and destination experiences, and expressing their opinions and judgements after the consumption process

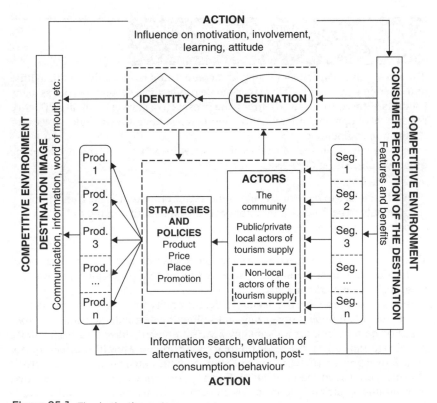

Figure 25.1 The destination system

(Um and Crompton, 1990). In the middle of this never-ending circle of images and perceptions is the destination, with its resources, the local actors (host community and public/private operators) and the other external actors (investors, tour operators, transport companies, etc.) whose strategies and policies affect the development and management of the destination product mix (Figure 25.1).

In this context, information and communications technologies (ICT) provide a driving force for cooperation at destination level and a critical tool for the development and management of the destination system (Bieger, 1997a). ICT contributes to enhance the interactions between local public/private operators, and between them and the potential customers and other external actors (e.g. tour operators), providing new tools for marketing and promotion (Keller, 2000; Pollock, 2000; World Tourism Organization, 2001b; Buhalis, 2003). Given all these elements, understanding the destination as a system requires the ability to give a strategic and operational solution to a number of issues, such as:

- targeting destination products for specific market segments
- matching the identity, image and perceptions of the destination to develop the right promotion
- identifying which actors are involved in which management strategies
- value generation by and for the destination system.

Targeting destination products for specific market segments

The rapid changes in demand, supply and competition have involved both mature and emerging destinations. There is no single product in a destination, but as many products as there are targeted current and prospective market segments. Effective product development, differentiation and management are strategic choices for destination competitiveness.

In his analysis on the re-engineering needs of Swiss destination marketing organizations, Bieger (1998) states it clearly:

> marketing has to be focused on products. Therefore tourism organizations
> have only to be funded, if they are covering an area that in the eyes of
> potential customers forms a product.

This new branding approach to destination marketing and the organization of destination resources should be applied to the whole production process and invest the whole marketing mix.

Branding implies, from the demand side, the ability to segment the market; on the supply side it implies organizing and selling the destination in specific products. Private tourism operators, mainly SMEs, frequently have insufficient skills, knowledge and budget to develop this marketing process. They have direct control of their own product (hotel, restaurant, sport activities, etc.) but not of the tourist's global experience at the destination. Furthermore, they may not be aware that their product contributes to form this global experience and thus tourists' satisfaction or dissatisfaction, with repercussions on their business. The destination positioning and branding has traditionally been managed by public tourism organizations (e.g. national or local tourist boards) who generally suffer lack of funds and do not have a direct control of final product mix. Consequently, they can only plan promotional strategies to develop image positioning and new market segments.

Due to globalization and an increasing competitive environment, a third method that is gaining consensus in many destinations is the creation of private or public–private consortia and agencies that combine the control of the product with the promotion of the destination image.

However, deciding which destination products to sell to which destination market segments requires, first of all, a market and product portfolio analysis. The former is usually (but not exclusively) carried out by local tourism organizations, while the latter should be managed both at global and business levels. Market and portfolio development should be planned, managed and controlled within and by the destination system, so as to ensure destination competitiveness.

Matching the identity, image and perceptions of the destination to develop the right promotion

Understanding the destination as a system (Figure 25.1) also implies planning accurate promotional strategies and actions. One of the main objectives of promotion should be not only to increase tourism flows and turnover, but also to differentiate the destination from those of competitors and position it in the tourist's evoked set – i.e. the set of potential destinations they consider as valid alternatives, according to their characteristics, attitudes and needs (Um and Crompton, 1990). Positioning is the most critical strategic decision for a destination, because it is central to determining visitors' perception and buying behaviour.

As stated by Gartner (1989), the traveller's final decision is based on the perceived benefit package expected from the destination experience/consumption. These expectations are the result of image formation. Thus, when judged correctly, a destination image may promote a destination in the traveller's evoked set. Destination image can be built both at the induced level and at the organic level (Gunn, 1972). At the induced level, commercial advertising, promotion, word of mouth, unsolicited messages, information searches etc. all influence the consumers' perception of the destination. At the organic level, i.e. when the consumer purchases and experiences the destination product and appraises the product attributes and benefits expected (image perception) against actual performance (identity perception), the marketer must act on the product delivery process and manage the product image in place.

In addition to the relationship between customer's perception and willingness to purchase, it is also important to analyse the destination's identity and its effects on product image. Furthermore, the contribution of each tourism supply actor to the destination image and how this contribution can be channelled towards a unique product positioning needs to be investigated. Both sides are needed in order to develop effective and efficient promotional strategies. Hence, destination product positioning and promotion must be planned and managed by and within the system, from the single product item to the whole product mix. This could be achieved through the development of accurate branding strategies, taking into account all the constraints previously discussed. Promotion must be carefully

Case study 25.1 Turin, Italy

Turin, located in northwest Italy in the Piedmont region, close to the Alps, was the first Italian capital city from 1861 to 1864, and is currently one of the most important industrial and business cities in the country. In 1998 a public–private consortium, the Turin Tourism Agency, was created in order to develop and manage tourism strategies, projects, products and promotion in Turin and its metropolitan area. The development of a detailed resource and market analysis allowed destination managers to understand the positioning of Turin in the consumers' mind and then to plan an accurate product mix. Even if the city cannot count on famous cultural attractions like, for example, Venice or Rome, it has developed a set of tourism programmes and packages targeted for specific market segments (cultural tourism, education tourism, gastronomic tours, business tourism, industrial tourism, etc.). This was done through a reorganization of local resources and the creation of new attraction opportunities (e.g. the Movie Museum, which in 2003 attracted more visitors than the Egyptian Museum – the second most important of its type in the world after that of Cairo). Turin will also host the 2006 Winter Olympiads, and many other initiatives are under way.

planned so as to match tourists' expectations with destination product features and benefits. It should be consistent with the destination identity and the destination product image for product positioning and, eventually, destination value creation. Case study 25.1 provides an example.

Identifying which actors are involved in which management strategies

Making a destination system work properly implies first identifying the complex set of public and private actors, their roles and competences. Secondly, projects must be developed around which diverging interests can be aggregated.

Regarding the first issue, public and private actors have different responsibilities and meet different costs/benefits during the 'use' of the destination. Each destination product combines goods and services produced by the market with the local natural and cultural resources that represent the reason why tourists choose this destination over competitors. The preservation of such public goods and attractions is vital for tourist activities, but the costs met to implement conservation measures are generally paid by tourists and the host community (e.g. through access fees, taxes, etc.) and only marginally by private operators, who receive the greatest economic benefits. Consequently, the public sector has a crucial role in ensuring optimal use of public tourism resources/services and a balanced sharing of costs and benefits among all the actors involved. This is critical in order to preserve the local environment, the residents' quality of life, the tourists' quality of experience, and the identity of the destination as a whole. Furthermore, the public sector must act as a 'development agent' and create the conditions to overcome all obstacles – cultural, legal and economic – to cooperation and networking. The private sector, on the other hand, should contribute to the destination

Case study 25.2 Switzerland

Switzerland is one of the most popular alpine tourism destinations in Europe. In the 1990s, the structure of tourism organizations was a hierarchical one. There were tourist organizations at national, state (Cantons), regional and local levels. At every level, some coordination work and political work was performed. At the national level, tasks were divided between the Swiss National Tourist Office (responsible for marketing strategies) and the Swiss Tourism Association (responsible for the political lobbying). At the other levels, many goal and role conflicts arose. Furthermore, all these organizations worked within political borders, while in most cases the area the tourist identifies as his or her destination is independent of such borders. This often led to inefficient coordination of the tourist product.

In 1997, an expert group formed by public and private tourism associations and the Universities of St Gallen and Bern worked out a new organizational structure that allows destinations to be managed as strategic business units by local DMOs. At national level, Switzerland Tourism (www.myswitzerland.com) is in charge of promoting and selling the country abroad. Tourism Switzerland has also created the Switzerland Destination Management Company (www.stc.ch) – the country's official holiday broker – in partnership with Swissair, the Swiss Hotel Association, Swiss Railways, Gastro-Suisse and Europcar.

preservation and development and become a 'market agent', matching demand and supply and making the tourism product available on the market.

The second issue relates to the planning of projects and initiatives around which diverging interests can be aggregated. Today, public and private operators' consensus should be achieved on market development strategies, the destination product development, branding, product promotion and distribution, taking into account the opportunities and constraints discussed above.

With this point of view, the creation process of a destination network implies a minimum degree of cooperation among local stakeholders, who should share goals regarding the growth and the development of the destination. The building of cooperation agreements even when in a competitive environment (co-opetition) is fundamental to acting efficiently (giving lower costs and increased margins) and effectively (achieving better attainment of key objectives) in the market.

The crucial question is: who acts as the catalyst of the destination network? Traditional public tourism organizations at local level are in many cases not powerful enough to coordinate action, and suffer from goal conflicts between political targets and marketing necessities. The creation of a Destination Management Organization (DMO) 'efficiently funded and provided with operational freedom to do a professional job' (Bieger, 1997b) can be the solution. Whatever the cooperation structure (association, consortium, etc.), its main functions are development planning, shaping supply, and coordination, marketing and political lobbying. A DMO is different from a Destination Management Company (DMC), which usually provides 'onsite coordination services for visiting groups' (Crouch, 2000).

Case study 25.2 describes how a new organizational structure has emerged in Switzerland.

Value generation by and for the destination system

The value generated by and for the destination system should be shown in two ways. The first one concerns the value deriving from each actor and to the destination as a whole from the interactions among tourism activities, resources, demand and the host community. This value can be positive or negative, and territorially distributed or concentrated, according to the characteristics of the destination and the type of stakeholder involved.

While the concentration of natural and cultural heritage gives each place a unique characterization and attracts tourism demand, the tourism activities that contribute to satisfy tourists' needs are generally distributed over a larger territory, extending beyond the geographic border of the destination (e.g. external actors, like tour operators or transport carriers). Consequently, the positive economic effects (in terms of revenues and employment) deriving from tourism development tend to be spread both within and outside the destination (leakage effects), while the impacts generated by excessive pressure of tourism demand (which are generally negative) are localized. In other words, a good performance in terms of tourism flows does not always imply a positive cost–benefit balance for the destination and the host community. The 'destination balance' is far from being easily reached, given the variety of factors that interfere with the destination's economic and social development. This situation characterizes the majority of traditional tourism destinations.

Creating value for the destination system also requires accurate development of human resources. Quality and value, at each level, come from people – their values and skills, their ability to interact with other actors, to understand tourists' needs, etc. The capacity to formulate strategic training/education projects coherently with local tourism and economic policies is of crucial importance for destination competitiveness and its sustainable growth. Promoting the operators' awareness of working in a systematic way, developing a culture of hospitality that involves the host community as a whole and supporting the development of new entrepreneurship, are strategic guidelines to achieve such success.

Product or destination management?

Tourism managers are currently faced with a strategic dilemma: do we need product management or destination management? According to the discussion in this chapter, the answer has to be destination management – which means not merely creating specific products for specific market segments, but also ensuring sustainable development of the destination as a whole, preserving local resources, the residents' quality of life and the tourists' quality of visit. The success of destination management does require deep understanding of the destination as a system of actors and actions, the development of a new branding approach, accurate destination positioning, and a clear identification of the roles, competences and responsibilities of different stakeholders. It implies the need for a set of methods and tools that can be used to analyse the competitive environment (on both the demand and supply side) and then to define effective strategic measures and policies.

Until now, many tourism destinations at national, regional and local levels still have a narrow view of their evolution process. However, in the future destination governance will be of crucial importance in order to gain, maintain or defend a competitive position sustainably in the global market.

It remains to be seen whether traditional tourism destinations, which are in the mature phase of their life cycle, will be more sensible to these changes and able to make an evolutionary leap – as, for example, occurred in Turin and Switzerland – or whether the competition will be driven by new emerging destinations that see tourism as an important factor of economic development and can learn from other territorial experiences. In any case, public organizations will be called to strengthen their coordinating role at local level. As stated by Keller (2000): 'without state support there would be no really effective destination organizations. No one would take the trouble to build up and to protect tourism brands.' Public branding policy and product management contribute to reduced transaction costs, and improve cooperation. In this context, public–private partnership and direct involvement of the local community in the planning and management of the destination will be key success factors for sustainable development.

Part Four: Conclusion

26

Conclusion: tourism futures

Carlos Costa and
Dimitrios Buhalis

Tourism Business Frontiers: Consumers, Products and Industry provides a comprehensive analysis of the way in which the core of the tourism industry, and particularly consumers, products and industry, will evolve in the future. The book demonstrates that the future of the tourism industry will emerge as a result of the evolution that is already taking place on the consumer's side, as customers are becoming more knowledgeable, informed, sophisticated and demanding. This requires new innovative products and alters both the operational and strategic management of tourism organizations, as well as the structure of tourism industry itself. It is evident that change is inevitable and it is influenced by a number of forces and factors in the external environment of tourism as well as the global competition emerging. With low barriers to entry, thousands of innovative businesses appear daily to capture market share, effectively enhancing the consumer bargaining power. Most chapters in the book demonstrate that innovative tourism organizations and destinations should explore consumer trends and design suitable offerings and experiences to entice consumers. They should modernize their management practices and processes, and develop links with compatible organizations to take advantage of the emerging opportunities.

Consumer transformation is one of the most critical factors in this process. Tourism demand is changing dramatically in terms of volume, characteristics, location, preferences and consumer behaviour. It is demonstrated that, in accordance with the 2020 WTO Tourism Forecasts, the world tourism market will more than double in two decades, reaching 1.6 billion consumers by 2020. Most of this growth will come from the amelioration of the living conditions of the world population, and it will be fuelled particularly by the maturing and strengthening of new tourism markets such as China and India (Chapter 3). The opening up and rapid economic growth of China and the benefits emerging from outsourcing and the IT developments in India create new travel demand for professionals in these countries. With better salaries, and in particular with more disposable income, the world population will proportionally spend less on 'deficiency needs'. Hence people will channel larger sums of their family's budget to the fulfilment of 'growth needs', such as travelling, leisure and tourism recreation.

Perhaps most importantly, transformation of tourism demand and consumer behaviour will gradually place customers in the driving seat of the industry and will require customer-centric strategies where consumers are empowered to build their experiences (Chapter 2). The changes operating in demographics and the maturing of some previously smaller market segments will bring about the creation of new destinations and the readjustment of well-established resorts. Exotic new destinations will boost the tourism market by bringing more diversity and new consumers into the tourism industry.

With more years to live and with almost unchanged retirement ages, people will have more time to travel, which will boost the expansion of senior tourism (Chapter 4). Particular needs and services will be required for this market, and often medical support and accessibility will be critical for attracting parts of this market. On the other side, motivation to travel and learn at younger ages, and the need for adventure, often in gap years between educational stages, in combination with the fact that education is getting more global and implying the movement of youngsters all around the world, will stimulate further the youth market. The rapid development of educational exchange programmes and the growing awareness that students must interact with life outside the classroom are good examples of how education will involve much more travelling in the future. In Europe, the Socrates exchange programme, involving teachers and pupils, is a good example of this trend. With the improvement in world living conditions, youngsters will have more available money and thus will have the chance of travelling more (Chapter 5). The domination of English as a global language and the availability of endless information on the Internet and the expansion of virtual communications will stimulate further demand.

The expansion of the tourism market will also arise from the steady global trend for people to travel with the motive of visiting friends and relatives (VFR). Urban routines, social mobility, the trend for people to find jobs away from their places of birth and the globalization that encourages immigration and international friendships support international travel. Therefore, the creation of global family and friendship networks will prompt a greater growth of the VFR market (Chapter 6). Business travel will continue to grow, mainly as a consequence of the way in which businesses are progressively becoming global with international collaborations or branches. The globalization of business is pushing industries to find places where they may obtain the best production conditions, leading to the migration of industry, lured by world honey pots consisting of labour, knowledge, geographical and political resources. Equally, the concentration of manufacturers that sell their products internationally as well as the expansion of the Meeting, Incentive, Conference and Exhibition (MICE) market will further extend the expansion of a growing legion of work travellers, and will support the development of dedicated facilities and services (Chapter 7).

The rapid expansion of the tourism market also brings a new intellectual and eclectic dimension to the industry. This will lead to growing efforts for the moralization of the sector. Better-educated citizens, widespread travelling and the search for new experiences and cultures is driving tourists to less developed and unspoiled territories. A better-regulated tourist industry will provide consumers with products capable of fulfilling their spiritual needs, and will also raise concerns about protecting locations and people that may collapse in the face of the development of unethical forms of tourism (Chapter 8).

The dynamics observed in the evolution of consumers requires the tourism industry to modernize its offerings, innovate, improve existing products, and develop new and exciting experiences. New and innovative products therefore emerge, at both micro-business and macro-destination levels. Some of the major changes that will be operated worldwide will involve the evolution, and the re-engineering, of old destinations (Chapter 9). Although the tourism industry has reached its present position due to the launching and development of mass tourism, this form of tourism is gradually losing popularity. By the late 1980s, most successful recreational tourist destinations were linked to seaside resorts and thus to the sun–sea–sand phenomenon. City and cultural tourism were the only exceptions. However, the world is undergoing major changes. The hole in the ozone layer, growing awareness of the link between sun exposure and skin cancer as well as other health problems, associated with better and more ecologically friendly customers, are driving the industry to new dimensions. Seaside resorts are increasingly concerned with their environmental impacts and are thus moving rapidly away from the ribbon developments well portrayed by mass tourism developments such as Praia da Rocha (Portugal), Hersonissos (Greece) and Torremolinos (Spain). These types of resorts are looking for opportunities to regenerate their physical infrastructure, re-launch their brand and attract new, more sophisticated and higher-spending customers. New recreational forms associated with cultural tourism, and with better integration of the landscape and the neighbouring regions, are often attempted. The dismantling of a number of blocks of apartments and hotels close to the shoreline and a greater concern to control the mushrooming number of beds is rapidly becoming important in the tourism planners' agenda. The new planning policies launched in Calvià, Mallorca, as well as the demolishing of several hotels in order to generate space for physically regenerating the resorts, will become a point of reference for other places.

The way consumers are progressing, the way new products are being designed and a progressing era of affluence are driving modern work society into a new leisure society. Geographical and technological accessibility are also allowing people to work remote from their offices, as well as increasing their mobility and flexibility. Hence, second-home tourism is flourishing worldwide and will become one of the major tourism businesses in the future (Chapter 10). Nevertheless, residential tourism demands particular attention from planners, since it increases the building pressure and creates forms of demands characterized by lower occupancy rates of the dwellings and high infrastructure costs. In addition, different types of services are required for this market, which are often provided by different industries.

The new emerging destinations (Chapter 11) will be more concerned with their capacity, and will increasingly offer a cultural dimension to the destination with a greater emphasis on the local resources. New destinations will be influenced by the improvement of the accessibility worldwide, cost and time reduction, and, generally speaking, globalization. Fashion will lead consumers to places for a period of time, and destinations will need to be able to manage demand fluctuations. New destinations will emerge all around the globe, but they will also be subject to strong pressure and competition from existing players.

A wider diversity of new products will become available in the marketplace, offering more sophisticated and rewarding experiences. New products associated with nature (Chapter 13), sports (Chapter 14), shopping (Chapter 15) and gastronomy (Chapter 16) will combine special interests, activities and experiences. 'Relaxation plus' products that include elements of education, knowledge development, training, wellness and internal exploration will boom worldwide, and these market segments will become part of the mainstream tourist industry in the future. Since the development of those products is dependent on a number of other sectors based both at the destination and at the place of origin, extensive value systems and clusters of activities need to be created to ensure the proper design and delivery of those products. From the macro-economic point of view, these products provide opportunities to integrate the resources available at destination regions and to ensure that tourist expenditure directly reaches the local community, increasing multiplier effects. Gradually, consumers are moving away from the consumption of products and are getting to enjoy experiences that they co-design and produce. Staging their own experience with the help of professionals and fellow travellers supports the development of more meaningful encounters and the exploration of cultures, resources and the inner soul. Hence, a new dimension will be brought into the tourist market by tourists seeking to be fulfilled and realized from a spiritual point of view. The concept of 'rewarding destinations' will then encompass matters related to the quality of the infrastructures, equipment and amenities alongside the fulfilment of a spiritual dimension (Chapter 17). Ultimately, space travel will emerge as a break to the last frontier. Travelling in orbit became reality not only with the achievement of Dennis Tito as the first space tourist, but also through the achievement of Prize-X and the launch of Virgin Galactica by Richard Branson (Chapter 18).

The dynamics observed in the new consumers and the creation of new products will push forward the management of each sector in the industry, as well as the structures of the tourism industry. Tourism organizations need to become better adjusted, more competitive, efficient, effective and rewarding, and therefore more profitable. As Neil Leiper's model emphasizes, the tourism system includes generating areas, transit regions and destinations.

Between the generating and the transit regions, intermediaries (Chapter 19) facilitate the meeting between consumers and producers. By providing information about what consumers expect and what places can offer, intermediaries ensure the link between hosts and guests. The wide availability of the Internet and of information and reservation capabilities is going to re-engineer the distribution channels dramatically in the future. Players will need to demonstrate the value they add to the system, and to justify any commissions or charges they apply. Ultimately intermediaries will be responsible for much of the personalization taking place in the marketplace, as they will be dynamically packaging all products, services and experiences according to individual preferences.

In the transit region, the future dynamics and success of tourism will be closely linked to transportation (Chapter 20) in terms of speed, comfort and costs. The tendency is for the transportation modes to evolve towards a new era. Although airlines and airports enjoy the highest profile of the transportation industry, the entire range of transportation vehicles (including private cars, coaches, trains and boats) as well as terminals and stations are increasingly developing facilities to support the traveller, whether on business or pleasure. Efficiency will be introduced through the development of multi-modal linkages assuring quick and comfortable connections between different modes of transportation. Less state involvement, concentration of transport operators, privatization and deregulation will become key trends. Environmental concerns and health issues will also dominate the debate regarding the transportation industry.

At the destination, the progress of the hospitality industry is becoming vital to cope with the forces that are driving the tourism market into the future (Chapter 21). The structure and organization of the tourism industry will include special attention to the concerns and profiles of the new consumers emerging in the leisure market, alongside the growing demands of emerging markets. The pressure created by wealthier and more demanding consumers and the mounting pressure for environmental and security measures will greatly increase in the hospitality industry. Pressure for differentiation and for providing a better experience will grow, calling for innovation and inventiveness. At the same time, the hospitality industry will need to improve its operations and production management in order to optimize its output and remain competitive.

The tendency to please, make more rewarding and also take more advantage of wealthier tourists will lead destinations to the creation of new forms of entertainment. Attractions (Chapter 22), cultural and heritage attractions (Chapter 23) and new forms of leisure and recreation (Chapter 24) will then emerge to provide better and more meaningful experiences for consumers. Destination management organizations (DMOs) (Chapter 25) are emerging as the catalyst that coordinates the entire range of stakeholders at the destination towards increasing the collective competitiveness. Their role will be to ensure that the tourists' visit is rewarding, while guaranteeing destinations the creation of business networks capable of linking tourism business and thus maximizing direct, indirect and induced economic impacts. DMOs will also play the role of providing investors with information regarding further investment, and thus will be responsible for making the investment opportunities more clear and available to all actors. DMOs will play a critical role in ensuring that business opportunities are planned and managed within the context of regional development, and therefore will be contributing to optimization of economic, physical and social impacts.

The future will be bright for those tourist organizations and destinations that explore trends, appreciate developments and develop suitable proactive and reactive strategies for enhancing their competitiveness. Tourists will continue to travel for business, health, leisure and recreation purposes. Businesses, destinations and governments will also get involved in tourism for the economic benefits it brings. However, it is increasingly becoming evident that only organizations and destinations that have the knowledge and the capacity to deal with tourism professionally will be able to develop their competitive advantage and achieve their objectives in the future. In spite of the growth rates expected for the tourism industry, destinations and businesses that fail to predict the future and to develop proactive and reactive strategies will be unable to benefit. It is within this framework that competitiveness, efficiency, effectiveness, long-term profitability, ethics and sustainability are the main themes that will ensure the long-term prosperity of tourism organizations and destinations.

Although predicting the future is always a hazardous occupation, *Tourism Business Frontiers*, together with its affiliate publication *Tourism Management Dynamics*, provides a comprehensive analysis of both supply and demand trends as well as of the emerging issues in the tourism external environment. The books also demonstrate a wide range of management mechanisms and tools that will enable tourism organizations and destinations to strengthen their competitiveness for the future.

References

ACI Europe (2002). *Financing Civil Aviation Security Costs in Europe.* Brussels: ACI Europe.

Acott, T., La Trobe, H. and Howard, S. (1998). An evaluation of deep ecotourism and shallow ecotourism. *Journal of Sustainable Tourism*, 6(3), pp. 238–253.

Adams, W. M. (2001). *Green Development: Environment and Sustainability in the Third World*, 2nd edn. London: Routledge.

Agarwal, S. (2002). Restructuring seaside tourism. The resort lifecycle. *Annals of Tourism Research*, 29(1), 25–55.

Alford, P. (2002). *EIBTM European Meetings and Incentive Report 2002.* London: Mintel International Group Ltd.

AlSayyad, N. (2001). Global norms and urban forms in the age of tourism: manufacturing heritage, consuming tradition. In: N. AlSayyad (ed.), *Consuming Tradition, Manufacturing Heritage: Global Norms and Urban Forms in the Age of Tourism.* London: Routledge, pp. 1–33.

Anderson, E. and Weitz, B. (1989). Determinants of continuity in conventional industrial channel dyads. *Marketing Science*, 8(4), 310–323.

Antarctica Flights Online (2004). http://www.AntarcticaFlights.com.au/ (accessed August 2004).

Ashford, D. M. (1990). Prospects for space tourism. *Annals of Tourism Research*, 11(2), 99–104.

Asplet, M. and Cooper, M. (2000). Cultural designs in New Zealand souvenir clothing: the question of authenticity. *Tourism Management*, 21(3), 307–312.

ATC (2001). *Australia's Olympics Special Post Games Tourism Report*. Sydney: Australian Tourist Commission.

Atchley, R. (2004). *Incorporating spirituality into professional work in aging*. San Francisco: American Society on Aging. Available at http://www.asaging.org/at/at-204/Atchley.htm.

Attix, S. (2002). New Age-oriented special interest travel: an exploratory study. *Tourism Recreation Research*, 27(2), 51–58.

Barber, B. (1995). *Jihad vs the World*. New York: Times Books.

Bardolet, E. (2001). The path towards sustainability in the Balearic Islands. In: D. Ioannides, Y. Apostolopoulos and S. Sonmez (eds), *Mediterranean Islands and Sustainable Tourism Development: Practices, Management, and Policies*. London: Continuum Press, pp. 193–213.

Barkham, P. and Gillan, A. (2004). Television chefs stir appetite for culinary change. *The Guardian*, 23 June: 7.

Barkin, D. (2001). Strengthening domestic tourism in Mexico: challenges and opportunities. In: K Ghimire (ed.), *The Native Tourist: Mass Tourism within Developing Countries*. London: Earthscan, pp. 30–54.

Bastakis, C., Buhalis, D. and Butler, R. (2004). The impact of tour operators' power on small and medium-sized tourism accommodation enterprises on the Mediterranean islands. *Tourism Management*, 25(2), 151–170.

Bayles, M. (1999). Tubular nonsense: how not to criticise television. In: A. M. Melzer, J. Weinberger and M. R. Zinman (eds), *Democracy and the Arts*. Ithaca: Cornell University Press, pp. 159–171.

BBC (2004). Virgin soars towards new frontier. http://news.bbc.co.uk/1/hi/sci/tech/3693518.stm (accessed December 2004).

Beedie, P. (2003). Adventure tourism. In: S. Hudson (ed.), *Sport and Adventure Tourism*. Binghampton: Haworth Hospitality Press, pp. 203–239.

Bennett, M. and Buhalis, D. (2003). Tourism and travel distribution: the travel agent's perspective. *Insights*, January, D25–D30.

Benton, N. (1995). Taking the waters. *The Leisure Manager*, 13(4), 40.

Bergoff, H., Korte, B., Schneider, R. and Harvie, C. (eds) (2002). *The Making of Modern Tourism: The Cultural History of the British Experience 1600–2000*. Basingstoke: Palgrave, pp. 109–131.

Bieger, T. (1997a). *Management von Destinationen und Tourismusorganisationen*, 3rd edn. Vienna: Verlag Oldenbourg.

Bieger, T. (1997b). *Reengineering Destination Structures as a Condition for Successful Tourist Products and Marketing*. St Gallen: IDT-HSG. Available at http://www.idt.unisg.ch/org/idt/main.nsf/.

Bieger, T. (1998). Reengineering destination marketing organisations – the case of Switzerland. *Tourist Review*, 53(3), 4–17.

Binder, J. (2004). The whole point of backpacking: anthropological perspectives on the characteristics of backpacking. In: G. Richards and J. Wilson (eds), *The Global Nomad: Backpacker Travel in Theory and Practice*. Clevedon: Channel View Press, pp. 92–108

Bitner, M. and Booms, B. (1982). Trends in travel and tourism marketing: the changing structure of distribution channels. *Journal of Travel Research*, 20(4), 39–44.

Blythe, M. A., Overbeeke, K., Monk, A. F. and Wright, P. C. (2003). *Funology – From Usability to Enjoyment*. Human–Computer Interaction Series, 3. Dordrecht: Kluwer Academic Publishers.

Boniface, P. and Fowler, P. J. (1993). *Heritage and Tourism in 'the Global Village'*. London: Routledge.

Bourgeois, J. C., Haines, G. H. and Sommers, M. S. (1987). Product market structure: problem, definition and issues. In: M. Houston (ed.), *Review of Marketing*. Chicago: American Marketing Association, pp. 327–384.

Bourrat, Y. (2000). La résidence secondaire. Obstacle ou tremplin au développement local? *Espaces*, 176, 16–21.

Boyd, S. W. (2002). Cultural and heritage tourism in Canada: opportunities, principles and challenges. *Tourism and Hospitality Research*, 3(3), 211–233.

Boyne, S. (2001). *VFR (Visiting Friends and Relatives) Tourism in Rural Scotland: A Geographical Case Study Analysis*. London: Continuum.

Bruce, D. and Cantallops, A. S. (1996). The walled town of Alcudia as a focus for an alternative tourism in Mallorca. In: L. Briguglio, W. W. Butler, D. Harrison and W. L. Filho (eds), *Sustainable Tourism in Islands and Small States*, Vol. 2. London: Pinter.

Buckley, R. C. (1994). A framework for ecotourism. *Annals of Tourism Research*, 21, 661–669.

Buckley, R. (2000). NEAT trends. Current issues in nature, eco- and adventure tourism. *International Journal of Tourism Research*, 2, 437–444.

Buhalis, D. (1998). Strategic use of information technologies in the tourism industry. *Tourism Management*, 19(3), 409–423.

Buhalis, D. (1999). Limits of tourism development in peripheral destinations: problems and challenges. *Tourism Management*, 20, 183–185.

Buhalis, D. (2000). Relationships in the distribution channel of tourism: conflicts between hoteliers and tour operators in the Mediterranean region. *International Journal of Hospitality and Tourism Administration*, 1(1), 113–139.

Buhalis, D. (2003). *eTourism: Information Technology for Strategic Tourism Management*. London: Prentice Hall.

Buhalis, D. (2004). eAirlines: strategic and tactical use of ICTS in the airline industry. *Information & Management*, 41(7), 805–825.

Buhalis, D. and Laws, E. (eds) (2001). *Tourism Distribution Channels: Practices, Issues and Transformations*. London: Continuum.

Buhalis, D. and Licata, M. C. (2002). The future eTourism intermediaries. *Tourism Management*, 23, 207–220.

Burton, R. (1995). *Travel Geography*. London: Pitman Publishing.

Burton, R. (1997). The sustainability of ecotourism. In: M. J. Stabler (ed.), *Tourism Sustainability. Principles to Practice*. Wallingford: CABI Publishing, pp. 357–374.

Butcher, J. (2003). *Sun, Sand … and Saving the World: The Moralisation of Tourism*. London: Routledge.

Butler, R. (1980). The concept of a tourist area cycle of evolution: implications for management of resources. *The Canadian Geographer*, 24(1), 5–12.

Butler, R. (2004). The tourism area life cycle in the twenty-first century. In: A. A. Lew, C. M. Hall and A. W. Williams (eds), *A Companion to Tourism*. Oxford: Blackwell Publishing, pp. 159–169.

Butler, R. W. (ed.) (2005). *Tourism Area Life Cycle* (2 volumes). Clevedon: Channel View Publications.

Calvia (2004). *Calvia Mallorca*. Available at http://www.calvia.com/Pages/Idiomas/Ingles/Pages/even/iespon.htm (accessed 25 August).

Cambridge Dictionaries (2000). *Cambridge International Dictionary of English* (available online at http://dictionary.cambridge.org/, accessed August 2004).

Canadian Tourism Commission (2002). *Acquiring a Taste for Cuisine Tourism: A Product Development Strategy*. Ottawa: Canadian Tourism Commission.

Canning, S. (2004). Grey blackout. *Australian*, 22 April, 15, 18.

Caraher, M., Lang, T. and Dixon, P. (2000). The influence of TV and celebrity chefs on public attitudes and behaviour among the English public. *Journal of the Association for the Study of Food and Society*, 4(1), 27–46.

Carmichael, B. and Smith, W. (2004). Canadian domestic travel behaviour: a market segmentation study of rural shoppers. *Journal of Vacation Marketing*, 10(4), 333–347.

Carson, R. L. (1963). *Silent Spring*. London: Hamilton.

Ceballos-Lascurain, H. (1998). Introduction. In: K. Lindberg, M. Epler Wood and D. Engeldrum (eds), *Ecotourism, A Guide for Planners and Managers*, Vol. 2. North Bennington: The Ecotourism Society, pp. 7–10.

CE Delft (2002). *Economic Incentives to Mitigate Greenhouse Gas Emissions from Air Transport in Europe*. Delft: CE Delft.

Cederholm, E. A. (1999). *The Attraction of the Extraordinary – Images and Experiences Among Backpacker Tourists*. Published PhD thesis. Lund: Arkiv Förlag (in Swedish with English abstract).

Chadwick, R. A. (1984). *Travel to Canada by Residents of the United Kingdom*. Ottawa: Tourism Canada.

Chandler, P. (2000). The UK outbound tour operating market – changing patterns of distribution. *Insights*, September, D5–D9.

Chandler, C., Holden, J. and Kolander, C. (1992). Counselling for spiritual wellness: theory and practice. *Journal of Counselling and Development*, 71(2), 168–175.

Christopher, M. (1992). *The Strategy of Distribution Management*. Oxford: Butterworth-Heinemann.

Cloke, P. and Perkins, H. (1998). Cracking the canyon with the awesome foursome: representations of adventure tourism in New Zealand. *Society and Space*, 16, 185–218.

Cloutier, R. (2003). The business of adventure tourism. In: S. Hudson (ed.), *Sport and Adventure Tourism*. Binghampton: Haworth Hospitality Press, pp. 241–272.

CNN (2004). Inflatable space module wins approval. http://www.cnn.com/2004/TECH/space/11/25/space.approve/index. html (accessed December 2004).

Collins, P. and Ashford, D. (1986). Potential economic implications of space tourism. In: *37th Congress of the International Astronautical Federation, Innsbruck, Austria*, 4–11 October. IAA-86-446. Innsbruck: IAF.

Collins, P., Iwasaki, Y., Kanayama, H. and Ohnuki, M. (1994). Commercial implications of market research on space tourism. *Journal of Space Technology and Science*, 10(2), 3–11.

Connolly, D. J., Olsen, M. D. and Moore, R. G. (1998). The Internet as a distribution channel. *Cornell Hotel and Restaurant Administration Quarterly*, August, 42–54.

Cooper, M., O'Mahony, K. and Erfurt, P. (2004). Backpackers: nomads join the mainstream? An analysis of backpacker employment on the 'Harvest Trail Circuit' in Australia. In: G. Richards and J. Wilson (eds), *The Global Nomad: Backpacker Travel in Theory and Practice*. Clevedon: Channel View Publications, pp. 180–195.

Cooper, C., Fletcher, J., Gilbert, D. *et al.* (2005). *Tourism Principles and Practice*, 3rd edn. Englewood Cliffs: Pearson.

Countryside Agency (2001). *Eat the View – Promoting Sustainable, Local Products.* Cheltenham: Countryside Agency.

Coward, R. (2001). Ten ways to give your guilt a holiday. *Guardian*, 5 February.

Crouch, G. I. (2000). Destination management company. In: J. Jafari (ed.), *Encyclopedia of Tourism.* London: Routledge, p. 146.

Crouch, G. (2001). The market for space tourism: early indications. *Journal of Travel Research*, 40, 213–219.

Crouch, G. I. and Ritchie, J. R. B. (1998). Convention site selection research: a review, conceptual model and propositional framework. *Journal of Convention and Exhibition Management*, 1(1), 49–69.

Cruise Industry News (2004). Market and brand growth. *Cruise Industry News*, Spring.

Daily Telegraph (2002). Majorca eco-tax an insult, say tourists. Available at http://traveltax.msu.edu/news/Stories/dailytelegraph9.htm (accessed 28 August 2004).

Dasse, M. E. and Aubert, B. (2000). Peut-on transformer les résidents secondaires en résidents permanents? L'exemple de la Vallée de l Ance. *Espaces*, 176, 22–27.

Davidson, R. (1998). *Tourism in Europe*, 2nd edn. Harlow: Longman.

Davidson, R. and Maitland, R. (1997). *Tourism Destinations.* London: Hodder and Stoughton.

Denman, R. (1988). *A Response to the VFR* Market. A Report to the English Tourist Board and Regional Tourist Boards. London: British Tourist Authority/English Tourist Board.

Dennis, N. (2004). The development of low cost airlines and the changing role of charters. Aviation and Tourism Seminar, March, London (unpublished).

Devas, E. (1986). Long haul travel from Europe to South America. Surveys of sources, destinations and the need to promotion. *Travel and Tourism Analyst*, October, 49–57.

Dimanche, F. (2003). The Louisiana tax-free shopping program for international visitors: a case study. *Journal of Travel Research*, 41(3), 311–314.

DKS (1999). *Pennsylvania Heritage Tourism Study*, prepared by D. K. Shifflet and Associates for the Pennsylvania Department of Conservation and Natural Resources.

Doganis, R. (2001). *The Airline Business in the 21st Century.* London: Routledge.

Dolnicar, S. and Mazanec, J. A. (1998). Destination marketing: reinventing the wheel or conceptual progress?. In: *AIEST, Destination Marketing, Reports 48th Congress, Marrakesh (Morocco).* St Gallen: AIEST Publications.

Eco, U. (1986). *Travels in Hyper-Reality.* London: Picador.

Economic Planning Group of Canada (EPG) (2002). *Wine and Culinary Tourism in Ontario – Executive Summary.* Toronto: Economic Planning Group of Canada.

Edensor, T. (2001). Performing tourism, staging tourism: (re)producing tourist space and practice. *Tourist Studies*, 1(1), 59–81.

Edvardsson, B. and Olsson, J. (1999). Key concepts for new service development. In: C. Lovelock, S. Vandermerwe and B. Lewis (eds) (1999). *Services Marketing. A European Perspective.* Berwick-upon-Tweed: Prentice Hall Europe, pp. 396–412.

Edvardsson, B., Gustafsson, A., Johnson, M. D. and Sanden, B. (2000). *New Service Development and Innovation in the New Economy*. Lund: Studentlitteratur.

Elliott, H. (1995). Test series gives big boost to West Indies tourism. *The Times*, 3 August, p. 19.

Elsrud, T. (2001). Risk creation in travelling – backpacker adventure narration. *Annals of Tourism Research*, 28(3), 597–617.

Emarketer (2004). *Search is still strong*. Available at http://www.emarketer.com/Article.aspx?1003002 (accessed 18 August 2004).

Enteleca Research and Consultancy (2000). *Tourist's Attitudes Towards Regional and Local Food*. Prepared for the Ministry of Agriculture, Fisheries and Food, and The Countryside Agency by Enteleca Research and Consultancy Ltd. London: Ministry of Agriculture, Fisheries and Food, and The Countryside Agency.

Ewert, A. and Hollenhorst, S. (1989). Testing the adventure model: empirical support for a model of risk recreation. *Journal of Leisure Research*, 21, 124–136.

Farrell, J. (2003). *One Nation under Goods: Malls and the Seductions of American Shopping*. Washington, DC: Smithsonian Institution.

Feifer, M. (1985). *Tourism in History: From Imperial Rome to the Present*. New York: Stein & Day.

Fennell, D. A. (2003). *Ecotourism: An Introduction*, 2nd edn. London: Routledge.

Fennell, D. and Dowling, R. (2003). Ecotourism policy and planning: stakeholders, management and governance. In: D. Fennell and R. K. Dowling (eds), *Ecotourism Policy and Planning*. Wallingford: CABI Publishing, pp. 331–344.

Fetzer Institute (1999). *National Institute on Aging Working Group: Multidimensional Measurement of Religiousness, Spirituality for Use in Health Research*. A Report of a National working group supported by the Fetzer Institute in Collaboration with the National Institute on Aging. Kalamazoo: Fetzer Institute.

Fleischer, A. and Pizam, A. (2002). Tourism constraints among Israeli seniors. *Annals of Tourism Research*, 29(1), 106–123.

Forer, P. (1978). A place for plastic space? *Progress in Human Geography*, 3, 230–267.

Forsyth, P. (2003). Air transport policy and the measurement of tourism benefits. Air Transport Research Society Conference, July, Toulouse(unpublished).

Framke, W. (2002). The destination as a concept: a discussion of the business-related perspective versus the socio-cultural approach in tourism theory. *Scandinavian Journal of Hospitality and Tourism*, 2, 93–108.

Frochot, I. and Morrison, A. (2000). Benefit segmentation: a review of its applications to travel and tourism. *Journal of Travel and Tourism Marketing*, 9(4), 21–45.

Futron (2004). *Space tourism report*. Available at www.futron.com (accessed December 2004).

Gallent, N., Mace, A. and Tewdwr-Jones, M. (2003). Dispelling a myth? Second homes in rural Wales. *Area*, 35(3), 271–284.

Gartner, W. C. (1989). Tourism image: attribute measurement of state tourism product using multidimensional scaling techniques. *Journal of Travel Research*, 27, 16–20.

Getz, D. (1993). Tourist shopping villages: development and planning strategies. *Tourism Management*, 14(1), 15–26.

Getz, D., Joncas, D. and Kelly, M. (1994). Tourist shopping villages in the Calgary region. *Journal of Tourism Studies*, 5(1), 2–15.

Ghimire, K. and Li, Z. (2001). The economic role of national tourism in China. In: K. Ghimire (ed.), *The Native Tourist: Mass Tourism within Developing Countries*. London: Earthscan, pp. 86–108.

Gibson, H. and Yiannakis, A. (1995). Some characteristics of sport tourism: a lifetime perspective. Paper presented at the Annual Conference of the North American Society for the Sociology of Sport, Savannah, Georgia.

Gilleard, C. and Higgs, P. (2002). Concept forum: the third age: class, cohort or generation? *Ageing & Society*, 22, 369–382.

Gillmor, D. and Kockel, U. (1994). Tourism development and impact in the Republic of Ireland. In: U. Kockel (ed.), *Culture Tourism and Development: The Case of Ireland*. Liverpool: Liverpool University Press, pp. 17–34.

Gilmore, J. H. and Pine II, J. B. (2002). *The Experience IS the Marketing*. Aurora: Strategic Horizons LLP.

Girard, T.C. and Gartner, W. C. (1993). Second home second view: host community perceptions. *Annals of Tourism Research*, 20(4), 685–700.

Go, F. and Pine, R. (1995). *Globalization Strategy in the Hotel Industry*. New York: Routledge.

Goodrich, J. N. (1987). Touristic travel to outer space: profile and barriers to entry. *Journal of Travel Research*, 16(2), 40–43.

Goodwin, H. (2000). Tourism and natural heritage, a symbiotic relationship? In: M. Robinson, N. Evans, P. Long et al. (eds), *Environmental Management and Pathways to Sustainable Development*. Sunderland: Business Education Publishers Limited, pp. 97–112.

Gottdiener, M. (1997). *The Theming of America: Dreams, Visions and Commercial Spaces*. Boulder, CO: Westview Press.

Graham, A. (2000). Transport and leisure. In: *Transport and Leisure*. Paris: ECMT, pp. 151–153.

Graham, A. (2003). *Managing Airports*, 2nd edn. Oxford: Elsevier.

Green, M. C. and Brock, T. C. (2002). In the mind's eye: transportation-imagery model of narrative persuasion. In: M. C. Green, J. J. Strange and T. C. Brock (eds), *Narrative Impact: Social and Cognitive Foundations*. Mahwah, NJ: Lawrence Erlbaum Associates, pp. 315–341.

Gretzel, U. and Fesenmaier, D. R. (2003). Experience-based Internet marketing: an exploratory study of sensory experiences associated with pleasure travel to the Midwest United States. In: A. J. Frew, M. Hitz and P. O'Connor (eds), *Information and Communication Technologies in Tourism 2003*, Vienna: Springer Verlag, pp. 49–57.

Griffiths, J. (2001). Tourism is bad for our health. *Guardian*, 8 February.

Grof, S. (1976). *Realms of the Human Unconscious*. New York: Dutton.

Grönroos, C. (2000). *Service Management and Marketing. A Customer Relationship Management Approach*. Chichester: John Wiley & Sons.

Guardian (2004). A well-earned break? Take five. *Guardian*, 16 June, p. 7.

Gunawan, M. P. (1996). Domestic tourism in Indonesia. *Tourism Recreation Research*, 21(1), 65–69.

Gunn, C. (1972). *Vacationscape*, Austin: Bureau of Business Research, University of Texas.

Gunn, C. (1988a). *Vacationscape: Designing Tourist Regions*, 2nd edn. New York: Van Nostrand Reinhold.

Gunn, C. (1988b). *Tourism Planning*. London: Taylor & Francis.

Gunn, C. (1994). *Tourism Planning: Basic, Concepts, Cases*, 3rd edn. New York: Taylor & Francis.

Gustafsson, A. and Johnson, M. D. (2003). *Competing in a Service Economy*. University of Michigan Business School Management Series. Michigan: John Wiley.

Hägerstrand, T. (1967). *Innovation Diffusion as a Spatial Process* (trans. A. Pred). Chicago: University of Chicago Press.

Hall, C. M. (1992). Adventure, sport and health. In: C. M. Hall and B. Weiler (eds), *Special Interest Tourism*. London: Belhaven Press, pp. 141–158.

Hall, C. M. (1994). Tourism and retail shopping development. *Australian Journal of Leisure and Recreation*, 4(3), 5–11.

Hall, C. M. (2003). *Tourism and Temporary Mobility: Circulation, Diaspora, Migration, Nomadism, Sojourning, Travel, Transport and Home*. International Academy for the Study of Tourism (IAST) Conference, 30 June–5 July, Savonlinna, Finland.

Hall, C. M. (2005a). *Tourism: Rethinking the Social Science of Mobility*. Harlow: Prentice-Hall.

Hall, C. M. (2005b). Space–time accessibility and the tourist area cycle of evolution: the role of geographies of spatial interaction and mobility in contributing to an improved understanding of tourism. In: R. Butler (ed.), *The Tourism Life Cycle: Conceptual and Theoretical Issues*. Clevedon: Channel View Publications (in press).

Hall, C. M. and Mitchell, R. (1998). 'We are what we eat': tourism, culture and the globalisation and localisation of cuisine. Paper presented at ATLAS Conference, Crete, October.

Hall, C. M. and Mitchell, R. (2000). We are what we eat: food, tourism and globalisation. *Tourism, Culture and Communication*, 2, 29–37.

Hall, C. M. and Mitchell, R. (2001). Wine and food tourism. In: N. Douglas, N. Douglas and R. Derrett (eds), *Special Interest Tourism: Context and Cases*. Brisbane: John Wiley & Sons, pp. 307–329.

Hall, C. M. and Muller, D. K. (eds) (2002). *Tourism, Mobility and Second Homes, Aspects of Tourism*. Clevedon: Channel View Publications.

Hall, C. M. and Sharples, E. (2003). The consumption of experiences or the experience of consumption? An introduction to the tourism of taste. In: C. M. Hall, E. Sharples, R. Mitchell *et al.* (eds), *Food Tourism Around the World: Development, Management and Markets*. Oxford: Butterworth-Heinemann, pp. 1–24.

Hall, C. M., Sharples, E. and Smith, A. (2003a). The experience of consumption or the consumption of experiences? Challenges and issues in food tourism. In: C. M. Hall, E. Sharples, R. Mitchell *et al.* (eds), *Food Tourism Around the World: Development, Management and Markets*. Oxford: Butterworth-Heinemann, pp. 314–335.

Hall, C. M., Mitchell, R. and Sharples, E. (2003b). Consuming places: the role of food, wine and tourism in regional development. In: C. M. Hall, E. Sharples, R. Mitchell *et al.* (eds), *Food Tourism Around the World: Development, Management and Markets*. Oxford: Butterworth-Heinemann, pp. 25–59.

Hand, D. J. (1996). *Practical Longtitudinal Data Analysis*. London: Chapman and Hall.

Hanink, D. M. and White, K. (1999). Distance effects in the demand for wildland recreation services: the case of national parks in the United States. *Environment and Planning A*, 31, 477–492.

Hannigan, J. (1999). *Fantasy City: Pleasure and Profit in the Postmodern Metropolis*. New York: Routledge.

Hawkins, D. E. (1986). The American tourist: different types of different trips. *Leisure Information Quarterly USA*, 13(2), 1–4.

Hawks, S. (1994). Spiritual health: definition and theory. *Wellness Perspectives*, 10, 3–13.

Heintzman, P. (2000). Leisure and spiritual well-being relationships: a qualitative study. *Society and Leisure*, 23(1), 41–69.

Heintzman, P. (2002). A conceptual model of leisure and spiritual well-being. *Journal of Park and Recreation Administration*, 20(4), 147–169.

Hinterkopf, E. (1998). *Defining the spiritual experience*. American Counselling Association. Available at http://www.focusing.org/defining.htm.

Hobson, P. and Christiansen, M. (2001). Cultural and structural issues affecting Japanese tourist shopping behavior. *Asian Pacific Journal of Tourism Research*, 6(1), 37–45.

Holbrook, M. B. (2000). The millennial consumer in the texts of our time: experience and entertainment. *Journal of Macromarketing*, 20(2), 178–192.

Honey, M. (1999). *Ecotourism and Sustainable Development: Who Owns Paradise?* Washington, DC: Island Press.

Honey, M. (ed.) (2002). *Ecotourism & Certification, Setting Standards and Practice*. Washington, DC: Island Press.

Horneman, L., Carter, R. W., Wei, S. and Ruys, H. (2002). Profiling the senior traveller: an Australian perspective. *Journal of Travel Research*, 41, 23–37.

Hossain, A. (2003). Senior travellers: their contribution to the domestic tourism market in Australia. *Journal of the Bureau of Tourism Research*, 5(1), 1–18.

Hu, Y. and Ritchie, J. R. B. (1993). Measuring destination attractiveness: a contextual approach. *Journal of Travel Research*, 32, 25–34.

Huang, L. and Tsai, H. (2003). The study of senior travel behaviour in Taiwan. *Tourism Management*, 24, 561–574.

Huang, C. T. Yuang, C. Y. and Huang, J. H. (1996). Trends in outbound tourism from Taiwan. *Tourism Management*, 17(3), 223–228.

Hudson, S. (2003). *Sport and Adventure Tourism*. Binghampton: Haworth Hospitality Press.

Hudson, S., Snaith, T., Miller, G. and Hudson, P. (2001). Travel retailing: 'switch selling' in the UK. In: D. Buhalis and E. Laws (eds), *Tourism Distribution Channels: Practices, Issues and Transformations*. London: Continuum, pp. 172–184.

ICEX, APCE (2002), *Turismo Residencial Español. Diagnóstico y Propuestas de Internacionalización*. Madrid: APCE.

IH&RA (1996). White Paper on the Global Hospitality Industry: Into the New Millennium. Paris: IH&RA.

International Association of Amusement Parks and Attractions (2003). *US amusement/theme parks & attractions industry – attendance & revenues*. Available at http://www.iaapa.org/ (accessed 15 June 2004).

Ioannides, D. (1994). The State, transnationals, and the dynamics of tourism evolution in small island nations. PhD Dissertation, Rutgers, State University of New Jersey.

Ioannides, D. and Holcomb, B. (2003). Misguided policy initiatives in small-island destinations: why do up-market tourism policies fail? *Tourism Geographies*, 5(1), 39–48.

IPCC (1999). *Aviation and the Global Atmosphere: Summary for Policymakers*. Geneva: IPCC.

Jackman, W. T. (1962). *The Development of Transportation in Modern England*, 2nd edn. London: Frank Cass.

Jackson, R. T. (1990). VFR tourism: is it underestimated? *Journal of Tourism Studies*, 1(2), 10–17.

Janelle, D. G. (1968). Central place development in a time-space framework. *Professional Geographer*, 20, 5–10.

Jansen-Verbeke, M. (1986). Inner-city tourism: resources, tourists and promoters. *Annals of Tourism Research*, 13(1), 79–100.

Jansen-Verbeke, M. (1987). Women, shopping and leisure. *Leisure Studies*, 6, 71–86.

Jansen-Verbeke, M. (1991). Leisure shopping: a magic concept for the tourism industry. *Tourism Management*, 11(1), 9–14.

Jessop, B. (1999). Reflections on globalisation and its (il)logic(s). In: K. Olds, P. Dicken, P. F. Kelly *et al.* (eds), *Globalisation and the Asia-Pacific: Contested Territories*. London: Routledge, pp. 19–38.

Johnston, C. S. (2001a). Shoring the foundations of the destination life cycle model, part 1: a case study of Kona, Hawaii. *Tourism Geographies*, 3(1), 2–28.

Johnston, C. S. (2001b). Shoring the foundations of the destination life cycle model, part 2. *Tourism Geographies*, 3(2), 135–164.

Jolley, R. and Curphey, M. (1994). Agents race for niche markets. *The Times*, 10 November, p. 35.

Jones, P. (1988). *Food Service Operations*, 2nd edn. London: Cassell.

Jones, P. (1996). The hospitality industry. In: P. Jones (ed.), *An Introduction to Hospitality Operations*. London: Cassell, pp. 1–17.

Jones, P. (2004). *Flight Catering*. Oxford: Elsevier.

Jones, P. and Lockwood, A. (1989). *The Management of Hotel Operations*. London: Cassell.

Jones, P. and Pizam, A. (1993). *International Hospitality Management – Organisational and Operational Issues*. London: Pitman.

Jones, C. B. and Robinett, J. (1998). *The future of theme parks in international tourism*. Available from Economic Research Associates, at http://wwww.hotel-online.com/Neo/Trends/ERA/ERARolethemeparks.html (accessed 18 August 2004).

Juan, F., Jesús, A. and Solsona, J. (2003). Las viviendas familiares y su uso turístico en la Comunidad Valenciana. *Estudios Turísticos*, 155/156, 159–177.

Katz, J. (2004). The future of Internet travel – building loyalty and making sites relevant. In: B. Dickson and A. Vladimir (eds), *The Complete 21st Century Travel and Hospitality Marketing Handbook*. Englewood Cliffs: Pearson, pp. 459–468.

Keller, P. (2000). Destination marketing: strategic areas of inquiry. In: M. Manente and M. Cerato (eds), *From Destination to Destination Marketing and Management. Designing and Repositioning Tourism Products*. Venice: Ca'Foscarina University, CISET Series, pp. 29–44.

Kerstetter, D., Confer, J. and Bricker, K. (1998). Industrial heritage attractions: types and tourists. *Journal of Travel and Tourism Marketing*, 7(2), 91–104.

Kim, J., Wei, S. and Ruys, H. (2003). Segmenting the market of West Australian senior tourists using an artificial neural network. *Tourism Management*, 24, 25–34.

King, B. E. M. and Gamage, H. A. (1994). Measuring the value of the ethnic connection. Expatriate travelers from Australia to Sri Lanka. *Journal of Travel Research*, 33(2), 46–50.

Kirstegs, T. (2003). Basic questions of 'sustainable tourism': does ecological and socially acceptable tourism have a chance? In: M. Lueck and T. Kirsges (eds), *Global Ecotourism. Policies and Case Studies. Perspectives and Constraints, Current Themes in Tourism*. Clevedon: Channel View Publications, pp. 1–20.

Klein, L. R. (1998). Evaluating the potential of interactive media through a new lens: search versus experience goods. *Journal of Business Research*, 41, 195–203.

Klemm, M. (1996). Langedoc Roussillon: adapting the strategy, *Tourism Management*, 17(2), 133–139.

Kleskey, A. and Kearsley, G. W. (1993). Mapping multiple perceptions of wilderness so as to minimize the impact of tourism on national environments. In: A. J. Veal, P. Jonson and G. Cushman (eds), *Leisure and Tourism: Social and Economic Change*. Sydney: University of Technology, pp. 104–119.

Koelle, D. E. (1997). *Technical Assessment of the Minimum 'Cost per Flight' Potential for Space Tourism. International Symposium on Space Tourism, Bremen, March 20–22*. Bremen: IAF.

Komppula, R. and Boxberg, M. (2002). *Product Development in a Tourism Enterprise*. (Matkailuyrityksen tuotekehitys). Helsinki: Edita Oyj.

Kotler, P., Bowen, J. and Makens, J. (1999). *Marketing for Hospitality and Tourism*, 2nd edn. Upper Saddle River: Prentice-Hall.

Krippendorf, J. (1999). *The Holiday Makers. Understanding the Impact of Leisure and Travel*. Oxford: Butterworth-Heinemann.

Ladkin, A. (2002). Research issues and challenges for the convention industry. In: K. Weber and K. Chon (eds), *Convention Tourism: International Research and Industry Perspectives*. Oxford: The Haworth Hospitality Press, pp. 101–118.

Ladkin, A. and Spiller, J. (2000). *The Meeting, Incentives, Conferences and Exhibitions Industry*. London: Travel and Tourism Intelligence.

Lancaster, K. J. (1966). A new approach to consumer theory. *Journal of Political Economy*, 14, 132–157.

Lang Research (2001). *Cuisine Tourism: Profiles*. Toronto: Ontario Tourism Marketing Partnership.

Lanzendorf, M. (2000). Social change & leisure mobility. *World Transport Policy & Practice*, 6(3), 21–25.

Laws, E. (1995). *Tourist Destination Management: Issues, Analysis and Policies*. London: Routledge.

Laws, E. (1997). *Managing Packaged Tourism: Relationships, Responsibilities and Service Quality in the Inclusive Holiday Industry*. London: International Thomson Business Press.

Laws, E. and le Pelley, B. (2000). Managing complexity and change in tourism – the case of a historic city. *International Journal of Tourism Research*, 2(4), 229–246.

Laycock, A. L. (2003). On the road again? A study of the changes in backpacking from the 1960s to the present day, from the perspective of institutionalisation. Unpublished BA (Hons) dissertation, Birmingham College of Food. Tourism and creative studies. Birmingham.

Le Bel, J., Sears D. and Dubé, L. (2004). Experiential Tourism: Preliminary scale development to assess pleasurable experiences. Paper presented at the

35th Annual Conference of the Travel and Tourism Research Association, Montreal, Canada, 20–23 June.

Lehto, X., Morrison, A. and O'Leary, J. T. (2001). Does the visiting friends and relatives' typology make a difference? A study of the international VFR market to the US. *Journal of Travel Research*, 40(2), 201–212.

Leiper, N. (1990a). Tourist attraction systems. *Annals of Tourism Research*, 17, 367–384.

Leiper, N. (1990b). *Tourism Systems*, Palmerston North: Massay University Press.

Leiper, N. (1995). *Tourism Management*. Melbourne: RMIT Press.

Leiper, N. (2000). Are destinations 'the heart of tourism'? The advantages of an alternative description. *Current Issues in Tourism*, 3, 364–368.

Liebman, N. (1997). *Miami Beach: a history of boom to bust to boom*. Available at http://www.state.fl.us/fdi/edesign/news/9704/beach.htm (accessed 25 August 2004).

Littrell, M., Baizerman, S., Kean, R. *et al.* (1994). Souvenirs and tourism styles. *Journal of Travel Research*, 33(1), 3–11.

Lloyd, K. (2003). Contesting control in transitional Vietnam: the development and regulation of traveller cafes in Hanoi and Ho Chi Minh City. *Travel Geographies*, 5, 350–366.

Long, N. (1998). Broken down by age and sex – exploring the ways we approach the elderly consumer. *Journal of Market Research Society*, 40(2), 73–92.

Lueck, M. (2003). Large-scale ecotourism – a contradiction in itself. In: M. Lueck and T. Kirsges (eds), *Global Ecotourism. Policies and Case Studies. Perspectives and Constraints, Current Themes in Tourism*. Clevedon: Channel View Publications, pp. 189–198.

Lukens, L. (1992). Focusing: another way to spirituality. *The Folio: A Journal for Focusing and Experiential Therapy*, 10, 65–72.

Lumsdon, L. (1997). *Tourism Marketing*. Oxford: International Thomson Business Press.

Lumsdon, L. and Page, S. (2004). Progress in transport and tourism research. In: L. Lumsdon and S. Page (eds), *Tourism and Transport: Issues and Agenda for the New Millennium*. Oxford: Elsevier, pp. 1–27.

MacCannell, D. (1976). *The Tourist: A New Theory of the Leisure Class*. New York: Schocken Books.

Mader, U. (1988). Tourism and the environment. *Annals of Tourism Research*, 1(2), 274–277.

Manente, M. and Cerato, M. (2000). Destination management. the conceptual framework. In: M. Manente and M. Cerato (eds), *From Destination to Destination Marketing and Management. Designing and Repositioning Tourism Products*. Venice: Ca'Foscarina University, CISET Series. pp. 15–27.

Mann, M. (for Tourism Concern) (2000). *The Community Tourism Guide*. London: Earthscan.

Maoz, D. (2004). The Conquerers and the Settlers: two groups of young Israeli backpackers in India. In: G. Richards and J. Wilson (eds), *The Global Nomad: Backpacker Travel in Theory and Practice*. Clevedon: Channel View Publications, pp. 109–122.

Markwell, K. (2001). 'An intimate rendezvous with nature'? Mediating the tourist-nature experience at three sites in Borneo. *Tourist Studies*, 1(1), 39–57.

Marobella, P. (2004). Contradictions in consumer trends. *Direct*, 15, 32.

Mason, P. and Mowforth, M. (1995). *Codes of Conduct in Tourism*. Plymouth: Occasional Papers, University of Plymouth.

McCabe, S. (2002). The tourist experience and everyday life. In: G. M. S. Dann (ed.), *The Tourist as a Metaphor of the Social World*. Wallingford: CABI Publishing, pp. 61–76.

McCabe, V., Poole, B., Weeks, P. and Leiper, N. (2000). *The Business and Management of Conventions*. Chichester: John Wiley & Sons.

McIntosh, A. J. and Prentice, R. C. (1999). Affirming authenticity: consuming cultural heritage. *Annals of Tourism Research*, 26(3), 589–612.

McKercher, R. (1998). *The Business of Nature Based Tourism*. Melbourne: Hospitality Press.

McKercher, B. (2001). Attitudes to a non-viable community-owned heritage tourist attraction. *Journal of Sustainable Tourism*, 9(1), 29–43.

McKercher, B. and du Cros, H. (2002). *Cultural Tourism: The Partnership between Tourism and Cultural Heritage Management*. Binghampton: The Haworth Press.

McNaught, T. (1982). Mass tourism and the dilemmas of modernisation in Pacific Island communities. *Annals of Tourism Research*, 9, 359–381.

Medina-Muñoz, D., García-Falcón, J. and Medina-Muñoz, R. (2002). Building the valuable connection: hotels and travel agents. *The Cornell Hotel and Restaurant Administration Quarterly*, 43(3), 46–52.

Meis, S., Joyal, S. and Trite, A. (1995). The US repeat and VFR visitor to Canada: Come again, Eh! *Journal of Tourism Studies*, 6(1), 27–37.

Middleton, V. (2001). Which way for tourist attractions? In: A. Lockwood and S. Medlik (eds), *Tourism and Hospitality in the 21st Century*. Oxford: Butterworth-Heinemann.

Middleton, V. T. C. and Clarke, J. (2001). *Marketing in Travel and Tourism*, 3rd edn. Oxford: Butterworth-Heinemann.

Mihalič, T. and Kaspar, C. (1996). *Umweltoekonomie im Tourismus*. Bern: Paul Haupt.

Mill, R. C. and Morrison, A. M. (1985). *The Tourism System*. Englewood Cliffs: Prentice Hall.

Miller, H. J. (1999). Measuring space–time accessibility benefits within transportation networks: basic theory and computational methods. *Geographical Analysis*, 31, 187–212.

Mitchell, R. and Hall, C. M. (2001a). Lifestyle behaviours of New Zealand winery visitors: wine club activities, wine cellars and place of purchase. *International Journal of Wine Marketing*, 13(3), 82–93.

Mitchell, R. and Hall, C. M. (2001b). The winery consumer: a New Zealand perspective. *Tourism Recreation Research*, 26(2), 63–75.

Mitchell, R. and Hall, C. M. (2003). Consuming tourists: food tourism consumer behaviour. In: C. M. Hall, E. Sharples, R. Mitchell *et al.* (eds), *Food Tourism Around the World: Development, Management and Markets*. Oxford: Butterworth-Heinemann, pp. 60–80.

Mitropolitski, S. (2004). United Arab Emirates: Dubai as Arab Singapore. *International Real Estate Digest*. Available at http://www.ired.com/news/mkt/dubai.htm (accessed 10 September 2004).

Monbiot, G. (1999). An unfair exchange. *Guardian*, 15 May.

Morgan, R., Pritchard, A. and Pride, R. (2002). *Destination Branding*. Oxford: Butterworth-Heinemann.

Morrison, M. A. and Sung, H. H. (2000). Adventure tourism. In: J. Jafari (eds.), *Encyclopedia of Tourism*. New York: Routledge, p. 11.

Moscardo, G. (2004). East meets west: a useful distinction or misleading myth? *Tourism*, 52(1), 7–20.

Moscardo, G., Faulkner, B. and Laws, E. (2000a). Moving ahead and looking back. In: B. Faulkner, G. Moscardo and E. Laws (eds), *Tourism in the Twenty First Century*. London: Continuum, pp. xviii–xxxii.

Moscardo, G., Pearce, P., Morrison, A. *et al.* (2000b). Developing a typology for understanding visiting friends and relatives markets. *Journal of Travel Research*, 38(3), 251–259.

Moseley, M. J. (1979). *Accessibility: The Rural Challenge*. London: Methuen.

Mowforth, M. and Munt, I. (1998). *Tourism and Sustainability: New Tourism in the Third World*. London: Routledge, Ch. 6.

MSS (2000). *Student Project*. Strasbourg: International Space University.

Mueller, H. and Fluegel, M. (1999). *Tourismus und Oekologie. Wechselwirkungen und Handlungsfelder*. Bern: Forschungsinstitut fuer Freizeit und Tourismus der Universitaet Bern.

Munro, D. (1994). Conference centres in the 21st century. In: A. V. Seaton (ed.), *Tourism: The State of the Art*. Chichester: John Wiley & Sons, pp. 200–203.

Murphy, P., Pritchard, M. P. and Smith, B. (2000). The destination product and its impact on traveller perceptions. *Tourism Management*, 21, 43–52.

Myers, R. (2000). SPACE.com Exclusive: *For Tom Hanks, Apollo 13 was a personal adventure*. Available at www.space.com (accessed August 2004).

Neale, G. (1999). *The Green Travel Guide*, 2nd edn. London: Earthscan.

Neirotti, L. D. (2003). An introduction to sport and adventure tourism. In: S. Hudson (ed.), *Sport and Adventure Tourism*. Binghampton: Haworth Hospitality Press, pp. 1–25.

Newlands, K. (2004). Setting out on the road less travelled: a study of backpacker travel in New Zealand. In: G. Richards and J. Wilson (eds), *The Global Nomad: Backpacker Travel in Theory and Practice*. Clevedon: Channel View Press, pp. 217–236.

NOP Market Research Ltd (1989). *Activities by the British on Holiday in Britain*. London: British Tourist Authority/English Tourist Board/National Opinion Poll.

Norton, D. W. (2003). *Why consumers want meaningful brand experiences*. Available at http://experience.yamamoto-moss.com/ (accessed 30 June 2004).

O'Brien, K. (1998). The future of the UK travel agent. *Insights*, March, D29–D35.

O'Connor, P. (2000). *Using Computers in Hospitality*, 2nd ed. London: Cassell.

O'Connor, P. (2001). The changing face of hotel electronic distribution. *EIU Travel and Tourism Analyst*, 5, 61–78.

O'Connor, P. (2003). Online intermediaries – revolutionizing travel distribution. *Travel and Tourism Analyst*, 2, 1–25.

O'Neil, D. (1997). *General Public Space Travel and Tourism – Volume 1 Executive Summary*. Huntsville: NASA & STA, Marshall Space Flight Center. Available at http://www.spacetransportation.org/genpub~2.pdf (accessed August 2004).

Oppermann, M. (1996). Convention destination images: analysis of association meeting planners' perceptions. *Tourism Management*, 17(3), 175–182.

Packer, R. and Jordan, K. (2001). *Multimedia: From Wagner to Virtual Reality*. New York, NY: W. W. Norton.

Page, S. (2003a). European rail travel – specific length focus. *Travel and Tourism Analyst*, April, pp. 1–53.

Page, S. (2003b). European bus and rail travel. *Travel and Tourism Analyst*, June, 1–36.

Page, S. and Dowling, R. K. (2002). *Ecotourism, Themes in Tourism*. London: Prentice Hall.

Palmer, M. (2002). Turn on, heat up, stay in. *Daily Telegraph*, 2 March.

Papatheodorou, A. (2002). Civil aviation regimes and leisure tourism in Europe. *Journal of Air Transport Management*, 8, 381–388.

Parasuraman, A., Berry, L. L. and Zeithaml, V. A. (1991). Refinement of and reassessment of the SERVQUAL scale. *Journal of Retailing*, 67(4), 420–450.

Pearce, P. (1993). Fundamentals of tourist motivation. In: D. G. Pearce and R. W. Butler (eds), *Tourism Research, Critiques and Challenges*. London: Routledge, pp. 113–134.

Pearce, P. (1998). Marketing and management trends in tourist attractions. *Asia Pacific Journal of Tourism Research*, 3(1), 1–8.

Pearce, P. L. (1999). Touring for pleasure. Studies of the senior self-drive travel market. *Tourism Recreation Research*, 24(1), 35–42.

Pedro, A. (2000). Dinámica inmobiliaria y sector turismo. In: A. Pedro and J. Sanchis (eds), *Problemas de acceso al mercado de la vivienda en la Unión Europea*. Valencia: Generalitat Valenciana, Universitat de València, Argentaria, Tirant Lo Blanch.

Pennington-Gray, L. (2003). Understanding the domestic VFR drive market in Florida. *Journal of Vacation Marketing*, 9(4), 354–367.

Pew Internet & American Life Project (2004). *Older Americans and the Internet*. Washington, DC: Pew Internet & American Life Project. Available at http://www.pewinternet.org/pdfs/PIP_Seniors_Online_2004.pdf (accessed 30 October 2004).

Pine II, B. J. and Gilmore, J. H. (1999). *The Experience Economy: Work is Theatre & Every Business a Stage*. Boston, MA: Harvard Business School Press.

Plog, S. C. (1974). Why destinations rise and fall in popularity. *Cornell Hotel and Restaurant Quarterly*, 15, 3–16.

Pollock, A. (2000). Intelligent destination management systems: the makings of a nervous system for tourism? In: M. Manente and M. Cerato (eds), *From Destination to Destination Marketing and Management. Designing and Repositioning Tourism Products*. Venice: Ca'Foscarina University, CISET Series, pp. 29–44, pp. 99–110.

Poon, A. (1993). *Tourism, Technology and Competitive Strategies*. Wallingford: CABI Publishing.

Poon, A. (2001). The future of travel agents. *Travel and Tourism Analyst*, 3, 57–80.

PricewaterhouseCoopers (2001). *New Europe and the Hotel Industry*. London: PricewaterhouseCoopers.

Prideaux, B. (2000). The role of the transport system in destination development. *Tourism Management*, 21, 53–63.

Priestley, G. and Mundet L. (1998). The post-stagnation phase of the resort cycle. Annals of Tourism Research, 25(1), 85–111.

Prosser, E. and Leisen, B. (2003). Determinants of on-board retail expenditures in the cruise industry. *Journal of American Academy of Business*, 3(1/2), 304–311.

Purves, L. (2001). Tourists should not travel light on morals. *Times*, 10 July.

Quark Expeditions (2000). *Explore Antarctica*. Available at http://www. quarkexpeditions.com/antarctic/nav/vavil_set.html (accessed August 2004).

Rao, N. and Suresh, K. T. (2001). Domestic tourism in India. In: K Ghimire (ed.), *The Native Tourist: Mass Tourism within Developing Countries*. London: Earthscan, pp. 198–228.

Redmond, G. (1990). Points of increasing contact: sport and tourism in the modern world. In: A. Tomlinson (ed.), *Sport in Society: Policy, Politics and Culture*. Eastbourne: Leisure Studies Association, pp. 158–169.

Reichert, M. (1999). *The Future of Space Tourism, 1.3.07*. 50th International Astronautical Congress, 4–8 October, Amsterdam. IAA-99-IAA. Amsterdam: IAF.

Reynolds, I. (1999). The changing face of the UK travel industry. *Journal of Vacation Marketing*, 6(1), 5–7.

Richards, G. (1995). Retailing travel products: bridging the information gap. *Progress in Tourism and Hospitality Research*, (1)1, 17–30.

Richards, G. (1996a). Production and consumption of European cultural tourism. *Annals of Tourism Research*, 23(2), 261–283.

Richards, G. (ed.) (1996b). *Cultural Tourism in Europe*. Wallingford: CABI Publishing.

Richards, G. (2002). Tourist attraction systems: exploring cultural behaviour. *Annals of Tourism Research*, 29(4), 1048–1064.

Richards, G. and Wilson, J. (2003). *Today's Youth Travellers: Tomorrow's Global Nomads*. Amsterdam: ISTC/ATLAS.

Richards, G. and Wilson, J. (2004). *The Global Nomad: Backpacker Travel in Theory and Practice*. Clevedon: Channel View Publications.

Richer, P. (2004). *Travel Agents Fighting Back*. Available at http://www.travel-mole.com/news_detail.php?news_id=100537.

Rifkin, J. (2000). *The Age of Access: The New Culture of Hypercapitalism where All of Life is a Paid-for Experience*. New York, NY: Penguin Putnam, Inc.

Rigg, J. and Lewney, R. (1987). The economic impact and importance of sport in the UK. *International Review for the Sociology of Sport*, 22(3), 149–169.

Ripe, C. (1996). *Goodbye Culinary Cringe*. Sydney: Allen & Unwin.

Ritchie, J. R. B. and Crouch, G. I. (2003). *The Competitive Destination: A Sustainable Tourism Perspective*. Wallingford: CABI Publishing.

Ritchie, J. and Lyons, M. (1990). Olympulse VI: a post-event assessment of resident reaction to the XV Olympic Winter Games. *Journal of Travel Research*, 28(3), 14–23.

Ritchie, B. W., Carr, N. and Cooper, C. (2003). *Managing Educational Tourism*. Clevedon: Channel View Publications.

Ritzer, G. (1996). *The McDonaldization of Society*. Thousand Oaks: Pine Forge Press.

Roberts, K. (1994). The role of leisure and recreational sport in Europe. In: J. Mester (ed.), *Sport Science in Europe 1993 – Current and Future Perspectives*. Aachen: Meyer & Meyer, pp. 113–125.

Robertson, G. (2002). Will Santa find me? Domestic Christmas travel 1998–2001. *BTR Tourism Research Report*, 4(2), 1–6.

Robinett, J. (1993). The American way. *Leisure Management*, 13(10), 52–54.

Rodríguez-Salmones, N., Aranda, E. and Garrido, B. (2003). El alojamiento turístico privado en el contexto del sistema de estadísticas de turismo. *Estudios Turísticos*, 155/156, 7–32.

Rogers, T. (2003). *Conferences and Conventions: A Global Industry*. Oxford: Butterworth-Heinemann.

Rojek, C. (1993). *Ways of Escape: Modern Transformations in Leisure and Travel*. London: Macmillan.

Rosa, J. A. and Malter, A. J. (2002). E-(Embodied) knowledge and E-commerce: how physiological factors affect on-line sales of experiential products. *Journal of Consumer Psychology, Special Issue on Consumers in Cyberspace*, 13(1&2), 63–75.

Rosenbloom, B. (1999). *Marketing Channels: A Management View*, 6th edn. New York: Dryden.

Sakai, M., Brown, J. and Mak, J. (2000). Population ageing and Japanese international travel in the 21st century. *Journal of Travel Research*, 38, 212–220.

Sarup, M. (1996). *Identity, Culture and the Postmodern World*. Edinburgh: Edinburgh University Press.

Schank, R. C. and Berman, T. R. (2002). The pervasive role of stories in knowledge and action. In: M. C. Green, J. J. Strange and T. C. Brock (eds), *Narrative Impact: Social and Cognitive Foundations*. Mahwah, NJ: Lawrence Erlbaum Associates, pp. 287–314.

Scheer, R. (1999). *What makes a place sacred*? Available at http://www.newagetravel.com/info/sacred.htm.

Scheyvens, R. (2002). *Tourism For Development: Empowering Communities*. London: Prentice Hall.

Schmitt, B. (1999). *Experiential Marketing*. New York, NY: The Free Press.

Seaton, A. V. (1994). Are relatives friends? Reassessing the VFR category in segmenting tourism markets. In: A. V. Seaton (ed.), *Tourism: The State of The Art*. Chichester: John Wiley & Sons, pp. 316–321.

Seaton, A. V. (1996). The marketing mix: the tourism product. In: A. V. Seaton and M. M. Bennet (eds), *Marketing Tourism Products. Concepts, Issues, Cases*. Falmouth: International Thomson Business Press, pp. 126–127.

Seaton, A. V. (1999). Book towns as tourism developments in peripheral areas. *International Journal of Tourism Research*, 1, 389–399.

Seaton, A. V. and Palmer, C. (1997). Understanding VFR tourism behaviour: the first five years of the United Kingdom tourism survey. *Tourism Management*, 18, 345–355.

Shackley, M. (2001a). Sacred world heritage sites: balancing meaning with management. *Tourism Recreation Research*, 26(1), 5–10.

Shackley, M. (2001b). *Managing Sacred Sites*. London: Continuum.

Shafranske, E. and Malony, H. (1990). Clinical psychologists' religious and spiritual orientations and their practice of psychotherapy. *Psychotherapy*, 27, 72–78.

Shaw, G. and Williams, A. (eds) (1997). *The Rise and Fall of British Coastal Resorts: Cultural and Economic Perspectives*. London: Mansell.

Shedroff, N. (2001). *Experience Design*. Indianapolis, IN: New Riders.

Sheldon, P. (1997). *Tourism Information Technology*. Wallingford: CABI Publishing.

Shepherd, N. (2003). How ecotourism can go wrong: the cases of SeaCanoe and Siam Safari, Thailand. In: M. Lueck and T. Kirsges (eds), *Global Ecotourism. Policies and Case Studies. Perspectives and Constraints, Current Themes in Tourism*. Clevedon: Channel View Publications, pp. 137–146.

Shoemaker, S. (2000). Segmenting the mature market: 10 years later. *Journal of Travel Research*, 39, 11–26.

Silberberg, T. (1995). Cultural tourism and business opportunities for museums and heritage sites. *Tourism Management*, 16(5), 361–365.

Silverstein, M. J. and Fiske, N. (2003). *Trading Up: The New American Luxury*. New York, NY: Portfolio.

Smith, S. L. J. (1995). *Tourism Analysis: A Handbook*, 2nd edn. Harlow: Longman.

Smith, V. (2000). Space tourism: the 21st century 'frontier'. *Tourism Recreation Research*, 25(3), 5–15.

Smith, M. (2003a). Holistic holidays: tourism and the reconciliation of body, mind, spirit. *Tourism Recreation Research*, 28(1), 103–108.

Smith, M. K. (2003b). *Issues in Cultural Tourism Studies*. London: Routledge.

Soja, E. W. (1989). *Postmodern Geographies: The Reassertion of Space in Critical Theory*. London: Verso.

Space Adventures (2004). http://www.spaceadventures.com (accessed August 2004).

Standeven, J. and De Knop, P. (1999). *Sport Tourism: An International Perspective*. Champaign: Human Kinetics Publishers.

Stansfield, C. A. (1978). Atlantic City and the resort cycle: background to the legalization of gambling. *Annals of Tourism Research*, 5(2), 238–251.

Steindl-Rast, D. (1984). *Gratefulness, The Heart of Prayer – An Approach to Life in Fullness*. New York: Paulist.

Stern, L., El-Ansary, A., and Coughlan, A. (1996). *Marketing Channels*, 5th edn. Upper Saddle River: Prentice Hall International.

Stevens, T. (2003). The future of visitor attractions. In: A. Fyall, B. Garrod and A. Leask (eds), *Managing Visitor Attractions*. Oxford: Butterworth-Heinemann, pp. 284–298.

Strapp, J. D. (1988). The resort cycle and second homes. *Annals of Tourism Research*, 15(4), 504–516.

Swarbrooke, J. (2002). *The Development and Management of Visitor Attractions*, 2nd edn. Oxford: Butterworth-Heinemann.

Symons, M. (1993). *The Shared Table: Ideas for Australian Cuisine*. Canberra: Australian Government Publishing Service.

Teare, R. and Olsen, M. (1992). *International Hospitality Management – Corporate Strategy in Practice*. London: Pitman.

Theuns, H. L. (1995). Tourism in Western Samoa: situation, policies, impacts and constraints. *Tourism Recreation Research*, 19(1), 149–158.

TIA (1998). *Adventure Travel Report*. Washington: Travel Industry Association of America.

Timothy, D. (1997). Tourism and the personal heritage experience. *Annals of Tourism Research*, 24(3), 751–754.

Timothy, D. (1999). Cross-border shopping: tourism in the Canada–United States borderlands. *Visions in Leisure and Business*, 17(4), 4–18.

Timothy, D. and Butler, R. (1995). Cross-border shopping: a North American perspective. *Annals of Tourism Research*, 22(1), 16–34.

Torres, E. (2003). El turismo residenciado y sus efectos en los destinos turísticos. *Estudios Turísticos*, 155/156, 45–70.

Travelmole (2004). *Over 40% of travel website visits come via search engines*. Available at http://www.travelmole.com/printable.php?news_id=102010 (accessed 29 October 2004).

Treloar, P., Hall, C. M. and Mitchell, R. (2004). Wine tourism and the Generation Y market: any possibilities? In: C. Cooper, C. Arcodia, D. Soinet and

M. Whitford (eds), *Creating Tourism Knowledge*, 14th CAUTHE International Research Conference, University of Queensland, St Lucia (CD ROM).

Tyrell, B. and Mai, R. (2001). *Leisure 2010 – Experience Tomorrow*. Henley: Jones Lang La Salle.

Ujma, D. (2002). The channel relationship between tour operators and travel agents in Britain and Poland. PhD thesis, University of Luton.

Um, S. and Crompton, J. L. (1990). Attitude determinants in tourism destination choice. *Annals of Tourism Research*, 25(2), 116–156.

UNEP (2001). *Industry and Environment, United Nations Environment Programme*, 24(3), 5.

Upchurch, R. S., Jeong, G. H., Clements, C. and Jung, I. (1999). Meeting planners' perceptions of site selection characteristics: the case of Seoul, Korea. *Journal of Convention and Exhibition Management*, 2(1), 15–35.

Urry, J. (1990). *The Tourist Gaze: Travel, Leisure and Society*. London: Sage.

Urry, J. (2002). *The Tourist Gaze: Leisure and Travel in Contemporary Societies*, 2nd edn. London: Sage.

Vacek, E. (1994). *Love, Human and Divine: The Heart of Christian Ethics*. Washington, DC: Georgetown University Press.

Vanier, J. (1999). *Becoming Human*. Mahwah: Paulist.

Van Kamm, A. (1986). *Fundamental Formation*. Formative Spirituality Series, 1. San Francisco: Crossroads.

Varela, B., López, A. and Martinez, A. (2003). Primeras aproximaciones al estudio estadístico del alojamiento privado con fines turísticos desde una perspectiva de oferta. *Estudios Turísticos*, 155/156, 87–109.

Villanueva, A. B. (2000). Review essay: population ageing and retirement issues in the next millennium. *The Social Science Journal*, 37(2), 321–325.

Virgin (2004). www.virgingallactic.com (accessed December 2004).

Vogt, C. and Fesenmaier, D. R. (1998). Expanding the functional tourism information search model: incorporating aesthetic, hedonic, innovation and sign dimensions. *Annals of Tourism Research*, 25(3), 551–579.

Vukonic, B. (1996). *Tourism and Religion* (trans. S. Matesic). New York: Elsevier.

Walley, L., Steinberg, M. and Warner, D. (1999). *Mature Age Labour Force*. Monograph series No. 2. Brisbane: Department of Employment, Training and Industrial Relations.

Walsh-Heron, J. and Stevens, T. (1990). The management of visitor attractions and events. Englewood Cliffs: Prentice-Hall.

Walton, J. (1994). *Fish and Chips and the British Working Classes 1870–1940*. Leicester: Continuum.

Wanhill, S. (2003). Interpreting the development of the visitor attraction product. In: A. Fyall, B. Garrod and A. Leask (eds), *Managing Visitor Attractions*. Oxford: Butterworth-Heinemann, pp. 16–36.

Waters, J. (2002). *Those who cruise the country in million-dollar motorcoaches will have country club near Palm Springs to call home*. Available at http://www.hotel-online.com/News/PR2002_3rd/Jul02_BusCntryClub.html (accessed May 2004).

Weber, K. and Ladkin, A. (2003). The conventions industry in Australia and the UK: key issues and competitive forces. *Journal of Travel Research*, 42(2), 125–132.

Weber, S. and Tomljenović (2004). *Reinventing a Tourism Destination*. Zagreb. Institute for Tourism.

Weiler, B. and Hall, C. M. (1992). *Special Interest Tourism*. London: Belhaven Press.

Wells, M. (2001). Travel shows portray Paradise and hide reality. *Guardian*, 28 August.

Wesley, S and LeHew, M. (2002). Tourist-oriented shopping centers: investigating customers' evaluation of attribute importance. *Journal of Shopping Center Research*, 9(2), 72–87.

Westerhausen, K. (2002). *Beyond the Beach: An Ethnography of Modern Travellers in Asia*. Bangkok: White Lotus.

Wheatcroft, S. and Seekings, J. (1995). *Europe's Youth Travel Market*. Brussels: European Travel Commission, ATI (Aviation and Tourism International).

White, P. (2002). Globalization in public transport. *Public Transport International*, 1, 4–7.

Whitford, M. (1998). *Seniors provide hoteliers with golden opportunities*. Available at http://www.hotel-online.com/SpecialReports1998/Senior Opportunities.html (accessed May 2004)

Windham, L. and Orton, K. (2000). *The Soul of the New Consumer*. New York: Allworth Press.

World Tourism Organization (2001a). *Tourism 2020 Vision – Global Forecasts and Profiles of Market Segments*. Madrid: World Tourism Organization.

World Tourism Organization (2001b). *eBusiness for Tourism: Practical Guidelines for Destinations and eBusinesses*. Madrid: World Tourism Organization.

World Tourism Organization (2003). *Chinese Outbound Tourism*. Madrid: World Tourism Organization.

X-Prize (2004). www.xprize.org (accessed August 2004).

Yiannakis, A. and Gibson, H. (1992). Roles tourists play. *Annals of Tourism Research*, 19, 287–303.

Yu, H. and Littrell, M. (2003). Product and process orientations to tourism shopping. *Journal of Travel Research*, 42(2), 140–150.

Zeithaml, V. A. and Bitner, M. J. (1996). *Services Marketing. Integrating Customer Focus Across the Firm*, 2nd edn. New York: McCraw-Hill Higher Education.

Index